BIG DATA

VOLUME 2

DR. MATTHEW N. O. SADIKU

BIG

DATA

VOLUME 2

DR. MATTHEW N. O. SADIKU

ARPress
ILLUMINATING IDEAS
EMPOWERING VOICES

ARPress
45 Dan Road Suite 15
Canton MA 02021
Hotline: 1(888) 821-0229
Fax: 1(508) 545-7580

Ordering Information:
Quantity sales. Special discounts are available on quantity purchases by corporations, associations, and others. For details, contact the publisher at the address above.

Printed in the United States of America.

ISBN-13:   Softcover   979-8-89676-676-6
           eBook   979-8-89676-677-3
           Hardback   979-8-89676-678-0

Library of Congress Control Number: 2025924885

DEDICATED TO MY WIFE

Janet Sadiku

Table of Contents

PREFACE

Data is one of the biggest byproducts of the 21st century. Almost everything we do produces data, from swiping credit cards to emailing. Every company generates data, whether consciously or unconsciously. Data can be a company's most valuable asset. For example, big data provides valuable insights into customers that companies can use to refine their marketing, advertising, and promotions to increase customer engagement and conversion rates. An organization can glean important insights, risks, patterns or trends from big data.

We are living in the era of big data, where businesses in every industry must deal with vast volumes of data. As its name implies, big data is a structured, semi-structured, and unstructured data, which is very big, fast, and comes in many forms. Big data refers to the huge volume of data that is being generated around the world and holds humongous information. It comes from a variety of sources such as sensors, social media sites, smart phones, Internet, emails, ecommerce transactions, weather data, medical records, insurance records, RFID devices, video sharing, etc. Due to its characteristics, big data requires new technologies and techniques to capture, store, and analyze. From healthcare to finance, big data is being used to transform how industries function, enabling business enterprises to create new revenue streams, enhance customer experiences, and increase operational efficiency.

Big data is drawing attention for its possible applications in industries that are ripe for digital transformation. It is an emerging technology that is on the verge of transforming many industries, including finance, architecture, pharmaceuticals, telecommunications, transportation, supply chain, media and entertainment, oil and gas, space exploration, maritime industry, and the military. The technology is already transforming industries and business processes, leading to completely new experiences and groundbreaking results.

This book is an extension or supplement to a former book,[+] where 16 applications of big data are covered. The brief Table of Contents of the book is provided in the Appendix. In this book, we cover 11 additional big data applications. The book is organized into twelve chapters that summarize big data and its applications in various sectors.

Chapter 1 - Introduction: This chapter provides an overview of big data and its applications. It serves as in introduction to the book. Big data applies to data sets of extreme size (e.g. exabytes, zettabytes) which are beyond the capability of the commonly used software tools. It involves situation where very large data sets are big in volume, velocity, veracity, and variability. Companies that act wisely on the insights gained from big data analytics are better poised to make the most of available opportunities as compared to those that do not apply big data solutions.

Chapter 2 - Finance: This chapter seeks to explore the current landscape of big data in banking and other financial services. The financial services industry is made up of banks, credit unions, insurance companies, wealth management companies, and credit card companies just to name a few. Big data is no longer a nice-to-have but a must-have for financial institutions aiming to stay competitive in today's data-driven world. In the financial services industry, big data can help businesses gain insights into customer behavior, optimize operations, and create new opportunities for growth. The future of big data in the finance sector appears promising, with numerous opportunities for innovation and improvement.

Chapter 3 - Architecture: This chapter examines the role of big data in architecture. Big data in architecture refers to the application of big data technologies and techniques within the field of architecture, where large volumes of data from building sensors, user interactions, and environmental factors are collected and analyzed to optimize building

---

[+]M. N. O. Sadiku, U. C. Chukwu, and P. O. Adebo, *Big Data and Its Applications*. Moldova, Europe: Lambert Academic Publishing, 2024.

design, performance, and operations. In the modern era of architecture, big data plays a crucial role in transforming design processes. While integrating big data into architecture promises impressive benefits, it also brings unique challenges.

Chapter 4 - Pharmaceuticals: This chapter provides an overview of recent developments in big data-related deals within the pharmaceutical industry. The pharma sector generates immense amounts of information. Clinical trial data, electronic health records, genomics information, real-world evidence, and patient-reported outcomes; all these data entries combined can be referred to as big data. Big data in the pharmaceutical industry have made positive changes throughout the years because they make the process of drug discovery more successful. When pharmaceutical companies collect large amounts of data at different stages of the value chain, they can leverage big data analytics to generate actionable insights for research and development.

Chapter 5 – Telecommunications: This chapter examines the roles of big data and big data analytics in telecommunications. In today's digital age, the telecom industry has become a crucial pillar for global connectivity and communication. The telecom industry is a leader in big data strategy because of the vast amount of data it gathers during normal business operations. Big data in the telecom industry encompasses a wide range of information, including customer profiles, call records, network logs, location data, social media interactions, and more. Telcos can leverage big data technologies to turn vast amounts of raw data into actionable insights. The application of big data in telecom companies is crucial for success in the current and future telecom industry.

Chapter 6 – Transportation: In this chapter, we focus on the applications of big data and big data analytics in the transportation industry. Transportation, as a means for moving goods and people between different locations, is a vital element of modern society. Big data has remarkably impacted the transportation industry. Organizations across various transportation and travel segments like airports, airlines, freight logistics, railways, hospitality, and others are enjoying the benefits of big data in managing a large amount of data that they handle.

Transportation professionals must make informed decisions based on current, reliable data, not on educated assumptions or the opinions of a few loud stakeholders.

Chapter 7 – Supply Chain: This chapter studies how big data is widely optimized and managed in the supply chain industry. The supply chain involves a series of systematic processes in converting the raw material into finished products and transporting it to the distributor, which is then made available to the consumers. Big data is altering how supply chain decision-makers make choices. Big data analytics has emerged as an integral force in the supply chain.. The use of big data in supply chain analysis and management projects is integral for optimized planning, operational efficiency, production, order fulfillment, and customer satisfaction.

Chapter 8 – Media and Entertainment: This chapter presents an overview of the state of the art of big data in the media and entertainment industry. Today, the term "media" encompasses not only television, radio, and print, but also phone calls, text messaging, social platforms, and video chatting — any channel through which information and entertainment is disseminated. The media and entertainment industry is all about art and employing big data in it. Big data plays a crucial role in the media and entertainment industry by enabling companies to understand audience behavior, personalize content, and optimize marketing efforts. With the influence of big data and analytics in media and entertainment on the rise, it is becoming evident that these technologies are pivotal to the industry's future trajectory.

Chapter 9 – Oil and Gas: This chapter reviews the utilization of big data and data analytics in the oil and gas industry. The oil and gas sector is one of the largest and most complex industries in the world, involving the exploration, extraction, refining, and distribution of hydrocarbon resources. There are ample opportunities for oil and gas companies to use big data to get more oil and gas out of hydrocarbon reservoirs, reduce capital and operational expenses, increase the speed and accuracy of investment decisions, and improve health and safety while mitigating environmental risks. Big data can be used to improve decision-making and operational efficiency by analyzing the data to uncover patterns and correlations. The future of big data in the oil and gas industry is promising, with the potential to drive efficiency, safety, and sustainability.

Chapter 10 – Space Exploration: In this chapter, we delve into the fascinating role of big data in space exploration. Space exploration has always been a primary goal for humanity, pushing the boundaries of our understanding and opening up new frontiers. Big data plays a central role in space exploration, where satellites, telescopes, rovers, and space probes collect and analyze colossal volumes of data from space and celestial bodies. The role of big data in space exploration is undeniable, revolutionizing the way we observe, analyze, and understand the universe. Big data analysis influences space exploration by enabling us to better understand space data, and unlock the mysteries of the universe. Big data has revolutionized the field of space technology, enabling us to explore the universe with unprecedented precision and efficiency.

Chapter 11 – Maritime Industry: This chapter explores big data as a tech trend that is shaping the maritime industry. The maritime industry is one of the largest and most important industries in the world, responsible for keeping global trade alive. Big data analytics is revolutionizing the maritime industry, enabling better decision-making, improved efficiency, and enhanced safety through the analysis of vast amounts of data generated by vessels and ports. Big data enables maritime companies to personalize their services, offer more targeted advertising and marketing campaigns, and improve customer satisfaction. It can provide valuable insights into various aspects of maritime trade, including vessel performance, route optimization, cargo tracking, and port operations.

Chapter 12 – Military: In this chapter, we delve into the role of big data in military operations and explore the realm of possibilities in military data analytics. The US military is currently witnessing a significant shift in warfare, predominantly propelled by advancements in technology. At the heart of this paradigm shift lies the capacity to effectively gather, analyze, and rapidly and securely distribute essential information to military units. Although the prospect of big data in revolutionizing the battlefield is promising, its effective integration into defense intelligence analysis poses a series of challenges and opportunities. Big data will play a key role in how the Army operates and wins its future combats. Big data has the potential not only to revolutionize the tools armed forces use to fight, but to transform members of the armed forces themselves.

This is a must-read book for anyone who wants to learn about the various applications of big data, which has become vital in many areas of life.

I am grateful for the support of Dr. Annamalia Annamalai, the department head of the Department of Electrical and Computer Engineering, and Dr. Pamela Obiomon, the dean of the College of Engineering at Prairie View A&M University, Prairie View, Texas. Special thanks to my wife, Dr. Janet Sadiku, for helping in various ways.

- M. N. O. Sadiku

ABOUT THE AUTHOR

Matthew N. O. Sadiku received his B. Sc. degree in 1978 from Ahmadu Bello University, Zaria, Nigeria and his M.Sc. and Ph.D. degrees from Tennessee Technological University, Cookeville, TN in 1982 and 1984 respectively. From 1984 to 1988, he was an assistant professor at Florida Atlantic University, Boca Raton, FL, where he did graduate work in computer science. In total, he received seven college degrees. From 1988 to 2000, he was at Temple University, Philadelphia, PA, where he became a full professor. From 2000 to 2002, he was with Lucent/Avaya, Holmdel, NJ as a system engineer and with Boeing Satellite Systems, Los Angeles, CA as a senior scientist. He is presently a Regents professor emeritus of electrical and computer engineering at Prairie View A&M University, Prairie View, TX.

He is the author of over 1,500 professional papers and over 160 books including "Elements of Electromagnetics" (Oxford University Press, 7th ed., 2018), "Fundamentals of Electric Circuits" (McGraw-Hill, 7th ed., 2020, with C. Alexander), "Computational Electromagnetics with MATLAB" (CRC Press, 4th ed., 2019), "Principles of Modern Communication Systems" (Cambridge University Press, 2017, with S. O. Agbo), and "Emerging Internet-based Technologies" (CRC Press, 2019). In addition to the engineering books, he has written Christian books including "Secrets of Successful Marriages," "How to Discover God's Will for Your Life," and commentaries on all the books of the New Testament Bible. Some of his books have been translated into ten languages: French, Korean, Chinese (and Chinese Long Form in Taiwan), Italian, Portuguese, Spanish, German, Dutch, Polish, and Russian.

He was the recipient of the 2000 McGraw-Hill/Jacob Millman Award for outstanding contributions in the field of electrical engineering.

He was also the recipient of Regents Professor award for 2012-2013 by the Texas A&M University System. He is a registered professional engineer and a life fellow of the Institute of Electrical and Electronics Engineers (IEEE) "for contributions to computational electromagnetics and engineering education." He was the IEEE Region 2 Student Activities Committee Chairman. He was an associate editor for IEEE Transactions on Education. He is also a member of Association for Computing Machinery (ACM). His current research interests are in the areas of computational electromagnetic, computer science/networks, engineering education, and marriage counseling. His works can be found in his autobiography, "My Life and Work" (Author's Tranquility Press, 2024) or his website: www.matthew-sadiku.com. He currently resides with his wife Janet in Westlake, Florida. He can be reached via email at sadiku@ieee.org

CHAPTER 1

INTRODUCTION

"Big data is at the foundation of all of the megatrends that are happening today, from social to mobile to the cloud to gaming." – Chris Lynch

1.1 INTRODUCTION

Data is the new gold. We produce a massive amount of data each day through every click on the Internet, every bank transaction, every video we watch on YouTube, and every email we send. Every company generates data, whether consciously or unconsciously. Data can be a company's most valuable asset. The data revolution initiated by the dawn of the Internet and further driven by the expansion of mobile technology is vastly considered as a significant innovation especially in developing nations around the world.

Big data is a combination of structured, semi-structured, and unstructured data that organizations collect, analyze, and mine for information and insights. These datasets are so huge and complex in volume, velocity, and variety, that traditional data management systems cannot store, process, and analyze them. Big data comes from many sources, including transaction processing systems, customer databases, documents, emails, medical records, Internet clickstream logs, mobile apps, and social networks. With the explosion of devices, sensors, online services, and digital platforms, data is now generated at an unprecedented rate [1]. Organizations that use and manage large data volumes correctly can reap many benefits. For example, big data provides valuable insights into customers that companies can use to refine their marketing, advertising, and promotions to increase customer engagement and conversion rates. An organization can glean important insights, risks, patterns or trends from big data. For example, companies such as Netflix and Procter & Gamble use big data to anticipate customer demand. Figure 1.1 shows the importance of big data [2].

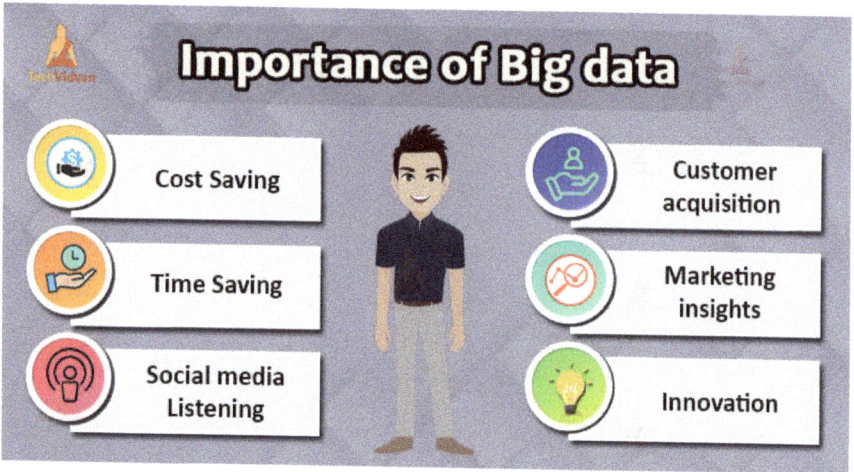

Figure 1.1 The importance of big data [2].t

Big data refers to extremely large and complex datasets that exceed the processing capacity of traditional data management systems. It is essentially about leveraging massive amounts of information to uncover patterns, trends, and insights that can inform better decision-making and drive innovation. Companies use big data in their systems to improve operational efficiency, provide better customer service, create personalized marketing campaigns and take other actions that can increase revenue and profits. By following a structured approach, businesses can extract valuable insights from the vast sea of data they possess. Organizations will be required to manage it appropriately for competitive advantage and durability in the modern digital market [3].

This chapter provides an overview of big data and its applications. It serves as in introduction to the book. It begins with describing big data and its characteristics. It provides some applications of big data. It highlights the benefits and challenges of big data. The last section concludes with comments.

1.2 WHAT IS BIG DATA?

Big data applies to data sets of extreme size (e.g. exabytes, zettabytes) which are beyond the capability of the commonly used software tools. It involves situation where very large data sets are big in volume, velocity, veracity, and variability [4]. The data is too big, too fast, or does not fit the regular database architecture. It may require different strategies and tools for profiling, measurement, assessment, and processing. Different components of big data are shown in Figure 1.2 [5]. The cloud word for big data is shown in Figure 1.3 [6].

Figure 1. 2 Different components of big data [5].

Figure 1.3 The cloud word for big data [6].

Big Data is essentially classified into three types [7]:

- *Structured Data*: This is highly organized and is the easiest to work with. Any data that can be stored, accessed, and processed in the form of fixed format is known as a structured data. It may be stored in tabular format. Due to their nature, it is easy for programs to sort through and collect data. Structured data has quantitative data such as age, contact, address, billing, expenses, credit card numbers, etc. Data that is stored in a relational database management system is an example of structured data.

- *Unstructured Data*: This refers to unorganized data such as video files, log files, audio files, and image files. Any data with unknown form or the structure is classified as unstructured data. Almost everything generated by a computer is unstructured data. It takes a lot of time and effort required to make unstructured data readable. Examples of unstructured data include Metadata, Twitter tweets, and other social media posts.

- *Semi-structured Data*: This falls somewhere between structured data and unstructured data, i.e., both forms of data are present. Semi-structured data can be inherited such as location, time, email address, or device ID stamp.

The different types of big data are depicted in Figure 1.4 [8].

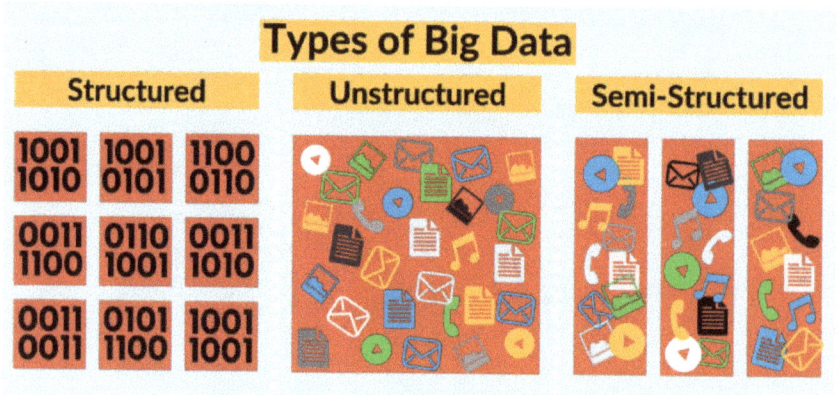

Figure 1.4 Types of big data [8].

The process of examining big data is often referred to big data analytics. It is an emerging field since massive computing capabilities have been made available by e-infrastructures [9]. Big data analytics is the application of advanced analytic techniques to large, heterogeneous data sets that comprise structured, semi-structured, and unstructured data from many sources with sizes ranging from terabytes to zettabytes.

It enables predictive analytics, which involves using historical data to forecast future outcomes. Analytics include statistical models and other methods that are aimed at creating empirical predictions. Data-driven organizations use analytics to guide decisions at all levels. Several techniques have been proposed for analyzing big data. These include the HACE theorem, cloud computing, Hadoop, and MapReduce [10]. Figure 1.5 shows big data analytics [11].

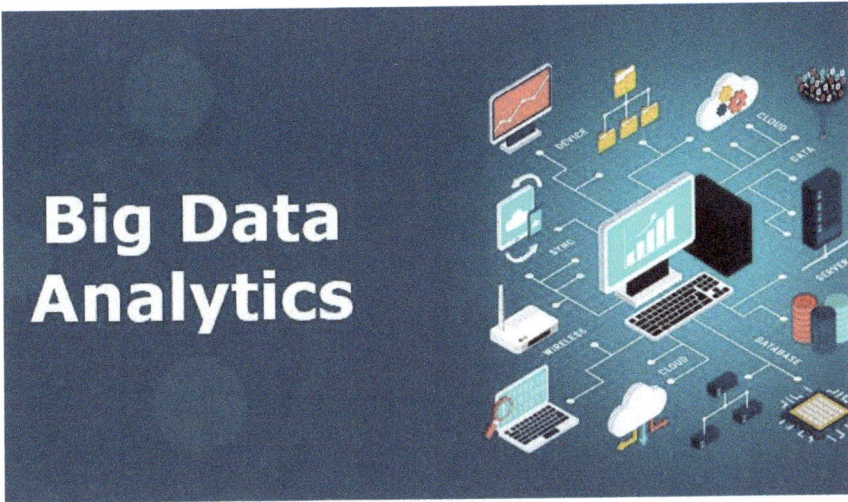

Figure 1.5 Big data analytics [11].

1.3 CHARACTERISTICS OF BIG DATA

Big data is growing rapidly and expanding in all science and engineering, including physical, biological, and medical services. Different companies use different means to maintain their big data. As shown in Figure 1.6 [12], big data is characterized by 42 Vs. The first five Vs are volume, velocity, variety, veracity, and value.

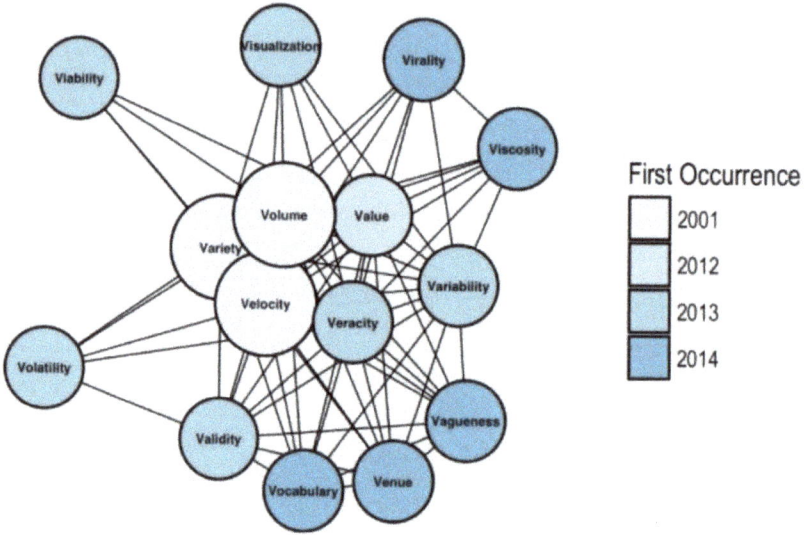

Figure 1.6 The 42 V's of big data [12].

- *Volume*: This refers to the size of the data being generated both inside and outside organizations and is increasing annually. Some regard big data as data over one petabyte in volume.

- *Velocity*: This depicts the unprecedented speed at which data are generated by Internet users, mobile users, social media, etc. Data are generated and processed in a fast way to extract useful, relevant information. Big data could be analyzed in real time, and it has movement and velocity.

- *Variety*: This refers to the data types since big data may originate from heterogeneous sources and is in different formats (e.g., videos, images, audio, text, logs). BD comprises of structured, semi-structured or unstructured data.

- *Veracity*: By this, we mean the truthfulness of data, i.e. weather the data comes from a reputable, trustworthy, authentic, and accountable source. It suggests the inconsistency in the quality of different sources of big data. The data may not be 100% correct.

- *Value*: This is the most important aspect of the big data. It is the desired outcome of big data processing. It refers to the process of discovering hidden values from large datasets. It denotes the value derived from the analysis of the existing data. If one cannot extract some business value from the data, there is no use managing and storing it.

On this basis, small data can be regarded as having low volume, low velocity, low variety, low veracity, and low value. Additional five Vs has been added [12]:

- *Validity*: This refers to the accuracy and correctness of data. It also indicates how up to date it is.

- *Viability*: This identifies the relevancy of data for each use case. Relevancy of data is required to maintain the desired and accurate outcome through analytical and predictive measures.

- *Volatility*: Since data are generated and change at a rapid rate, volatility determines how quickly data change.

- *Vulnerability*: The vulnerability of data is essential because privacy and security are of utmost importance for personal data.

- *Visualization*: Data needs to be presented unambiguously and attractively to the user. Proper visualization of large and complex clinical reports helps in finding valuable insights.

Instead of the 10V's above, some suggest the following 5V's: Venue, Variability, Vocabulary, Vagueness, and Validity) [13].

Industries that benefit from big data include the healthcare, financial, airline, travel, restaurants, automobile, sports, agriculture, and hospitality industries. Big data technologies are playing an essential role in farming: machines are equipped with sensors that measure data in their environment. The analysis of both structured and unstructured data is crucial in the shipping industry to gain insights into customer behavior, improve operational efficiency, and make informed business decisions.

1.4 APPLICATIONS OF BIG DATA

The potential applications for big data are essentially unlimited, and it is already being used across multiple industries. Common applications include the following [5,14-17]:

- *Healthcare*: The healthcare industry can combine numerous data sources internally, such as electronic health records, patient wearable devices, and staffing data, and externally, including insurance records and disease studies, to optimize both provider and patient experiences. Medical researchers use big data to identify disease signs and risk factors. Doctors use it to help diagnose illnesses and medical conditions in patients. In addition, a combination of data from electronic health records, social media sites, the web, and other sources gives healthcare organizations and government agencies up-to-date information on infectious disease threats and outbreaks. For example, big data facilitated in the storage mechanism of the vaccine, since they were kept and stored within precise temperature range.

- *Education*: The educational system is one of the main civilization pillars. Its development can characterize the advancement level of any society. Big data has played a vital role in restructuring the educational system. It enabled educational institutes and professionals to personalize the educational experience for students. Big data can analyze, find correlation between the data, highlight patterns, provide insights and predict for the ultimate teaching-learning process. Hence, educators and professionals in the educational field will provide intelligent decisions to enhance the educational regime. For example, big data can improve the learning process, by optimizing the selection, of the prior teaching techniques and newly proposed ones to meet the student actual needs and interests.

- *Government*: Government digital archiving rates and data generation are on the rise. Government offices can potentially collect data from many different sources, such as DMV records, traffic data, police/firefighter data, public school records, and more. This can drive efficiencies in many different ways, such as detecting driver trends for optimized intersection management and better resource allocation in schools. Governments can also post data publicly, allowing for improved transparency to bolster public trust. Government agencies can leverage big data insights in inventive ways. They can leverage big data and analytics to unlock key information, and improve transparency and efficiency in public management. The use of big data in government and public sector is illustrated in Figure 1.7 [17].

Figure 1.7 Use of big data in government and public sector [17].

- *Finance*: Financial institutions leverage big data for fraud detection and risk management. By analyzing transaction patterns and detecting anomalies, banks can prevent fraudulent activities in real time. Big Data is revolutionizing the finance industry by providing real-time insights into market trends and customer behavior. In the financial sector, big data analytics helps in fraud detection, risk management, customer segmentation, personalized banking services, and trading analytics.

- *Manufacturing*: Big data is being used in the manufacturing industry to improve efficiency, reduce costs, and optimize supply chain operations. Big data applications in manufacturing include predictive maintenance, quality control, and supply chain optimization. By monitoring machinery and equipment data, manufacturers can predict failures and schedule maintenance proactively, reducing downtime and improving operational efficiency.

- *Transportation*: Millions of citizens use public roads every day, whether driving or walking. Many factors contribute to safety on the road, such as the state of the roads, police officers, vehicle safety, and weather conditions. With these factors in play, it is almost impossible to control everything that might lead to an accident. Big data allows governments to oversee the transportation sector to ensure safer roads. Route optimization and fleet management are driven by big data. Analyzing traffic patterns and fleet data helps optimize routes, improve fuel efficiency, and schedule maintenance, leading to cost savings and improved service delivery. For example, big data plays a vital role in predicting the cause effect relation between the driving restriction policies and traffic congestion.

- *Fraud Detection*: One of the most feared challenges of running a business is encountering financial frauds and claims. This was an alarming global problem among organizations before the advent of big data. However, with the emergence of big data, companies can now detect, prevent, and also eliminate any fraudulent risks. Data analysts utilize artificial intelligence and machine learning algorithms to find abnormalities and transaction trends. These irregularities in transaction patterns show that something is out of place or that there is a mismatch, providing us with hints regarding potential frauds. By spotting fraud before they cause problems, a company may provide superior customer service, avoid losses, and stay compliant.

- *Accounting*: The accounting industry is using big data, especially in auditing. Big data is incredibly valuable for accounting firms that need to sell their services; providing accurate and actionable information to clients is a great way to boost firm value. At the moment, accounting firms typically use "audit sampling" to detect issues or trends in transactions or invoices. However, big data analytics can excel at identifying exceptions and outliers within a larger trend. Accounting firms can then focus their efforts on those exceptions for further analysis. For example, big data sets can allow accounting firms to aggregate performance metrics across an entire industry and present them to a client, pointing out specific reasons the competition may be outperforming the client rather than relying on outdated methods such as ratios or guesswork. Even better, big data can allow accounting professionals to look at the big picture of a particular industry and see shifts in consumer behavior or trends.

- *Marketing*: Big data is notable in marketing due to the constant "datafication" of everyday consumers of the Internet, in which all forms of data are tracked. The datafication of consumers can be defined as quantifying many of or all human behaviors for the purpose of marketing. The increasingly digital world of rapid datafication makes this idea relevant to marketing because the amount of data constantly grows exponentially. Big data in marketing is a highly lucrative tool that can be used for large corporations, its value being as a result of the possibility of predicting significant trends, interests, or statistical outcomes in a consumer-based manner. Big data provides customer behavior pattern spotting for marketers, since all human actions are being quantified into readable numbers for marketers to analyze and use for their research.

1.5 BENEFITS

Organizations that use and manage large data volumes correctly can reap many benefits. Unlike traditional data management solutions, big data technologies and tools are made to help you deal with large and complex datasets to extract value from them. Big data can be used to identify solvable problems, such as improving healthcare or tackling poverty in a certain area. Other benefits include the following [19,20]:

- *Better Decision-making*: Big data applications and analytics are vital in proposing ultimate strategic decisions. Big data is the key element to becoming a data-driven organization. When you can manage and analyze your big data, you can discover patterns and unlock insights that improve and drive better operational and strategic decisions. An organization can glean important insights, risks, patterns or trends from big data. Large data sets are meant to be comprehensive and encompass as much information as the organization needs to make better decisions.

Big data insights let business leaders quickly make data-driven decisions that impact their organizations.

- *Better Insights*: When organizations have more data, they are able to derive better insights. With better insights, organizations can make data-driven decisions with more reliable projections and predictions. Big data that covers market trends and consumer habits gives an organization the important insights it needs to meet the demands of its intended audiences. Product development decisions, in particular, benefit from this type of insight.

- *Better Customer Experience*: Big data has made an unblemished customer experience more relevant and workable. Combining and analyzing structured data sources together with unstructured ones provides you with more useful insights for consumer understanding, personalization, and ways to optimize experience to better meet consumer needs and expectations. Big data allows organizations to build customer profiles through a combination of customer sales data, industry demographic data, and related data such as social media activity and marketing campaign engagement.

- *Cost Savings*: Big data can be used to pinpoint ways businesses can enhance operational efficiency. For example, analysis of big data on a company's energy use can help it be more efficient.

- *Higher Efficiency*: Every company generates data. Using big data analytics tools and capabilities allows you to process data faster and generate insights that can help you determine areas where you can reduce costs, save time, and increase your overall efficiency.

- *Competitive Advantage*: In today's competitive landscape, organizations that harness the power of big data analytics gain a significant advantage. This competitive advantage enables organizations to stay ahead of the curve and drive sustainable growth. By making data-driven decisions, businesses can stay ahead of the curve and adapt to changing market dynamics quickly.

- *Poverty Eradication*: There is a lot of poverty in the world that many governments have tried to eradicate for many years. Big data gives governments the necessary tools to uncover better and innovative ideas on how to reduce poverty levels across the globe. This data makes it easier to identify the areas with urgent needs and how to meet those needs.

1.6 CHALLENGES

While big data has many advantages, it does present some challenges that organizations must be ready to tackle when collecting, managing, and taking action on such an enormous amount of data. Big data is big and complex, making it difficult to manage. Big data technology is changing at a rapid pace. Although the term "big data" has been around for some time now, there is still quite a lot of confusion about what it actually means. Other challenges include the following [13,19-21]:

- *Data Privacy*: Data privacy is a critical issue in big data projects, as large amounts of personal data are often collected and analyzed. Organizations must ensure that they comply with data privacy regulations and take appropriate measures to protect sensitive data. The big data we now generate contains a lot of information about our personal lives, much of which we have a right to keep private. Increasingly, we are asked to strike a balance between the amount of personal data we divulge, and the convenience that big data-powered apps and services offer.

- *Data Security*: Data security is an important consideration in big data projects, as large amounts of data can be a target for cyber attacks. Big data contains valuable business and customer information, making big data stores high-value targets for attackers. Since these datasets are varied and complex, it can be harder to implement comprehensive strategies and policies to protect them.

- *Data Discrimination*: When everything is known, will it become acceptable to discriminate against people based on data we have on their lives? We already use credit scoring to decide who can borrow money, and insurance is heavily data-driven. We can expect to be analyzed and assessed in greater detail, and care must be taken that this is not done in a way that contributes to making life more difficult for those who already have fewer resources and access to information.

- *Data Growth*: Big data, by nature, is changing and increasing exponentially. Without a solid infrastructure in place that can handle your processing, storage, network, and security needs, it can become extremely difficult to manage.

- *Data Quality*: Ensuring data quality is a critical component of big data projects. Poor data quality can lead to inaccurate analysis and incorrect decisions. Data quality directly impacts the quality of decision-making, data analytics, and planning strategies. Raw data is messy and can be difficult to curate. Having big data does not guarantee results unless the data is accurate, relevant, and properly organized for analysis. This can slow down reporting, but if not addressed, you can end up with misleading results and worthless insights.

- *Data Storage*: The collected data then needs to be stored in a way that it can be easily accessed and analyzed later. Big data needs big storage, whether in the cloud, on-premises, or both. Data must also be stored in whatever form required. It also needs to be processed and made available in real time. Increasingly, companies are turning to cloud solutions to take advantage of the unlimited compute and scalability.

- *Data Governance*: This involves establishing policies and procedures for managing and protecting data. It includes defining data standards, ensuring data quality, and compliance with data privacy regulations.

- *Data Integration*: Big data projects often involve integrating data from multiple sources, which can be a complex and challenging. Data integration requires careful planning and consideration of data formats, schemas, and structures. Big data allows you to integrate automated, real-time data streaming with advanced data analytics. However, the process of integrating sets of big data is complicated, particularly when data variety and velocity are factors. Big data collects terabytes, and sometimes even petabytes, of raw data from many sources that must be received, processed, and transformed into the format that business users and analysts need to start analyzing it. Integrating disparate data sources and making data accessible for business users is complex, but vital, if you hope to realize any value from your big data.

- *Accessibility*: Among the main challenges in managing big data systems is making the data accessible to data scientists and analysts, especially in distributed environments that include a mix of different platforms and data stores. To help analysts find relevant data, data management and analytics teams are increasingly building data catalogs that incorporate metadata management and data lineage functions.

- *Skill Shortage*: One of the biggest obstacles to benefiting from your investment in big data is not having enough staff with the necessary skills to analyze your data. Deploying and managing big data systems also requires new skills compared to the ones that database administrators and developers focused on relational software typically possess. Data scientists, data analysts, and data engineers are in short supply. Lack of big data skills and experience with advanced data tools is one of the primary barriers to realizing value from big data environments.

- *Regulation*: Standardizing your approach will allow you to manage costs and leverage resources. To ensure that they comply with the laws that regulate big data, businesses need to carefully manage the process of collecting it. Controls must be put in place to identify regulated data and prevent unauthorized employees and other people from accessing it. Big data contains a lot of sensitive data and information, making it a tricky task to continuously ensure data processing and storage meet data privacy and regulatory requirements, such as data localization and data residency laws.

- *Scalability*: Scalability is a key consideration in big data projects, as the amount of data being processed and analyzed can quickly grow beyond the capacity of traditional systems. Organizations must select tools and platforms that can scale to meet their needs. Cloud platforms like AWS, Azure, and Google Cloud offer scalable solutions for big data storage and processing.

1.7 CONCLUSION

The amount and availability of data is growing rapidly, spurred on by digital technology advancements, such as connectivity, mobility, the Internet of things (IoT), and artificial intelligence (AI). Big data refers to the huge volume of both structured and unstructured data that is being generated around the world and holds humongous information. It describes large and diverse datasets that are huge in volume and also rapidly grow in size over time. Companies that act wisely on the insights gained from big data analytics are better poised to make the most of available opportunities as compared to those that do not apply big data solutions. The future of big data is filled with exciting possibilities, including applications in fields such as agriculture, transportation, and energy. More information about big data can be found in the books in [22-27] and the following related journals:

- *Journal of Big Data*
- *Big Data and Cognitive Computing*

REFERENCES

[1] "What is big data?" August 2025,
https://www.geeksforgeeks.org/data-engineering/what-is-big-data/
[2] "Why big data – Benefits and importance of big data,"
https://techvidvan.com/tutorials/why-big-data/
[3] M. N. O. Sadiku, P. A. Adekunte, and J. O. Sadiku, "Big data: An overview," to appear.
[4] M. N. O. Sadiku, M. Tembely, and S.M. Musa, "Big data: An introduction for engineers," *Journal of Scientific and Engineering Research*, vol. 3, no. 2, 2016, pp. 106-108.
[5] "Big data: What it is and why it matters?" August 2024,
https://www.inventateq.com/top-stories/big-data-what-it-is-and-why-it-matters/
[6] L. Rembert, "How accounting teams can leverage big data,"
https://tdwi.org/articles/2020/03/03/adv-all-how-accounting-teams-can-leverage-big-data.aspx

[7] "The complete overview of big data," https://intellipaat.com/blog/tutorial/hadoop-tutorial/big-data-overview/

[8] R. Allen, "Types of big data | Understanding & Interacting with key types (2024)," https://investguiding-com.custommapposter.com/article/types-of-big-data-understanding-amp-interacting-with-key-types

[9] P. Baumann et al., "Big data analytics for earth sciences: The earthserver approach," *International Journal of Digital Earth*, vol. 19, no. 1, 2016, pp.3-29.

[10] X. Wu et al., "Knowledge engineering with big data," *IEEE Intelligent Systems*, September/October 2015, pp.46-55.

[11] "Comprehensive guide to big data analysis," May 2024, https://www.sprinkledata.com/blogs/comprehensive-guide-to-big-data-analysis

[12] "The 42 V's of big data and data science," https://www.kdnuggets.com/2017/04/42-vs-big-data-data-science.html

[13] P. K. D. Pramanik, S. Pal, and M. Mukhopadhyay, "Healthcare big data: A comprehensive overview," in N. Bouchemal (ed.), *Intelligent Systems for Healthcare Management and Delivery*. IGI Global, chapter 4, 2019, pp. 72-100.

[14] "Big data," https://botpenguin.com/glossary/big-data

[15] M. Kour, "A deep dive into big data fundamentals and uses," June 2024, https://www.applify.co/blog/what-is-big-data

[16] "Big data," *Wikipedia*, the free encyclopedia, https://en.wikipedia.org/wiki/Big_data

[17] A. Subramanian, "Big data analytics in government: How the public sector leverages data insights," November 2024, https://www.datasciencecentral.com/big-data-analytics-in-government-how-the-public-sector-leverages-data-insights/

[18] Z. A. Al-Sai et al., "Explore big data analytics applications and opportunities: A review," *Big Data and Cognitive Computing*, vol. 6, no. 4, 2022.

[19] C. Hashemi-Pour, "Big data," March 2024,

https://www.techtarget.com/searchdatamanagement/definition/big-data

[20] "What is big data?"
https://cloud.google.com/learn/what-is-big-data

[21] B. Marr, "What is big data?"
https://bernardmarr.com/what-is-big-data/

[22] M. N. O. Sadiku, U. C. Chukwu, and P. O. Adebo, *Big Data and Its Applications*. Moldova, Europe: Lambert Academic Publishing, 2024.

[23] N. Crepalde, *Big Data on Kubernetes: A Practical Guide to Building Efficient and Scalable Data Solutions*. Packt Publishing, 2024.

[24] J. S. Cook and R. S. Segall (eds.), *Handbook of Research on Big Data Storage and Visualization Techniques*. IGI Global, 2018.

[25] L. M. Goyal et al. (eds.), *Big Data Processing Using Spark in Cloud*. Springer, 2018.

[26] S. Govindappa, *Ultimate Big Data Analytics with Apache Hadoop: Master Big Data Analytics with Apache Hadoop Using Apache Spark, Hive, and Python (English Edition)*. Orange Education Pvt. Ltd, 2024.

[27] A. E. Hassanien et al. (eds.), *Big Data in Complex Systems: Challenges and Opportunities*. Springer, 2015.

CHAPTER 2

✧⁓✧

BIG DATA IN FINANCE

"The world is one big data problem." – Andrew McAfee

2.1 INTRODUCTION

The financial services industry is made up of banks, credit unions, insurance companies, wealth management companies, and credit card companies just to name a few. Community-based financial institutions, such as credit unions and cooperatives, frequently cater to local communities by offering financial services to individuals who may lack access to traditional commercial banks. Historically, financial institutions have been collecting data in the form of addresses, names, and demographic data from credit cards, loan applications, and bank accounts. Traditionally, number crunching was done by humans, and decisions were made based on inferences drawn from calculated risks and trends. However, in recent times, such functionality is usurped by computers.

Big data comes from both internal and external sources and is collected in different ways. Internal sources of big data include invoices, payments, delivery receipts, storage, demographic data, and sensor data, while external sources include social media, data from government agencies, and search engine data. Big data in the financial services industry can help businesses gain insights into customer behavior, optimize operations, and create new opportunities for growth. It is a powerful tool that can help companies make more informed decisions and gain competitive advantages. Big data technologies are instrumental in making the financial industry strengthen their efficiencies, protect their companies, and provide better service to their customers [1].

Big data refers to extremely large data sets that may be analyzed computationally to reveal patterns, trends, and associations, especially relating to human behavior and interactions. It is a term used to describe the large and complex datasets that are generated by businesses, organizations, and individuals. Big data in finance refers to large, diverse (structured and unstructured) and complex sets of data that can be used to provide solutions to long-standing business challenges for financial services and banking companies around the world. Big data analytics is transforming financial services by enabling institutions to analyze vast datasets, identify patterns, and make more informed decisions. Businesses across industries are using this technology for a wide range of purposes, including fraud detection, predictive analysis, and market research. Financial institutions leverage big data to personalize services, offer tailored products, and predict future outcomes [2].

This chapter seeks to explore the current landscape of big data in banking and other financial services. It begins with describing big data. It explains big data in finance and provides some examples. It covers some applications of big data in finance. It highlights some benefits and challenges of big data in finance. The last section concludes with comments.

2.2 WHAT IS BIG DATA?

Big data applies to data sets of extreme size (e.g. exabytes, zettabytes) which are beyond the capability of the commonly used software tools. It involves situation where very large data sets are big in volume, velocity, veracity, and variability [3]. The data is too big, too fast, or does not fit the regular database architecture. It may require different strategies and tools for profiling, measurement, assessment, and processing. Different components of big data are shown in Figure 2.1 [4].

Figure 2.1 Different components of big data [4].

Big data is essentially classified into three types [5]:

- *Structured Data*: This is highly organized and is the easiest to work with. Any data that can be stored, accessed, and processed in the form of fixed format is known as a structured data. It may be stored in tabular format. Due to their nature, it is easy for programs to sort through and collect data. Structured data has quantitative data such as age, contact, address, billing, expenses, credit card numbers, etc. Data that is stored in a relational database management system is an example of structured data.

- *Unstructured Data*: This refers to unorganized data such as video files, log files, audio files, and image files. Any data with unknown form or the structure is classified as unstructured data. Almost everything generated by a computer is unstructured data. It takes a lot of time and effort required to make unstructured data readable. Examples of unstructured data include Metadata, Twitter tweets, and other social media posts.

- *Semi-structured Data*: This falls somewhere between structured data and unstructured data, i.e., both forms of data are present.

Semi-structured data can be inherited such as location, time, email address, or device ID stamp.

The different types of big data are depicted in Figure 2.2 [6]. Structured and unstructured data are generated in various types [7-10].

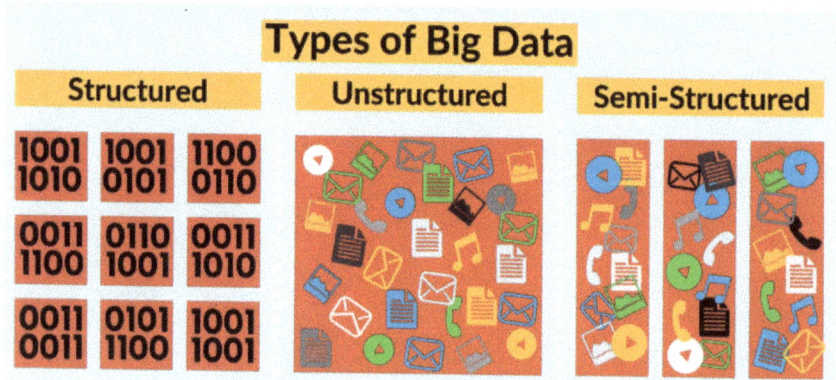

Figure 2.2 Types of big data [6].

The process of examining big data is often referred to big data analytics. It is an emerging field since massive computing capabilities have been made available by e-infrastructures [11]. Big data analytics is the application of advanced analytic techniques to large, heterogeneous data sets that comprise structured, semi-structured, and unstructured data from many sources with sizes ranging from terabytes to zettabytes.

Analytics include statistical models and other methods that are aimed at creating empirical predictions. Data-driven organizations use analytics to guide decisions at all levels. Several techniques have been proposed for analyzing big data. These include the HACE theorem, cloud computing, Hadoop, and MapReduce [12].

2.3 BIG DATA IN FINANCE

In the age of technological innovation, various types of data are available with the advance of information technologies, and data is seen as one of the most valuable commodities in managing automation systems. Big data is an emerging issue in almost all areas of business. Big data technology has become an integral part of the financial services industry and will continue to drive future innovation. It effects a variety of facility, such as financial management, risk management, financial analysis, and managing the data of financial applications. Big data in finance refers to the petabytes of organized and unstructured data that may be utilized by banks and financial institutions to predict client behavior and develop strategies. Financial institutions are not digital natives and have had to go through a lengthy conversion process that necessitated behavioral and technological changes.

Big data is the ability to retain, process, and understand data like never before. It is when you have challenges that cannot be handled by traditional database systems. Big data is one of the most recent business and technical issues in the age of technology. Big data solutions are increasingly being used within the financial services industry. Big data in finance encompasses the profound impact and influence of data within the realms of finance, financial products, and financial services. It is the large amount of structured and unstructured data that companies and financial institutions can use for their business: analyzing future trends, getting to know customers better, saving costs, etc. This data can come from various sources, such as credit card purchases, loan applications, social media interactions, and even mobile app usage. Big data in financial services empowers companies to be more agile, customer-focused, and efficient in a competitive marketplace. Harnessing big data to formulate best practices and drive financial decisions is key in achieving multiple missions [13]. Big data in finance is illustrated in Figure 2.3 [14].

Big Data In Finance And Companies

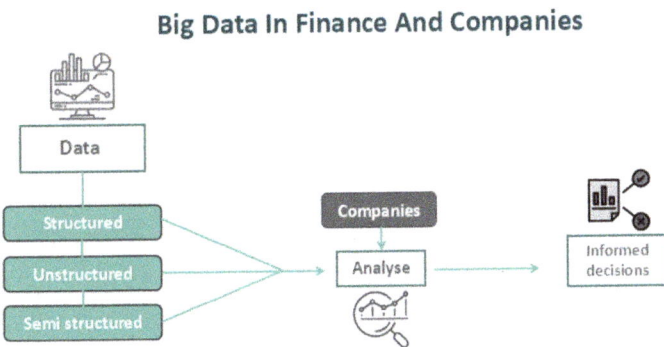

Figure 2.3 Big data in finance [14].

Organizations use big data tools to store vast amounts of big data, so it is available for data analysis. Financial companies are increasingly using big data because of its many-core strengths. Some good ways to use big data include real-time insights, fraud detection, risk analysis, accelerating processes, decreasing instances of human errors, increased customer satisfaction, and analyzing company performance. The financial services sector has also started using big data to enhance risk management, detect fraud and track consumer behavior in order to keep up with compliance standards and increase customer satisfaction and revenues.

2.4 EXAMPLES OF BIG DATA IN FINANCE

Big data has been extensively utilized in finance for a significant period. There are numerous successful big data use cases to explore. The following real-life examples demonstrate the power of big data in financial analysis [15-17]:

- *Capital One*: This leading financial institution leverages Big data analytics to enhance risk management and improve customer experience. By analyzing vast amounts of customer data, Capital One can personalize credit card recommendations, offer customized rewards, and detect potential fraud attempts proactively.

- *Goldman Sachs*: This US company has been at the forefront of leveraging big data in finance to find better investment opportunities, gain a competitive edge, and provide better client services. It provides investment banking and financial services and uses big data to detect investment opportunities. To identify the best possibilities, the institution developed data-driven investment algorithms that assess thousands of businesses worldwide.

- *JP Morgan and Chase*: JPMorgan, which offers various financial services worldwide, uses analytics tools to integrate transaction data with information from other sources to gain deeper insights and accurately assess clients' creditworthiness. The company uses big data analytics to gain insights into market trends and make informed investment decisions. It utilizes predictive analytics to help its customers manage their working capital and cash forecasting needs. It also uses big data technologies to detect patterns in client behavior, helping identify potential revenue opportunities and market risks.

- *Wells Fargo and Company*: This US-based financial services company offers retail, wholesale banking, and wealth management services to individuals, businesses, and institutions. It turned to big data to improve business operations and customer service. It has enhanced customer experience and boosted revenue creation by improving risk management, customization, and segmentation. The bank has embraced big data analytics to optimize business operations, make data-driven decisions, and provide better client services.

- *American Express*: American Express is an American financial services company that offers credit, charge cards, and insurance services to individuals and businesses. The firm operates in more than 110 countries across the globe. The company utilizes big data in finance to enhance its fraud detection and prevention capabilities. By processing big data, it comprehensively views the cardholder's spending behavior.

- *Morgan Stanley*: Morgan Stanley, an American multinational investment and wealth management bank, utilizes big data technology to optimize its portfolio analysis, improve its financial operations, and offer better services to its clients. The banking stalwart collects massive amounts of data from various sources, including customer data, market data, economic data, news articles, social media posts, and others. Utilizing big data, they extract insights, trends, and hidden patterns to help financial advisors and clients make the right investment decisions to achieve their financial goals.

2.5 APPLICATIONS OF BIG DATA IN FINANCE

Big data applications help with gaining insights, measuring processes, managing costs, and elevating customer service. Big data and its applications work as indicators of organizations' ability to innovate to respond to market opportunities. Such applications include financial markets, banking risk and lending, Internet finance, financial management, financial growth, financial analysis, predictive analysis, data mining and fraud detection, and risk management. Figure 2.4 shows various use cases of big data in finance [17]. From risk management to regulatory compliance, the applications of big data analytics in financial services are numerous. Below are some of the common applications [17-20]:

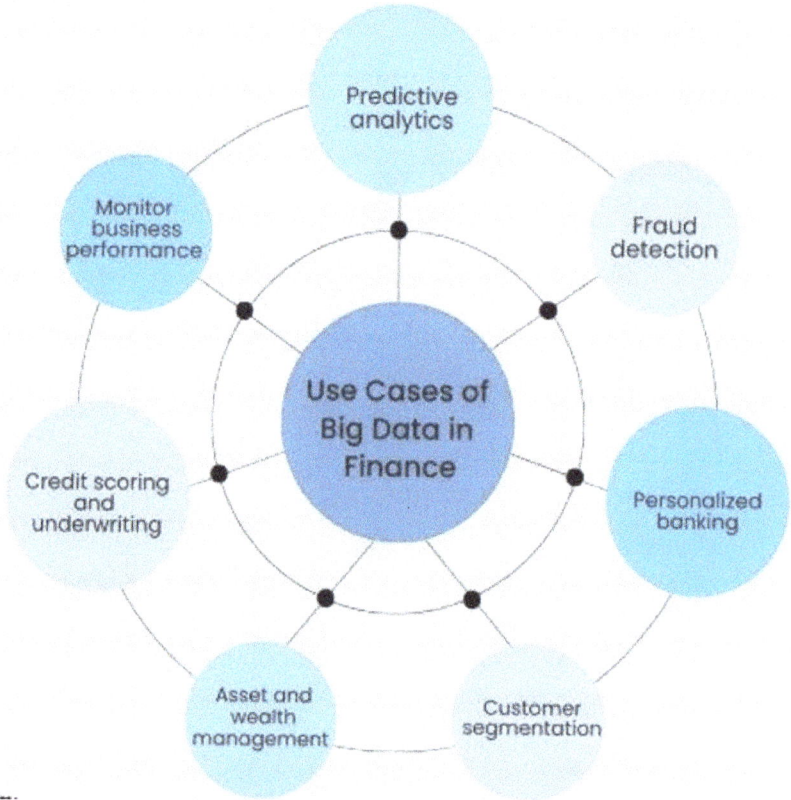

Figure 2.4 Use cases of big data in finance [17].

- *Banking Industry*: The banking industry has significantly transformed from traditional brick-and-mortar establishments to modern data-driven financial institutions. This shift has been propelled by the advent of big data technologies that enable banks to analyze vast amounts of data for better decision-making. With the help of big data analytics, banks will find it easier to expand into new markets. For example, the Oversea-Chinese Banking Corporation (OCBC) analyzed huge amounts of historical customer data to determine individual customer preferences to design an event-based marketing strategy. Big data becomes increasingly crucial in any area of the banking industry. Figure 2.5 shows big data in banking [21].

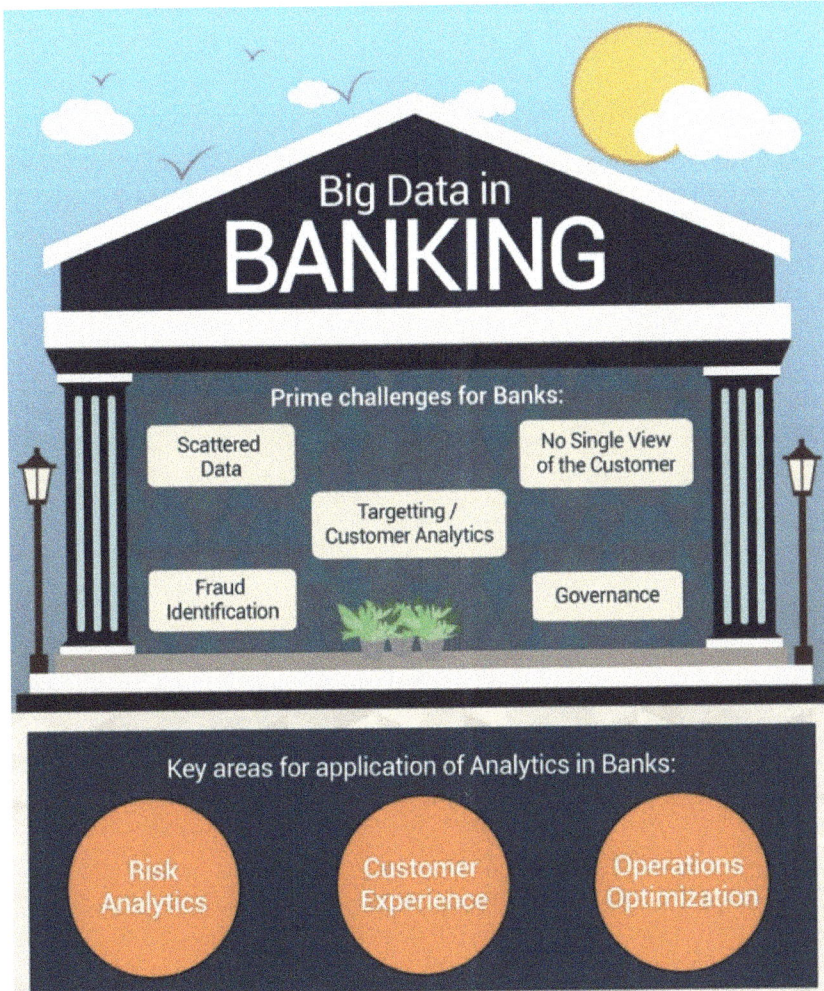

Figure 2.5 Big data in banking [21].

- *Open Banking*: The concept of open banking, which allows third-party developers to create applications and services around a financial institution, is gaining traction. Big data will be at the core of this ecosystem, enabling more seamless and integrated services for customers.

- *Personalized Banking*: In a competitive market, providing a high-quality user experience is critical. There is a need to know who your clients are and, in some cases, to anticipate their wants. As a result, financial institutions are shifting from a business-centric to a customer-centric business strategy. Offering personalized banking is critical for financial institutions as it improves customer satisfaction and loyalty by tailoring financial services to individual needs and preferences. This allows banks to offer tailored lending solutions, insurance policies, and investment options that align with their customers' requirements and risk tolerance.

- *Fintech*: The word "fintech," stands for "financial technology," and refers to the application of various forms of technology to enhance and automate financial services. This can cover a wide variety of applications, ranging from investment management and insurance to mobile banking and digital payments. Big data's application in financial technology (fintech) has increased dramatically over the past several years, and it is anticipated to keep growing in significance. Big data is essential to fintech because it allows businesses to instantly evaluate vast amounts of financial data. As a result, they may spot patterns and trends that help them make smarter judgments, like figuring out which clients are most likely to default on loans or spotting fraud. Fintech businesses can spot possible hazards and take action to reduce them by analyzing vast amounts of data on market trends and client behavior. The use of big data in financial technology is shown in Figure 2.6 [22].

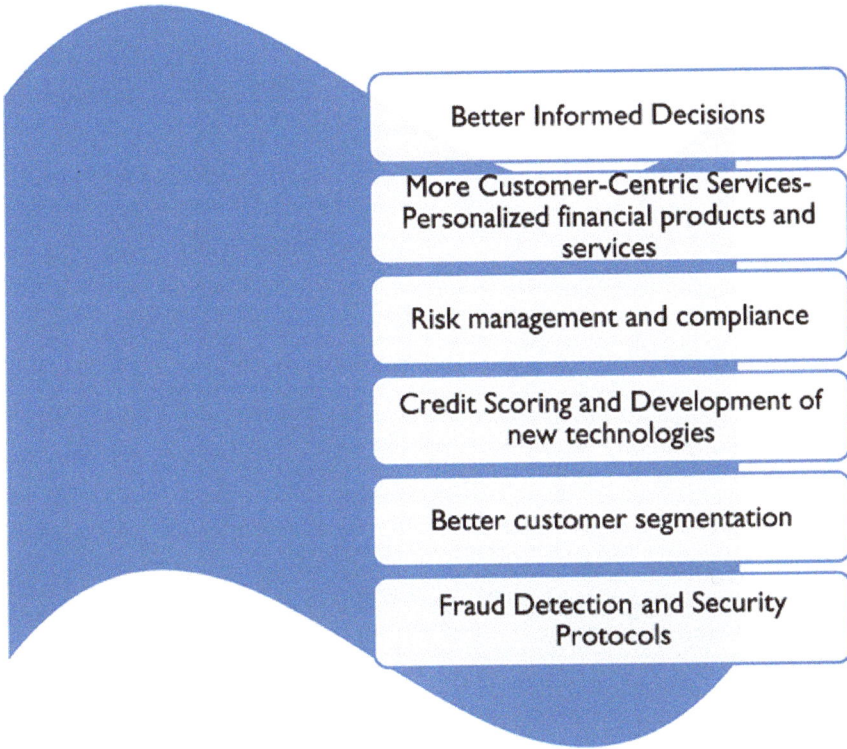

Figure 2.6 The use of big data in financial technology [22].

- *Accounting*: Big data in finance describes the enormous volume of data (structured, unstructured, and semi-structured data) that financial institutions produce daily. Businesses use this data for accounting, finance, and auditing needs. As a result, businesses have increased efficiency and performance to get the best possible results in their operational activities by utilizing data in the audit and accounting departments.

- *Fraud Detection*: One of the most pressing issues in banking is fraud detection and prevention. Big data can be used to detect and prevent fraudulent activities by analyzing transaction patterns, identifying unusual behavior, and flagging potential risks. Big data analytics can monitor customer spending patterns and identify unusual behavior, thereby preventing unauthorized transactions. Big data and statistical computing empower banks to detect potential fraud before it even occurs. Specialized algorithms track and analyze spending and behavioral patterns, allowing banks to identify individuals who may be at risk of committing fraud. When credit card information that is both secure and valuable is stolen, banks can now immediately freeze the card and the transaction, as well as warn the consumer of the security danger. TD Bank has implemented up-to-date security standards to protect its systems and users' information against unauthorized access. By analyzing transactions and behavioral data, the system can flag potential fraud immediately, allowing TD to take immediate action to prevent financial losses.

- *Predictive Analysis*: Another massive benefit that big data tools have to offer is predictive analysis. Techniques like predictive analytics, machine learning, and artificial intelligence are used to forecast market trends, detect fraud, and personalize customer services. One of the key advantages of big data for banking is the ability to predict future trends before they occur. Using a non-biased equation to spot trends in numbers is a fool-proof way to estimate future earnings and losses. Big data analytics presents an exciting opportunity to improve predictive modeling to better estimate the rates of return and outcomes on investments. Businesses today leverage big data in finance for predictive analysis since it uses historical and real-time data to forecast future trends, risks, and opportunities. This predictive analysis helps lenders decide when to approve or deny their loan applications. Moreover, financial analysts can use big data to predict market trends and make investment decisions. Predictive risk models can anticipate potential financial crises or market downturns.

- *Customer Segmentation*: Big data in financial services can be used to identify different types of customers based on their spending habits and other demographic information. Segmenting customers based on their behavior and preferences allows financial institutions to proactively address the needs of different customer groups, helping them retain customers and reducing churn rate. Big data analytics is pivotal in segmenting customers based on their financial behavior and preferences.

Big data can help businesses distinguish customers in different groups.

- *Asset Management*: Big data analytics offers a wealth of benefits to financial institutions in asset and wealth management. It enhances decision-making by providing insights into market trends and customer behavior while bolstering risk management through predictive analysis. The ability to analyze individual client data enables the provision of personalized services and investment advice.

- *Risk Management*: Big data improves risk management capabilities by providing organizations with the tools they need to identify, assess, and mitigate the risks. Big data techniques help to measure credit banking risk in home equity loans. Financial organizations use big data to mitigate operational risk and combat fraud while achieving regulatory and compliance objectives. With access to large amounts of historical market data, banks and other financial institutions can better assess risk associated with investments or loans by using predictive analytics models. This allows them to make more informed decisions about how many resources they should allocate toward certain assets or businesses.

- *Financial Inclusion*: Financial inclusion is a complex notion that encompasses the objective of guaranteeing universal access to a diverse array of inexpensive and suitable financial services and products offered by established financial institutions, for both individuals and enterprises. Financial inclusion encompasses a diverse array of initiatives, such as the provision of fundamental banking services including savings accounts and checking accounts, as exemplified by basic banking services. In the rapidly evolving landscape of financial technology (fintech), big data stands as a cornerstone, driving significant transformations. Big data has the potential to bring about financial inclusion by helping banks understand the needs of underserved communities. Tailored financial products can be developed to cater to these identified requirements, thereby promoting economic equality. Big data catalyzes the development of novel financial products and services, enhances risk management, and boosts operational efficiency, thereby fostering financial inclusion. Big data's capability to offer insightful customer behavior analytics is highlighted as a key driver for creating inclusive financial services.

2.6 BENEFITS

The investment management company uses big data in finance to analyze vast amounts of financial data, economic indicators, and market trends. By leveraging large datasets, companies can gain valuable insights into customer behavior and preferences, optimize their operations, reduce costs, and improve customer experience. Big data is completely revolutionizing how the stock markets worldwide are functioning and how investors are making their investment decisions. Other benefits include the following [18]:

- *Automation*: Automating tasks increases productivity and makes the work of financial services analysts, managers, and associates easier. You may manage every financial process with greater speed, performance, and value with the help of automation. Big data technologies can automate up to 30% of all work within banks, leading to significant cost savings and reduced risk of human error. Big data boosts operational efficiency by automating data analysis processes, leading to cost reductions and improved service delivery. As a result of advanced automation, banks can experience significant cost savings and reduce the risk of failure by eliminating the human factor from some critical processes. JP Morgan Chase & Co. is one of the automation pioneers in the banking services industry. It has significantly decreased the human error associated with loan-servicing.

- *Cost Reduction*: Big data can automate several manual tasks, such as compliance checks, fraud detection, and risk management. Businesses can also use big data analytics to improve efficiency in various areas, such as customer service, risk management, and marketing. Big data can also help businesses reduce costs.

- *Customer Profiling*: Big data plays a crucial role in customer profiling within banking institutions. Banks can offer individualized plans and financial solutions by analyzing a customer's banking history and personal and transactional information, and monitoring customer spending patterns over time. Big data enables financial institutions to personalize customer experiences by analyzing customer data, such as their financial history, preferences, and behavior. This enhances the customer experience and enables banks to differentiate their services, increasing customer retention.

- *Enhanced Customer Experience*: Customer satisfaction is at the forefront of everyone's minds in this current financial climate. Big data in banking and financial services is pivotal to improving the level of client satisfaction. Customer preferences and needs are changing fast in this age of digital transformation. Big data is crucial in improving user experience by providing insights that enable businesses to understand their customers better, engage with them, and meet their needs. Big data technologies enable banks to understand their customers on a granular level. Banks can offer personalized banking solutions by analyzing various customer data points like investment habits, shopping behaviors, and financial backgrounds.

- *Scalability*: Scalability is a feature of data integration solutions that allows them to grow as business needs change. Big data solutions must be able to scale up or down depending on the needs of the financial services organization. Solutions should be able to handle large amounts of data and complex calculations quickly and efficiently, while also being flexible enough to accommodate changing business requirements.

- *Social Responsibility*: Big data will play a major role in helping banks become more socially responsible. Analytics can help financial institutions understand their investments' environmental and social impact, leading to more sustainable business practices.

- *Improved Decision-making*: The success of every business in the financial space hinges on the ability to make decisions that increase the company's business while shielding it from risk. Big data in finance can significantly improve decision-making by providing valuable insights into market trends and customer behavior, allowing them to predict future outcomes. Big data analytics in financial services provides access to vast amounts of information that can be used to make more informed decisions. This helps businesses improve risk management processes as well as product development strategies.

- *Competitive Advantage*: The implementation of big data analytics is key to maintaining a competitive edge in the financial sphere. Big data is a key driver for gaining a competitive edge in the financial industry, enabling institutions to better understand markets, minimize risks, and deliver value to their customers, improving client satisfaction and long-term loyalty. Taking advantage of the vast amounts of data available from different sources, financial companies can keep their competitive edge, make stronger, data-driven decisions, and increase the efficiency of business operations. Big data analytics allows financial institutions to make data-driven decisions, giving them a competitive edge. Companies can gain insights into market trends, customer behavior, and risk factors by analyzing vast amounts of data.

- *Operational Efficiency*: Big data in financial services enhances operational efficiency and reduces costs by process automation. Big data in financial services can automate such processes as loan approvals, customer onboarding, and compliance checks. Big data analytics tools can identify unprofitable branches and initiatives, helping financial enterprises boost efficiency. In addition, big data analytics solutions can automate processes such as fraud detection, credit scoring, customer segmentation, and feedback analysis, speeding up operations and saving resources. Automation reduces human error, speeds up workflows, and cuts operational costs. This also improves customer satisfaction as customers are offered a better, smoother experience.

- *Regulatory Compliance*: Regulatory compliance is a critical aspect of businesses, especially in finance. Fraud undoubtedly costs the industry a lot of losses, but failure to comply with regulations creates a potential for even greater liabilities in the form of hefty fines from governing authorities. Big data analytics and business intelligence (BI) tools significantly streamline the process of regulatory compliance. It can help financial institutions comply with complex regulations by monitoring transactions, identifying potential risks, and reporting data to regulatory agencies. This includes complying with anti-money laundering regulations, KYC (Know Your Customer) requirements, and other regulatory obligations.

- *Cybersecurity*: AI and big data technologies are instrumental in identifying fraud and preventing internal risks. Banks are leveraging big data analytics and AI tools to bolster their cybersecurity measures in the face of increasing cyber threats. These tools can track customer behavior and internal activities, helping to identify potential security risks.

Figure 2.7 shows some of these benefits [17].

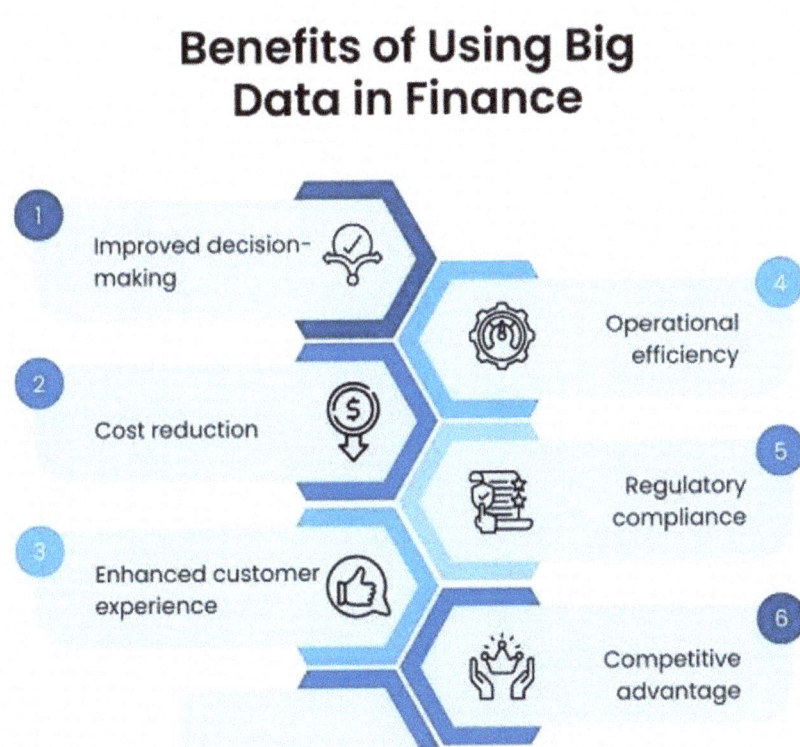

Figure 2.7 Some benefits of big data in finance [17].

2.7 CHALLENGES

While big data offers many benefits to the banking sector, it also presents its own challenges and concerns. Addressing ethical concerns related to data bias, algorithmic fairness, and data misuse is important. Other challenges include the following [18]:

- *Privacy Concerns*: One of the major challenges with big data is privacy concerns. In many places, banks are the second-biggest hoarders of personal information after the government. Financial services companies are required to protect customer information from unauthorized access or misuse. Big data in fintech requires large amounts of personal information which can be vulnerable if not properly secured.

- *Ethical Concerns*: Using big data analytics to profile banks' target customers raises ethical questions about discrimination and fairness. Banks need to be cautious to ensure that their use of data does not result in unfair or biased outcomes.

- *Data Security*: The financial industry is a prime target for cyberattacks. The more extensive the data, the higher the risk of cybersecurity threats. Protecting sensitive customer information remains a significant concern, especially when banks collect and apply users' data. The financial service industry must invest heavily in robust cybersecurity measures to mitigate these risks.

- *Data Quality*: Ensuring data quality and integrity is crucial for accurate financial analysis. Poor data quality can lead to incorrect analysis, which in turn can result in flawed decision-making. With the sheer volume and variety of data, financial institutions may face challenges related to data completeness, accuracy, and consistency. Ensuring the data's quality, management, and integrity is a constant challenge. Data cleansing techniques, such as data validation and data normalization, are essential to remove duplicates, errors, and inconsistencies.

- *Data Silos*: The inability to connect data across department and organizational silos is now considered a major business intelligence challenge, leading to complicated analytics and standing in the way of big data initiatives. Financial institutions have large volumes of data scattered across various systems. This creates data silos, which can prevent comprehensive analysis. Addressing this issue requires a multilayered approach that includes creating centralized data repositories, standardizing data formats, and establishing data governance frameworks.

- *Complexity*: The data's complexity is a significant challenge. Data is collected through various activities with distinct goals, which is the cause of these errors and difficulties. Specifying how filters should be applied is vital so that no crucial information is lost. There are billions of pieces of data being produced from diverse sources; missing data is a major concern, and data quality and dependability are also important issues.

- *Anomaly Detection*: Big data analytics enables financial institutions to identify anomalies and unusual patterns in transaction data. By analyzing historical transaction records, banks can build models that highlight deviations from normal behavior. These models can flag suspicious activities, such as unusually large transactions, multiple transactions from different locations, or transactions outside the customer's usual spending patterns.

- *Regulatory Compliance*: Financial institutions must comply with data privacy laws and regulations, and managing big data while complying with these regulations can be challenging. Banks must adhere to various data storage, usage, and sharing regulations. Compliance becomes increasingly complex with the growing volume of data being processed, and non-compliance can result in severe penalties.

- *High Implementation Costs*: Implementing big data technologies requires substantial hardware, software, and skilled personnel investment. Smaller financial institutions may find these costs prohibitive, thereby creating a competitive disadvantage.

- *Skill Gap*: Another challenge associated with big data is the lack of skilled personnel who understand how to effectively utilize it within the financial services industry. Finding and retaining skilled data scientists and analysts is a significant challenge.

The specialized skills required for big data analytics are in high demand, but they also require more supply. The demand for skilled professionals can slow the implementation process and affect the quality of insights derived from the existing data.

- *Customer Trust*: Customers are increasingly concerned about how their data is used. Transparency in data usage policies is essential to maintain customer trust, but achieving this transparency can be very challenging.

2.8 CONCLUSION

Big data is no longer a nice-to-have but a must-have for financial institutions aiming to stay competitive in today's data-driven world. It has completely transformed the fintech industry. Banks and other financial institutions are using big data to improve their operational performance, make better decisions, and provide more personalized services to their customers. Big data is playing an increasingly important role in the financial services industry. It is completely revolutionizing how stock markets across the world are functioning and how investors are making their investment decisions.

The maximum potential of big data in banking and finance is yet to be harnessed. The future of big data in the finance sector appears promising, with numerous opportunities for innovation and improvement. It will be shaped by the ability of financial institutions to extract and deliver more customer value from data. As big data technology develops, financial institutions can build innovative products and services that will cater to the evolving needs of consumers and investors. More information about big data in the financial services can be found in the books in [23-26] and the following related journals:

- *Journal of Big Data*
- *International Journal of Logistics Research and Applications.*

REFERENCES

[1] D. Chen, "Big data use cases: How to use big data for financial services," May 2022,
https://inrix.com/blog/big-data-use-cases-finance/

[2] M. N. O. Sadiku, P. A. Adekunte, and J. O. Sadiku, "Big data in finance," *International Journal of Trend in Scientific Research and Development*, vol. 9, no. 2, March-April 2025, pp. 1385-1397.

[3] M. N. O. Sadiku, M. Tembely, and S.M. Musa, "Big data: An introduction for engineers," *Journal of Scientific and Engineering Research*, vol. 3, no. 2, 2016, pp. 106-108.

[4] A. Slamecka, "Big data explosion," April 2022, https://blogs.cisco.com/financialservices/big-data-explosion

[5] "The complete overview of big data," https://intellipaat.com/blog/tutorial/hadoop-tutorial/big-data-overview/

[6] R. Allen, "Types of big data | Understanding & Interacting with key types (2024)," https://investguiding-com.custommapposter.com/article/types-of-big-data-understanding-amp-interacting-with-key-types

[7] J. Moorthy et al., "Big data: Prospects and challenges," *The Journal for Decision Makers*, vol. 40, no. 1, 2015, pp. 74–92. https://www.grandviewresearch.com/industry-analysis/industrial-wireless-sensor-networks-iwsn-market

[8] A. K. Tiwari, H. Chaudhary, and S. Yadav, "A review on big data and its security," *Proceedings of IEEE Sponsored 2nd International Conference on Innovations in Information Embedded and Communication Systems*, 2015.

[9] M. B. Hoy, "Big data: An introduction for librarians," *Medical Reference Services Quarterly*, vol. 33, no 3. 2014, pp. 320-322.

[10] M. Viceconti, P. Hunter, and R. Hose, "Big data, big knowledge: Big data for personalized healthcare," *IEEE Journal of Medical and Health Informatics*, vol. 19, no. 4, July 2015, pp. 1209-1215.

[11] P. Baumann et al., "Big data analytics for earth sciences: The earthserver approach," *International Journal of Digital Earth*, vol. 19, no. 1, 2016, pp.3-29.

[12] X. Wu et al., "Knowledge engineering with big data," *IEEE Intelligent Systems*, September/October 2015, pp.46-55.

[13] "Big data in finance," https://corporatefinanceinstitute.com/resources/data-science/big-data-in-finance/#:~:text=Time%204%20minutes-,What%20is%20Big%20

Data%20in%20Finance?,organizations%2C%20and%20the%20
entire%20industry.

[14] A. Jayachandran, "Big data in finance," June 2023,
https://www.wallstreetmojo.com/big-data-in-finance/

[15] "Big data in financial services," Unknown Source. p.139

[16] "Harnessing the power of big data in financial analysis," April
2025,
https://fastercapital.com/content/Harnessing-the-Power-of-Big-Data-
in-Financial-Analysis.html#Enhancing-Customer-Insights-with-Big-
Data-Analytics\

[17] S. Dutta, "Big data in finance: Benefits, use cases, & examples,"
September 2023,
https://www.turing.com/resources/big-data-in-finance

[18] V. Zubenko, "How big data changes the scope of modern
banking," September 2023,
https://www.avenga.com/magazine/how-big-data-changes-banking/

[19] "Big data for financial services: Benefits, challenges, and use
cases," February 2023,
https://www.n-ix.com/big-data-for-financial-
services/#:~:text=What%20is%20Big%20Data%20
and,strategies%2C%20and%20customer%20service%20initiatives.

[20] M. Hasan, J. Popp, and J. Oláh, "Current landscape and
influence of big data on finance," *Journal of Big Data*, vol. 7, 2020.

[21] "How big data is redefining the banking and financial industry,"
March 2017,
https://tgdaily.com/technology/how-big-data-is-redefining-the-
banking-and-financial-industry/

[22] D. Mhlanga, "The role of big data in financial technology toward
financial inclusion," *Front. Big Data*, vol. 7. May 2024.

[23] M. N. O. Sadiku, U. C. Chukwu, and P. O. Adebo, *Big Data
and Its Applications*. Moldova, Europe: Lambert Academic Publishing,
2024.

[24] B. Alareneni (ed.), *Big Data in Finance: Transforming the
Financial Landscape (Volume 1)*. Springer, 2025.

[25] I. Aldridge and M. Avellaneda, *Big Data Science in Finance*.
Wiley, 2021.

[26] T. Guida, *Big Data and Machine Learning in Quantitative
Investment*. Wiley, 2019.

CHAPTER 3

~~~
∞
~~~

BIG DATA IN ARCHITECTURE

"Time and the world do not stand still. Change is the law of life. And those who look only to the past or present are certain to miss the future." – John F. Kennedy

3.1 INTRODUCTION

Big data has been a buzzword in recent years. The increasing amount of data raises both the opportunities and the challenges of managing it. Figure 3.1 shows Google's data center in Mayes County, Oklahoma, USA, where data is stored [1]. When properly analyzed, big data can reveal patterns, trends, and relationships related to human behavior and interaction in the built environment. Today's organizations depend on data and insights to make most of their decisions.

Figure 3.1 Google's data center [1].

Big data in architecture refers to the application of big data technologies and techniques within the field of architecture, where large volumes of data from building sensors, user interactions, and environmental factors are collected and analyzed to optimize building design, performance, and operations. It also refers to the extensive datasets collected from various technologies, such as IoT sensors, social media, and satellite imaging, which provide valuable insights into design practices and urban planning. In the architecture industry, big data can be utilized to analyze vast amounts of information like building usage patterns, environmental data, construction costs, and design trends, allowing architects to make data-driven decisions for more efficient, sustainable, and user-centric building designs.

Big data is a broad term for the collection of both structured and unstructured data. Data is one of the biggest byproducts of the 21st century. Almost everything we do produces data, from swiping credit cards to emailing. Our production of data is exploding. Increasingly, the value of a business is tied to its ability to mine data. In the field of architecture, data is having a similar impact. In the modern era of architecture, big data plays a crucial role in transforming design processes. Big data and architecture are a combination worth exploring in depth [2].

This chapter examines the role of big data in architecture. It begins with explaining what big data is all about. It explains big data in architecture and provides some of its applications. It highlights the benefits and challenges of big data in architecture. The last section concludes with comments.

3.2 WHAT IS BIG DATA?

Big data applies to data sets of extreme size (e.g. exabytes, zettabytes) which are beyond the capability of the commonly used software tools. It involves situation where very large data sets are big in volume, velocity, veracity, and variability [3]. The data is too big, too fast, or does not fit the regular database architecture. It may require different strategies and tools for profiling, measurement, assessment, and processing.

Big Data is essentially classified into three types [4]:

- *Structured Data*: This is highly organized and is the easiest to work with. Any data that can be stored, accessed, and processed in the form of fixed format is known as a structured data. It may be stored in tabular format. Due to their nature, it is easy for programs to sort through and collect data. Structured data has quantitative data such as age, contact, address, billing, expenses, credit card numbers, etc. Data that is stored in a relational database management system is an example of structured data.

- *Unstructured Data*: This refers to unorganized data such as video files, log files, audio files, and image files. Any data with unknown form or the structure is classified as unstructured data. Almost everything generated by a computer is unstructured data. It takes a lot of time and effort required to make unstructured data readable. Examples of unstructured data include Metadata, Twitter tweets, and other social media posts.

- *Semi-structured Data*: This falls somewhere between structured data and unstructured data, i.e., both forms of data are present. Semi-structured data can be inherited such as location, time, email address, or device ID stamp.

The different types of big data are depicted in Figure 3.2 [5]. Structured and unstructured data are generated in various types [6-9].

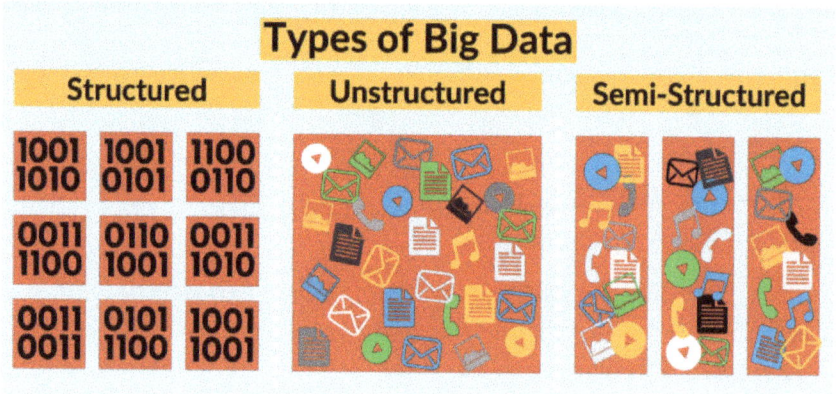

Figure 3.2 Types of big data [5].

The process of examining big data is often referred to big data analytics. It is an emerging field since massive computing capabilities have been made available by e-infrastructures [6]. Big data analytics is the application of advanced analytic techniques to large, heterogeneous data sets that comprise structured, semi-structured, and unstructured data from many sources with sizes ranging from terabytes to zettabytes.

Analytics include statistical models and other methods that are aimed at creating empirical predictions. Data-driven organizations use analytics to guide decisions at all levels. Several techniques have been proposed for analyzing big data. These include the HACE theorem, cloud computing, Hadoop, and MapReduce [10].

3.3 BIG DATA IN ARCHITECTURE

Big data in architecture and design leverages vast datasets to enhance and personalize user experiences, optimize product functionalities, and streamline design processes through data-driven insights. An increasing number of gadgets in the built environment, such as thermostats and refrigerators, are bolstering the Internet of things and relaying the data that they gather. Data has even manifested a physical presence. In New York, a new type of architecture is emerging in which large skyscrapers are being retrofitted into digital warehouses that accommodate computers rather than people. An example is 375 Pearl Street in New York, shown in Figure 3.3 [1]. Similar buildings are popping up across the United States for the purpose of storing and analyzing data.

Figure 3.3 A building in New York for storing and analyzing data [1].

When architects embark on a project, they gather data from a variety of sources, most often directly from the client. They determine which data points will help them create buildings that will have the greatest impact on their end users. They also tailor data analysis to every new project. Architects must gather as much data as possible in the early stages of the design process, because even small details can impact the efficiency of an entire building.

Data sources for big data in architecture include data on HVAC systems, lighting, and other building systems such as connected devices like smart meters and wearable technology. It also includes environmental sensors that monitor air quality, temperature, humidity, and other environmental parameters. Key aspects of big data in architecture:

Data collection: Sensors embedded in buildings gather data on energy consumption, temperature, humidity, occupancy levels, lighting conditions, and more. Data collection is now part of our daily lives, from the temperature set on our thermostat to the time we walk down the sidewalk.

Data analysis: Advanced analytics tools are used to process and interpret the collected data, identifying patterns and trends to inform design decisions.

Data integration: Combining data from various sources (sensors, building management systems, weather data) can be complex.

Data is changing architecture in the following three ways [1]:

1.*Clients are demanding data from architects*: Clients are starting to ask architects to deliver more than just drawing sets. They are eyeing the data-rich BIM models that companies use to document projects as a way to supply data for downstream applications, such as facilities management. For architects, this means that their data needs to be as rigorous as their drawings.

2. *Clients are demanding data from buildings*: Clients have also become interested in the data generated by the buildings. This data enables building owners to measure and improve their facilities' performance quantitatively. Architects also need to recognize that clients are going to use this data to measure their own performance. Performance-based contracts, where a portion of an architect's fee is withheld until post-occupancy data validates its prescribed design performance, are gaining popularity.

3. *Data is changing the process as much as it is changes the output*: The abundance of data may give rise to data warehouses, but the much more profound changes for architects will be procedural. If architects are to harness data from the built environment, even more significant procedural changes may be coming.

3.4 APPLICATIONS OF BIG DATA IN ARCHITECTURE

In architecture, big data applications can be used for various purposes including facility performance monitoring, predictive maintenance, energy optimization, space utilization analysis, design optimization through data-driven insights, construction project management, and even urban planning. Common applications of big data in architecture include the following [11]:

- *Building Performance Monitoring* (BPM): Sensors deployed throughout a building collect data on energy consumption, temperature, humidity, CO2 levels, and occupancy patterns, which can be analyzed to identify areas for improvement and optimize energy usage. This involves analyzing energy usage data to identify areas for improvement, optimizing HVAC systems, and adjusting lighting based on occupancy. It may monitor energy usage, indoor air quality, and occupant comfort levels in real-time to identify areas for improvement. Real-time data can be used to optimize building performance while studying occupants can be useful for user-centered design.

- *Predictive Maintenance*: By analyzing sensor data from building systems, potential failures can be predicted before they occur, allowing for proactive maintenance and preventing costly breakdowns. This may entail identifying potential issues in building systems before they occur, preventing costly breakdowns.

- *Space Utilization Analysis*: Data from occupancy sensors and building management systems can be used to understand how spaces are being used, leading to improved space planning and allocation.

- *Design Optimization*: Analyzing large datasets on climate patterns, building materials, and user behavior can inform design decisions to create more sustainable and user-friendly buildings. This may also involve analyzing user behavior to optimize building layout, lighting, and ventilation for occupant comfort. It may identify potential delays and optimize construction schedules using data from past projects.

- *City Planning*: Cities use big data to improve urban planning and urban development. Analyzing demographic data, traffic patterns, and environmental factors can help urban planners design more sustainable and resilient cities. This data-driven approach to urban planning can guide decision-making processes not only for architects and urban planners but also for city officials to create policies for more livable cities. New York City, for example, developed an initiative known as NYC Open Data, a public platform that provides over 1,300 datasets from housing and construction, education, health, and safety, to transportation. Figure 3.4 shows Manhattan in New York [11]. Another example is MX3D Bridge, a smart 3D-printed bridge in the City of Amsterdam to analyze pedestrian and crowd behavior. The smart bridge uses a sensor network to collect data from its users. The goal is to predict future behaviors to improve its 3D-printed manufacturing technique.

Figure 3.4 Manhattan in New York [11].

- *Smart City Design*: Heavily connected "smart cities" are becoming more prominent in society and are no longer the stuff of future-oriented dreams. Although some of them are built from scratch, other city officials bring in architects and similar professionals. Although smart cities rely on architects to design physical buildings, they also depend on data architects to develop big data-based infrastructures that coincide with the easily visible structures. Smart cities use big data for advertising purposes. They use data from traffic, pollution, and transport to optimize urban planning.

- *Synthesis Design*: Big data analytics was used to design an interior feature wall for the Watson Experience Center in San Francisco. They used data from the influence of mobile phones on monthly consumer spending to create a precise screen material that defines the wall. Figure 3.5 shows a synthetic wall design [12]. Without any explanation, the design gives little indication that it represents a massive data set.

Figure 3.5 A synthetic wall design [13].

3.5 BENEFITS

The application of big data in architecture brings numerous benefits that significantly influence the quality and efficiency of projects. In architecture, big data is used to improve design decisions, operational efficiency, and overall building performance. Integrating big data into architecture can lead to more informed, sustainable, and efficient design solutions. By collecting and analyzing data on past projects, construction companies can use predictive analytics to identify potential risks. Other benefits of big data in architecture include the following [11]:

- *Clash Detection*: With the help of big data, we can anticipate potential design problems before construction begins. For example, using building information modeling (BIM) it is now common practice to do collision detection to check all areas. This reduces costs for our clients and much less headaches for architects as there are fewer design changes during construction.

- *Energy Efficiency*: Another area where big data shines is improving energy efficiency. Using data sets of weather patterns, solar trajectories, wind direction, and strength, we can design better buildings that maximize natural light, ventilation, and heating for a more sustainable future.

- *Project Management*: Tracking progress on construction sites using sensors and data analytics can help identify potential delays, optimize resource allocation, and improve overall project efficiency.

- *Parametric Design*: Parametric design in architecture involves the use of parameter-based algorithms to design buildings that automatically adapt to changing variables, allowing for customizable and flexible structures.

- *Enhanced Decision-Making*: Data provides the foundation for evidence-based design decisions. Big data is transforming architectural design processes by enabling more informed decision-making through data-driven insights. It allows architects to analyze user behavior, environmental conditions, and urban trends, improving design accuracy and sustainability. The data-driven approach facilitates informed decision-making, reducing waste, and enhancing sustainability in architecture.

- *Anticipate the Future*: The architects of the past had to largely rely on guesswork when calculating things like population growth or the effects of climate change. Big data aids architects in understanding places and people, then incorporating the associated revelations into their designs. Datasets and modeling could help architects test the viability of design concepts before constructing them in real life.

- *Waste*: Waste is a major practical and political concern. It also becoming an increasingly public issue as news outlets publish pieces about pollution, plastics in the ocean, and whales killed by car parts. Figure 3.6 shows waste [13]. Recycling is viewed as the responsible way of dealing with waste. By embracing big data, however, businesses can streamline their disposal practices where it really matters. Data systems all play a role in moving the US towards being a zero waste system.

Figure 3.6 Waste [13].

- *Sustainable Design*: Utilizing data to design buildings that minimize environmental impact through energy efficiency and resource optimization. Big data informs sustainable architectural design by analyzing environmental impacts, optimizing resource use, and predicting energy efficiency. It allows architects to assess site conditions, climate, and material performance to create eco-friendly buildings.

3.6 CHALLENGES

Although big data has tremendous impact on industries, it is not without challenges. The challenges of integrating big data into architectural design include managing and analyzing large volumes of data, ensuring data privacy and security, the need for specialized skills and technology, and bridging the gap between data insights and creative design processes. Opting for a big-data enabled data analytics solution is not straightforward. It requires vast technology land space for components to ingest data from numerous sources. It is also essential to have proper synchronization between these components. Keeping up with varying use cases of big data is a significant challenge for many organizations. Other challenges in using big data in architecture include the following [13]:

- *Data Security*: Although big data can provide great insight for decision-making, protecting data from theft is challenging.

- *Data Privacy*: Data collected may contain personal information. It is necessary to ensure user data is protected when collecting information about building occupants.

- *Data Visualization*: Presenting complex data insights in a clear and understandable way for architects and building owners.

- *Data Integration*: Combining data from various sources can be complex.

- *Data Interpretation*: Another challenge is the interpretation and application of data. The architect are liable for making the final decision. Misinterpretation can lead to wrong decisions, leading to ineffective architectural solutions.

- *Data Storage*: Data volume remains a significant challenge because data volumes are doubling in size about every two years. Besides data size, the number of file formats used to store data is also growing. As a result, effectively storing and managing information is often a challenge for an organization.

- *Data Analytics*: Data analysis in architecture is a complicated process. Design teams must not only gather the most accurate data, but also analyze it and locate hidden patterns that predict how people will most efficiently use a building.

- *Data Quality*: Data quality aspects include accuracy, consistency, relevance, completeness, and use fitness. Data quality is a challenge anytime working with diverse data sources. Consequently, obtaining useful data requires a significant effort to clean the data before bringing it for analysis.

- *Learning New Data Tools*: Despite its transformative potential, it can be challenging for firms to incorporate big data into architecture due to the sheer volume and complexity of data. Architects often do not have the skill set required to understand complex data and algorithms. This means they have to constantly learn new tools to implement big data in our practice.

- *Scaling*: Big data solutions are used to handle large volumes of data. It can cause issues if the planned architecture is unable to scale. This may degrade the application performance and efficiency.

- *Complexity*: Big data systems can be challenging to implement since they must deal with various data types from various sources.

- *Collaboration*: This is essential during the design process, especially when architects and their clients gather data simultaneously. It is crucial to use data analysis tools that foster collaboration between all parties involved in the building's development.

- *Skillset*: Big data technologies are highly specialized, and they use frameworks and languages that are not common in more general application architectures. To operate these modern technologies and data tools, skilled data professionals are required. These will include data scientists, analysts, and engineers to operate tools and get data patterns. A shortage of data experts is one of the challenges that companies face.

- *Emerging Technologies*: Emerging technologies such as artificial intelligence, machine learning, and Internet of things are expected to play an increasingly important role in analyzing and interpreting big data. Architects need to learn about these technologies and harness the power of big data to become better designers of buildings and cities.

- *Cost*: This can also be a challenge when performing data analysis in architecture. Third-party data formatting can be a long, expensive process, depending on the scope of the project.

Some of these challenges are displayed in Figure 3.7 [14].

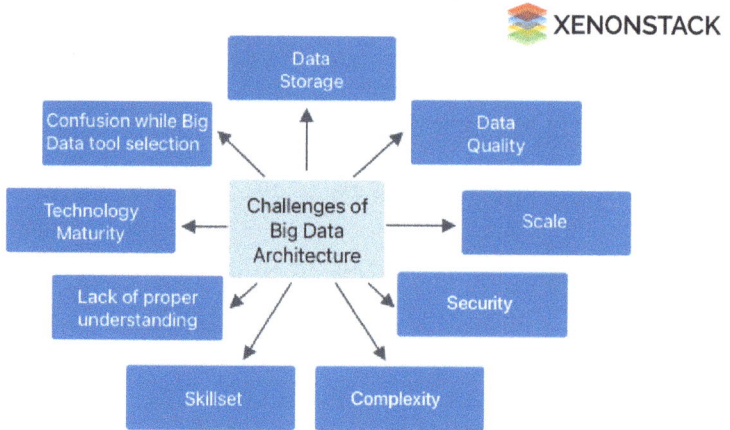

Figure 3.7 Some of the challenges of big data in architecture [14].

3.7 CONCLUSION

Data analytics in architecture is vital. Data analytics in architecture can be used to improve wayfinding at a facility. But in order to use data effectively, we must first understand what types of data to gather and how to analyze it properly. While integrating big data into architecture promises impressive benefits, it also brings unique challenges. Despite the challenges, big data is here to stay. Those who can harness big data will undoubtedly lead the charge toward more responsive and responsible built environments. More information about big data in the architecture industry can be found in the books in [15,16].

REFERENCES

[1] D. Davis, "How big data is transforming architecture," April 2015, https://www.architectmagazine.com/technology/how-big-data-is-transforming-architecture_o

[2] M. N. O. Sadiku, U. C. Chukwu, and J. O. Sadiku, "Big data in architecture," *Innovative Mult-disciplinary Journal of Applied Technology*, vol. 3, no. 1, 2025, pp.28-39.

[3] M. N. O. Sadiku, M. Tembely, and S.M. Musa, "Big data: An introduction for engineers," *Journal of Scientific and Engineering Research*, vol. 3, no. 2, 2016, pp. 106-103.

[4] "The complete overview of big data," https://intellipaat.com/blog/tutorial/hadoop-tutorial/big-data-overview/

[5] R. Allen, "Types of big data | Understanding & Interacting with key types (2024)," https://investguiding-com.commapposter.com/article/types-of-big-data-understanding-amp-interacting-with-key-types

[6] P. Baumann et al., "Big data analytics for earth sciences: The earthserver approach," *International Journal of Digital Earth*, vol. 19, no. 1, 2016, pp.3-29.

[7] A. K. Tiwari, H. Chaudhary, and S. Yadav, "A review on big data and its security," *Proceedings of IEEE Sponsored 2nd International Conference on Innovations in Information Embedded and Communication Systems*, 2015.

[8] M. B. Hoy, "Big data: An introduction for librarians," *Medical Reference Services Quarterly*, vol. 33, no 3. 2014, pp. 320-326.

[9] M. Viceconti, P. Hunter, and R. Hose, "Big data, big knowledge: Big data for personalized healthcare," *IEEE Journal of Medical and Health Informatics*, vol. 19, no. 4, July 2015, pp. 1209-1215.

[10] X. Wu et al., "Knowledge engineering with big data," *IEEE Intelligent Systems*, September/October 2015, pp.46-55.

[11] "The promises and pitfalls of big data in architecture," July 2024, https://slantis.com/blog/the-promises-and-pitfalls-of-big-data-in-architecture

[12] "Big data becomes architecture in this CNC-milled screen wall for IBM," April 2017, https://www.archdaily.com/870095/big-data-becomes-architecture-in-this-cnc-milled-screen-wall-for-ibm

[13] L. Alton, "Facing environmental crisis, data is reshaping waste management,"

https://www.smartdatacollective.com/facing-environmental-crisis-data-is-reshaping-waste-management/#google_vignette

[14] C. Gaur, "Top 9 challenges of big data architecture and its solutions | Overview," January 2023, https://www.xenonstack.com/insights/challenges-of-big-data-architecture

[15] M. N. O. Sadiku, U. C. Chukwu, and P. O. Adebo, *Big Data and Its Applications*. Moldova, Europe: Lambert Academic Publishing, 2024.

[16] S. M. F. Akhtar, *Big Data Architect's Handbook: A Guide to Building Proficiency in Tools and Systems Used by Leading Big Data Experts*. Packt Publishing, 2013.

CHAPTER 4

BIG DATA IN PHARMACEUTICALS

"The goal is to turn data into information, and information into insight."
– Carly Fiorina

4.1 INTRODUCTION

Advances in data science and digitalization are transforming the world, including the pharmaceutical industry. In this technology era, like every other industry, things are changing very fast in the pharma sector. We live in an age where there is too much information for one single person to analyze. Big data is a term for analyzing massive data sets. It refers to the massive and varied datasets generated by recording digital touchpoints everywhere. The use of big data has been on the rise in recent years because they offer a better way for companies to analyze customer needs and wants than ever before.

The pharma sector generates immense amounts of information. Clinical trial data, electronic health records, genomics information, real-world evidence, and patient-reported outcomes; all these data entries combined can be referred to as big data. Multiple sensor-equipped manufacturing processes and laboratory analysis are the main sources of primary data. Big data is voluminous and diverse information of any format and from any source that can be converted into insights via analytics. With the hope of the world pinned on the pharmaceutical industry more than ever before, big data analytics plays a crucial role in drug and vaccine development. Big data in the pharmaceutical industry have made positive changes throughout the years because they make the process of drug discovery more successful.

Big data is the datasets that are so large and complex that conventional methods and hardware for collecting, sharing, and analyzing them are impossible. The use of big data is a trend that results in amassing massive amounts of information and data from digital platforms and applications generated in a wide variety of industries such as healthcare, pharmaceuticals, business analytics, and advertising. By adopting big data, the pharma sector can drive improvements at each step of the drug development process. In pharmaceuticals, the importance of big data has boomed over the past decade due to the incorporation of high performing automation processes. Big data is changing the way drugs are developed [1].

This chapter provides an overview of recent developments in big data-related deals within the pharmaceutical industry. It begins with explaining what big data is all about. It presents some information on pharmaceutics. It describes some applications of big data in pharmaceutics. It highlights some benefits and challenges of big data in pharmaceutics. The last section concludes with comments.

4.2 WHAT IS BIG DATA?

Big data applies to data sets of extreme size (e.g. exabytes, zettabytes) which are beyond the capability of the commonly used software tools. It involves situation where very large data sets are big in volume, velocity, veracity, and variability [2]. The data is too big, too fast, or does not fit the regular database architecture. It may require different strategies and tools for profiling, measurement, assessment, and processing.

Big Data is essentially classified into three types [3]:

- *Structured Data*: This is highly organized and is the easiest to work with. Any data that can be stored, accessed, and processed in the form of fixed format is known as a structured data. It may be stored in tabular format. Due to their nature, it is easy for programs to sort through and collect data. Structured data has quantitative data such as age, contact, address, billing, expenses, credit card numbers, etc. Data that is stored in a relational database management system is an example of structured data.

- *Unstructured Data*: This refers to unorganized data such as video files, log files, audio files, and image files. Any data with unknown form or the structure is classified as unstructured data. Almost everything generated by a computer is unstructured data. It takes a lot of time and effort required to make unstructured data readable. Examples of unstructured data include Metadata, Twitter tweets, and other social media posts.

- *Semi-structured Data*: This falls somewhere between structured data and unstructured data, i.e., both forms of data are present. Semi-structured data can be inherited such as location, time, email address, or device ID stamp.

The different types of big data are depicted in Figure 4.1 [4]. Structured and unstructured data are generated in various types [5-7].

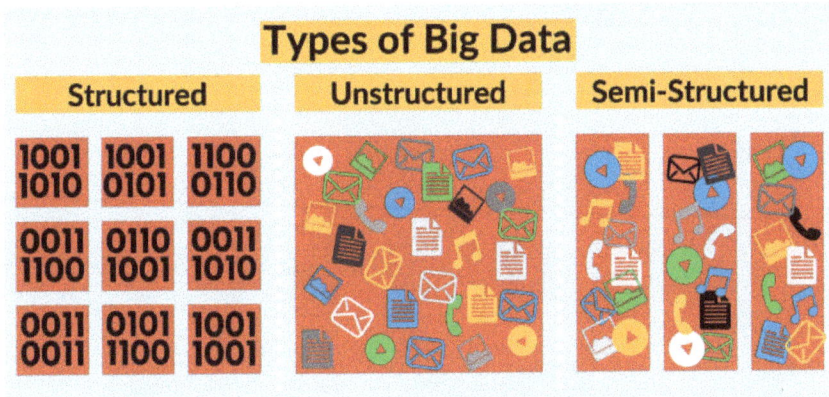

Figure 4.1 Types of big data [4].

The process of examining big data is often referred to big data analytics. It is an emerging field since massive computing capabilities have been made available by e-infrastructures [8]. Big data analytics is the application of advanced analytic techniques to large, heterogeneous data sets that comprise structured, semi-structured, and unstructured data from many sources with sizes ranging from terabytes to zettabytes.

Analytics include statistical models and other methods that are aimed at creating empirical predictions. Data-driven organizations use analytics to guide decisions at all levels. Several techniques have been proposed for analyzing big data. These include the HACE theorem, cloud computing, Hadoop, and MapReduce [9].

4.3 PHARMACEUTICALS

Medicines have evolved from crude herbal and botanical preparations into more complex manufacturing of sophisticated drug products and dosage forms. Figure 4.2 shows a typical drug [10]. The pharmaceutical industry is really complex, and this complexity has translated to the pharma needing better management of their data. Constantly growing, sheer amount of data generated by the pharma companies has also made data management and interpretation a daunting task. The largest pharmaceutical companies in North America are shown in Figure 4.3 [10].

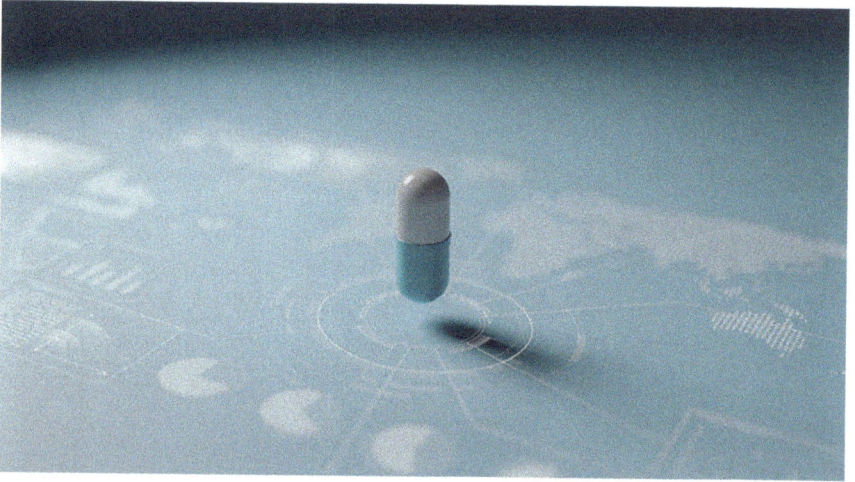

Figure 4.2 A typical drug [10].

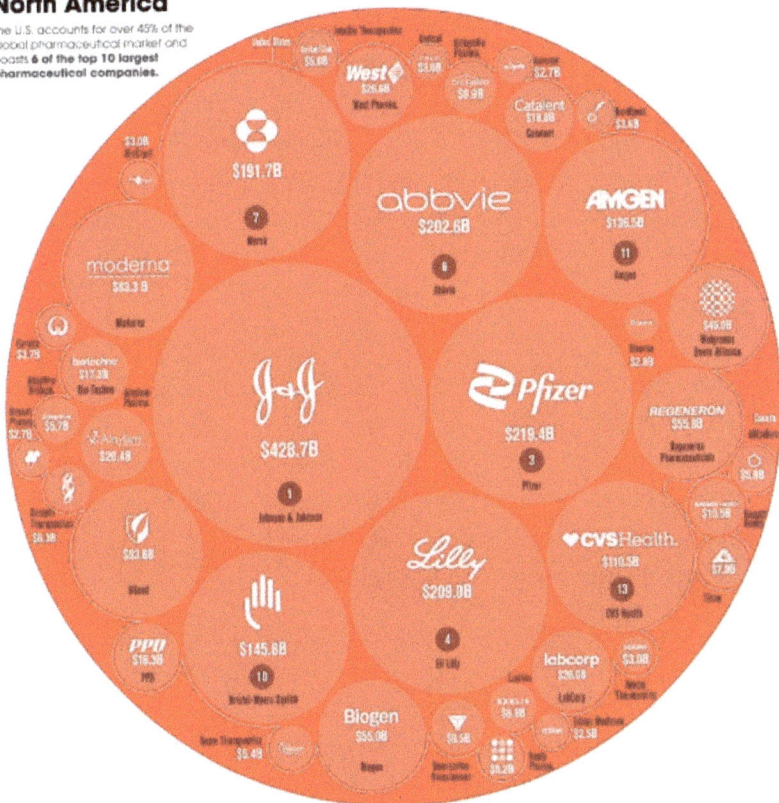

Figure 4.3 The largest pharmaceutical companies in North America [10].

The pharma sector has access to a lot of data: electronic health records, genomic information, real-world evidence, and more. The emergence of big data is providing pharmaceutical companies with an opportunity to gain novel insights that can enhance and accelerate drug development. Pharmaceutical companies are increasingly leveraging big data technologies to enhance innovation and operational efficiency. The proper application of big data to business problems requires employing data scientists who have a cross-disciplinary ability to translate domain-specific needs into analytical solutions.

Data can be unstructured, semi-structured, or structured, and each format has its place in the pharmaceutical industry. But real-world data comes in a variety of different formats, is often highly unstructured. Unstructured data includes physicians' notes, scans and images, and pathology reports. Unstructured data can also alert drug manufacturers about potential safety issues culled from social media posts and Google searches that report possible adverse reactions. Supervised learning can include methods such as ANN or multivariate regression and classification analysis, which learn from and connect input data and outcomes. Supervised learning methods are commonly associated with process design and controls. Semi-structured data is a hybrid of both the unstructured and structured data.

4.4 APPLICATIONS OF BIG DATA IN PHARMACEUTICALS

In recent years, the pharma industry has invested heavily in "data lake" style technologies. Real-world data is used extensively for crafting deterministic models to measure the incidences of adverse drug reactions in patients. Here, we want to analyze some decisive applications of big data in the pharmaceutical sector, with their advantages. Such applications include the following [12,13]:

- *Drug Development:* Drug development is a long and risky road. Very few drug candidates make it to the market. The process of drug development is lengthy and complex combined with several processes, applications, and approvals. At every step of the drug development process, pharmaceutical big data can come in handy. Drug discovery starts with researchers understanding the process behind a disease at a cellular or molecular level. With potential targets identified, the process follows by searching for compounds that can interact with the target and interfere with its activity. In drug discovery, gene expression is one of the most widely used molecular features that has been used to inform target selection. Traditionally, researchers used plant or animal compounds to test candidate drugs. With big data in the pharmaceutical industry, targets can also be directly discovered by analyzing public big data. Figure 4.4 illustrates drug development [14].

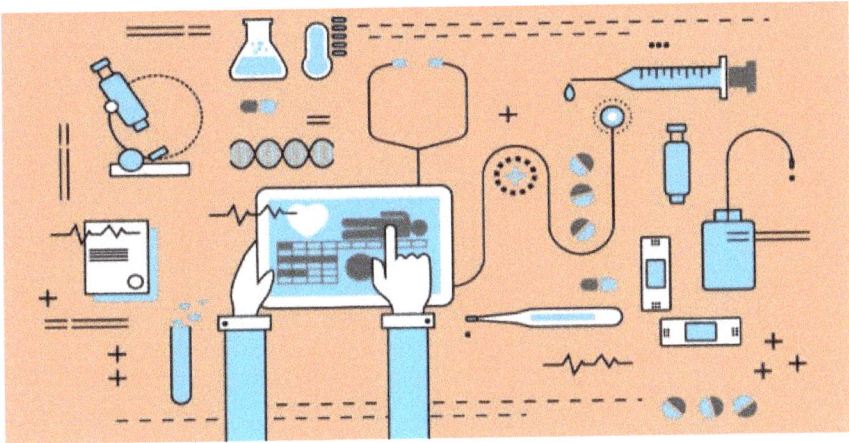

Figure 4.4 Illustration of drug development [14].

- *Pharmaceutical Manufacturing*: Along with the evolution of medicines, the manufacturing practices for their production have advanced from small-scale manual processing with simple tools to large-scale production as part of a trillion-dollar pharmaceutical industry. Today's pharmaceutical manufacturing technologies continue to evolve as the Internet of things, artificial intelligence, robotics, and advanced computing begin to challenge the traditional approaches, practices, and business models for the manufacture of pharmaceuticals. The application of these technologies has the potential to dramatically increase the agility, efficiency, flexibility, and quality of the industrial production of medicines.

- *Precision Medicine*: It can be defined as an approach aiming to provide the right treatment to the right person at the right time. It is a data-driven approach to disease prevention and treatment that takes into account a person's medical history, genome, lifestyle, and other information. It supports the development of unique drugs that target specific patients. Traditionally, precision strategies remained mostly aspirational for most clinical problems. Patients with a similar cancer subtype often respond differently when they receive the same chemotherapeutics. Using big data is becoming a popular way to study the complex relationship between genomics and chemotherapeutic resistance, toxicity, and sensitivity. Big data can be a key factor in precision medicine, where a disease is diagnosed and treated using appropriate data on a patient's genetic makeup, environmental factors, and behaviors.

- *Personalized Medicine*: Medical practitioners and facilities are leveraging big data to determine individualized treatment for specific patients. They do this by looking at a patient's genetics and using their information to prescribe medications working for them. If a person's DNA is found to be highly responsive to a drug, the doctor can prescribe the medicine to them as this may have better odds of success. On the other hand, if the DNA reacts adversely or none at all, then doctors can look for alternatives.

- *Digital Health*: This is the use of digital technologies for the health and well-being of individuals. It is a field that straddles the line between pharma and fitness. It is a sector that is booming and feeds on big data. For example, Takeda Pharmaceuticals is designing an app with Apple Watch to fight depressive disorders. An industry giant like Roche has developed a sensor to be implanted under the skin, which constantly monitors the blood glucose level of diabetic patients.

- *Clinical Trials*: Clinical trials are crucial in the pharmaceutical and life sciences world as it is used to test whether a specific treatment is effective and safe for human subjects. Clinical trials are costly and time-consuming to run and several clinical trials fail as recruiting the right patient for the trial is quite difficult. The goal of a clinical trial is to tell whether a treatment is safe and effective for humans. Usually, it follows in three sequential stages: (1) a drug is tested on a small group of healthy individuals, (2) the drug is tested on a larger group of people showing a specific condition being targeted, (3) that involves a larger number of patients. The process has always been time consuming and tedious. However, with the wider adoption of big data in pharma, clinical trials are changing. Using big data in pharma can change the way clinical trials are designed and managed. Now researchers can track and detect drug exposure levels, the immunity provided by the medicine, the tolerability and safety of the treatment, and other factors that are crucial for recruits' safety in real time. Analyzing pharmaceutical big data can facilitate adaptive trial design and let researchers change trial parameters based on interim results. Clinical trial information grouped by demographics and genetic factors can be accessed and used to create more personalized treatment options. Figure 4.5 shows a medical practitioner [14].

Figure 4.5 A medical practitioner [14].

- *Monitoring Prescribed Drugs*: When doctors prescribe medication to patients, there is a likelihood not all of them may follow the prescription. This situation used to be almost impossible to track until big data analytics came. Experts can now analyze data from pharmacies and pharmaceutical insurance on the number of patients not taking their prescribed medication. These results are then used in formulating policies and practices to resolve these issues. Also, prescription drug abuse is also one of the trends and problems identified with the help of big data. Records from a pharmacy, insurance claims and many more can be used to track patterns of healthcare professionals overprescribing. They may also be used to assess how many patients consume more than their advisable dosage of medication.

4.5 BENEFITS

Big data has emerged as a powerful tool for solving some of the most pressing scientific research and drug discovery challenges. Big data can improve the patient's safety on medication by assessing the risk and side effects of drugs accurately according to the population health statistics on medication. One of the greatest benefits of big data and advanced analytics is that they enable physicians to better match patients with treatments. The pharmaceutical and healthcare industry has experienced a watershed moment in its evolution for treatment, as more and more hospitals look towards big data methods to resolve issues. Other benefits include the following [13,17]:

- *Marketing*: By using pharmaceutical big data, companies can predict industry trends and anticipate the sales of specific medicine based on demographic factors. This can help tailor pharma marketing campaigns to customer behavior. With the help of algorithms, information can be catalogued and structured, providing a baseline for future formulations.

- *Compliance Management*: Big data in pharma plays an important role in facilitating regulatory compliance. Companies in the pharmaceutical industry are subject to a complex web of regulations as well as strict data privacy laws. Pharma companies can minimize regulatory risks by detecting anomalies, deviations, and non-compliant activities early on by using automated monitoring systems and big data analytics solutions.

- *Personalized Medicine*: With the advent of personalized medicine, the patient is moving more and more into the spotlight. Biomarkers are essential for personalized medicine. In recent years, it has become evident that developing new medicines cannot rely on the "one size fits all" approach. Patient stratification is becoming a prerequisite not only in the real world but also in the design of successful development programs.

- *Predictive Modelling*: This enables researchers to predict drug interactions, toxicity, and inhibition and thus speeds up the whole process. With the help of data analytics, researchers can utilize predictive modelling for drug discovery.

- *Pharmacovigilance*: Pharmacovigilance or drug safety monitoring is a branch of pharmacological studies that intends to minimize the effects and reactions of drug intake by studying consumption trends in sample populations. Big data is making an impact in pharmacovigilance, which shed light on adverse events and safety concerns associated with drugs. Pharmacovigilance processes make it imperative to establish a solid clinical data management strategy. Big data approaches in pharmacovigilance refers to utilizing large-scale, real-world data from various sources to identify potential adverse drug events and safety signals. To obtain useful data for pharmacological studies and pharmacovigilance at a glance, analysts prescribe a battery of characteristic studies. As shown in Figure 4.6, big data approaches in pharmacovigilance is creating decision relevant evidence [18].

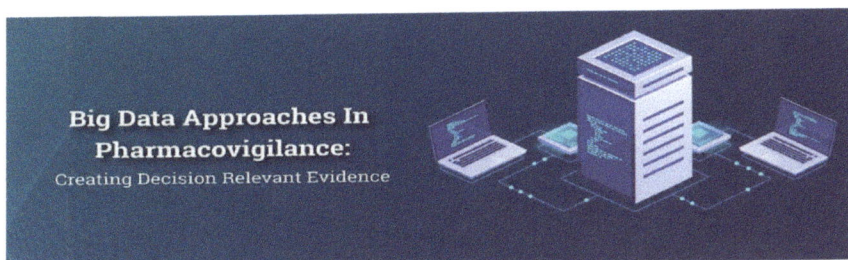

Big Data Approaches In Pharmacovigilance:
Creating Decision Relevant Evidence

Figure 4.6 Big data in pharmacovigilance [18].

Figure 4.7 shows the advantages of big data in pharma R&D [15].

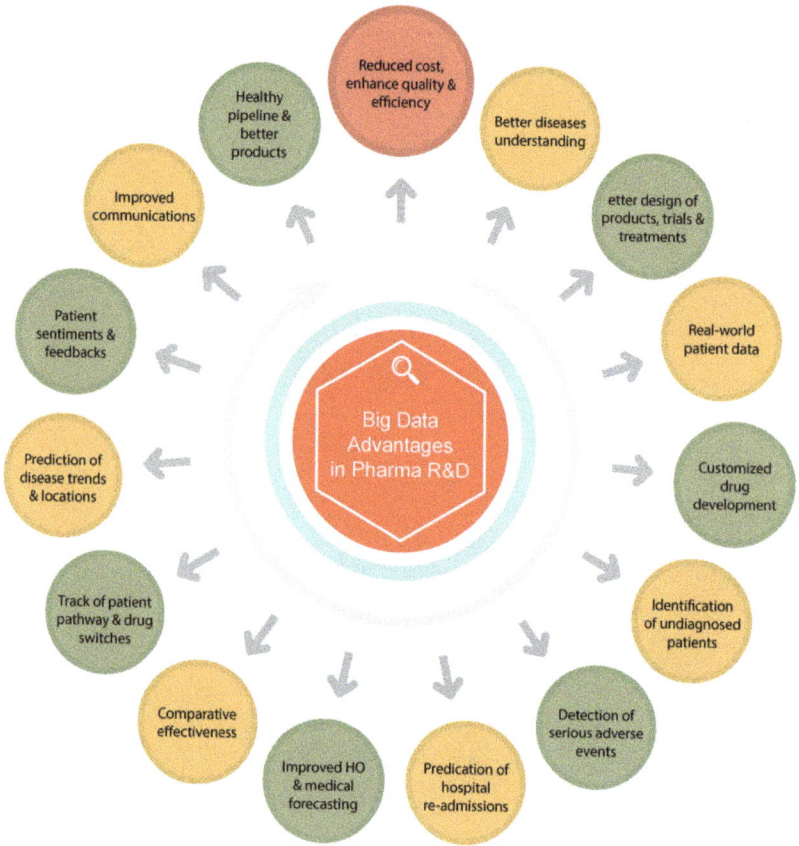

Figure 4.7 Advantages of big data in pharma R&D [15].

4.6 CHALLENGES

Adopting big data in the pharma sector is a challenging enterprise that will require companies to overcome organizational silos, seamlessly integrate disparate data sources, and ensure regulatory compliance. The main challenges the industry is facing are associated with the variety of data. While big data has been around for some time, data sets in the pharmaceutical industry have always been complex. Other challenges include the following [13,17]:

- *Privacy Concerns*: Despite its significant usage, big data can still negatively affect pharmacy practice in different ways. This includes privacy and data validity. The problem is that big data can collect information about any person without their consent or knowledge. It means there could be a public access to a person's private information such as their health status and what illnesses they have.

- *Integrating Sources*: Having all data sources well linked is one of the key challenges for the pharma sector to overcome to reap the benefits of big data. Effectively using big data in the pharmaceutical sector requires integrating data generated at all stages of the drug development process, from discovery to regulatory approval to real-world application.

- *Crisis Management*: Pharma companies can no longer afford reactive crisis management. New paradigms should emerge that can help the industry battle long-overdue issues. Industry players may invest in emerging markets and diversify their product portfolios to battle those issues.

- *Regulatory Compliance*: Adopting big data in pharma and rolling out centralized data management systems, you must make sure the data is handled safely and securely. The FDA requires software used in the sector to meet a number of requirements, including access control procedures, user identity verification, tracking of performed actions, and more. When planning your project, make sure to carefully study relevant compliance requirements and incorporate them into the design of your data management solution.

- *Lack of Talent*: The biggest challenge by far has been talent: upgrading skill sets from those sufficient to analyze relatively small amounts of clinical trial data to those required to gain insights from the vast amount of real-world data. The pharma sector has traditionally been a slow adopter of technology, so many companies are still lacking the needed talent to realize their ambitious plans. Pharma industry players must think of an appropriate way to close the knowledge gap, be it breeding in-house talent or turning to external teams.

- *Productivity*: Over the last 20 years, productivity in the pharmaceutical industry has been diminishing because of constantly increasing costs while output has overall been stagnant. Despite many efforts, productivity remains a challenge within the industry. With the implementation of big data initiatives trying to integrate data from disparate data sources and disciplines that are available in life science, the industry has identified a new frontier that might provide the insights needed to turn the ship around and allow the industry to return to sustainable growth.

- *Collaboration*: No single organization or company has all of the data available. It is therefore important for companies, the healthcare sector, and also the academic community to work together. This has been recognized, and many pre-competitive or non-competitive collaborations are taking shape. Big data enabled collaboration among different internal and external healthcare stakeholders will benefit pharma companies by breaking the silos that separate internal functions and enhance integrated, consistent research, and care management.

- *Data Corruption*: This can completely spoil AI models and prediction results, costing pharma companies millions of dollars and making their AI and machine learning unreliable. Bad data produces bad results. Getting good data begins by eliminating these factors and keeping a close vigilance on the effects that matter most. It is therefore essential to have clean curated data before any analytics and insight engines can interpret the data. This data problem underscores the need for data observability from the very earliest stages in creating a data lake. Ensuring data integrity will help the company to acquire a smaller number of warning letters. Figure 4.8 shows data integrity [17].

Figure 4.8 Data integrity [17].

4.7 CONCLUSION

Big data in pharma presents vast opportunities for innovation, efficiency, and improved patient outcomes. The pharmaceutical industry is only starting to implement big data initiatives, and a long road still lies ahead. While many pharma manufacturers have both the right tools and growing access to data, relatively few thus far have developed the capabilities to leverage big data fully. The use of big data is still an untapped asset in the pharma industry. Reaping the rewards is still a matter of clear goal setting, strategy, and execution. When pharmaceutical companies collect large amounts of data at different stages of the value chain, they can leverage big data analytics to generate actionable insights for research and development. More information about big data in the pharmaceutical industry can be found in the books in [19,20] and the following related journals:

- *Intelligent Pharmacy*
- *International Journal of Pharmaceutics*

- *International Journal of Research in Pharmaceutical Sciences*

REFERENCES

[1] M. N. O. Sadiku, M. Oteniya, J. O. Sadiku, and S. Abunene, "Big data in pharmaceutical industry," *International Journal of Trend in Scientific Research and Development*, vol. 8, no. 6, November-December 2024, pp. 922-931.

[2] M. N.O. Sadiku, M. Tembely, and S.M. Musa, "Big data: An introduction for engineers," *Journal of Scientific and Engineering Research*, vol. 3, no. 2, 2016, pp. 106-108.

[3] "The complete overview of big data,"
https://intellipaat.com/blog/tutorial/hadoop-tutorial/big-data-overview/

[4] R. Allen, "Types of big data | Understanding & Interacting with key types (2024),"
https://investguiding-com.custommapposter.com/article/types-of-big-data-understanding-amp-interacting-with-key-types

[5] A. K. Tiwari, H. Chaudhary, and S. Yadav, "A review on big data and its security,"
Proceedings of IEEE Sponsored 2nd International Conference on Innovations in Information Embedded and Communication Systems, 2015.

[6] M. B. Hoy, "Big data: An introduction for librarians," *Medical Reference Services Quarterly*, vol. 33, no 4. 2014, pp. 320-326.

[7] M. Viceconti, P. Hunter, and R. Hose, "Big data, big knowledge: Big data for personalized healthcare," *IEEE Journal of Medical and Health Informatics*, vol. 19, no. 4, July 2015, pp. 1209-1215.

[8] P. Baumann et al., "Big data analytics for earth sciences: The earthserver approach," *International Journal of Digital Earth*, vol. 19, no. 1, 2016, pp.3-29.

[9] X. Wu et al., "Knowledge engineering with big data," *IEEE Intelligent Systems*, September/October 2015, pp.46-55.

[10] J. Alea, "The benefits of big data in drug development,"
https://www.contractpharma.com/issues/2024-01-02/view_features/the-benefits-of-big-data-in-drug-development/

[11] A. Deshmukh, "Visualizing the world's biggest pharmaceutical companies," September 2021,

https://www.visualcapitalist.com/worlds-biggest-pharmaceutical-companies/#google_vignette

[12] "How big data is affecting pharmacy practice," May 2021, https://bigdataanalyticsnews.com/big-data-affecting-pharmacy-practice/#google_vignette

[13] V. Shashkina, "From drug development to marketing: the potential of big data in pharma," June 2023, https://itrexgroup.com/blog/big-data-in-pharma-definition-use-cases/

[14] "How big data is affecting pharmacy practice," May 2021, https://bigdataanalyticsnews.com/big-data-affecting-pharmacy-practice/#google_vignette

[15] "The big data magic for pharma," https://www.wipro.com/pharmaceutical-and-life-sciences/the-big-data-magic-for-pharma/https://www.wipro.com/pharmaceutical-and-life-sciences/the-big-data-magic-for-pharma/

[16] P. Sahoo and R. Kamaraj, "Review of data integrity in pharmaceutical industry," *International Journal of Research in Pharmaceutical Sciences*, vol. 11. No. SPL4, 2020.

[17] P. Tormay, "Big data in pharmaceutical R&D: Creating a sustainable R&D engine," *Pharmacist Med*, vol. 29, no. 2, March 2015, pp. 87-92.

[18] A. Govil, "Big data approaches in pharmacovigilance: Using big, real-world data to create decision-relevant evidence," July 2019, https://www.cuelogic.com/blog/big-data-approaches-in-pharmacovigilance

[19] M. N. O. Sadiku, U. C. Chukwu, and P. O. Adebo, *Big Data and Its Applications*. Moldova, Europe: Lambert Academic Publishing, 2024.

[20] M. Johannes, *Big Data for Big Pharma: An Accelerator for The Research and Development Engine?* ibidem, 2016.

CHAPTER 5

BIG DATA IN TELECOMMUNICATIONS

"We are surrounded by data, but starved for insights." – Jay Baer

5.1 INTRODUCTION

Every day, massive amounts of data are collected using various methods, and that amount is sometimes so large that it is hard to process and analyze using traditional means. Data consumption by users and data generation by corresponding software systems are steadily growing year to year. This huge trove of data is now presented under the umbrella term "big data." We are in the big data age, where businesses in every industry must deal with vast volumes of data. Several experts and practitioners have lately emphasized the need of understanding how, why, and when big data applications may be a valuable resource for businesses seeking a competitive edge. The cloud word for big data is shown in Figure 5.1 [1].

Figure 5.1 The cloud word for big data [1].

In today's digital age, the telecom industry has become a crucial pillar for global connectivity and communication, noted for its complex infrastructure, as shown in Figure 5.2 [2]. Big data in the telecom industry encompasses a wide range of information, including customer profiles, call records, network logs, location data, social media interactions, and more. The telecom industry is a leader in big data strategy because of the vast amount of data it gathers during normal business operations. The integration of big data analytics has revolutionized various facets of the telecom industry, from enhancing customer experiences to ensuring regulatory compliance and optimizing network operations [3].

Figure 5.2 The telecom industry is noted for its complex infrastructure [2].

The world has seen a digital revolution where more and more work is being conducted online. Storing this activity has led to the concept of big data, i.e., large datasets that are otherwise difficult to manage. Because of these characteristics, big data requires new technologies and techniques to capture, store, and analyze. Telecom companies generate huge volumes of data from mobile phone usage, call detail records, server logs, network equipment, social networks, and billing. The number of data sources is growing as well. Typical sources of big data are shown in Figure 5.3 [4].

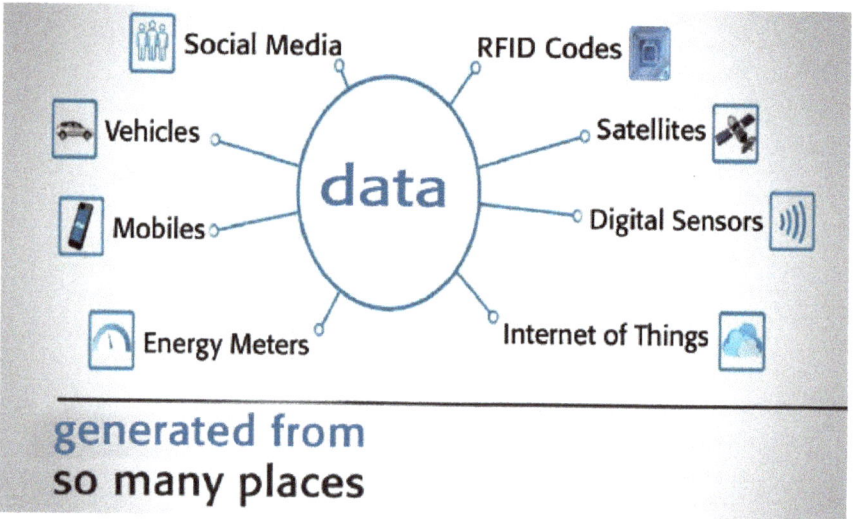

Figure 5.3 Typical sources of big data [4].

Big data and the technologies it rely on, such as AI and ML, are the driving force behind progress in the telecommunications industry. Telecommunications companies have always managed enormous volumes of network activity data and find ways they can put it to good use. Big data for telecom is the fuel that can and will drive the entire industry toward higher revenues and better customer service. Telecom companies must be able to collect this massive amount of data from different sources, analyze it, and distribute the insights to disparate databases [5].

This chapter examines the roles of big data and big data analytics in telecommunications. It begins with describing what big data is all about. It discusses the role of big data in telecommunications. It highlights the benefits and challenges of big data in telecommunications. The last section concludes with comments.

5.2 WHAT IS BIG DATA?

Big data applies to data sets of extreme size (e.g. exabytes, zettabytes) which are beyond the capability of the commonly used software tools. It involves situation where very large data sets are big in volume, velocity, veracity, and variability [6]. The data is too big, too fast, or does not fit the regular database architecture. It may require different strategies and tools for profiling, measurement, assessment, and processing.

Big Data is essentially classified into three types [7]:

- *Structured Data*: This is highly organized and is the easiest to work with. Any data that can be stored, accessed, and processed in the form of fixed format is known as a structured data. It may be stored in tabular format. Due to their nature, it is easy for programs to sort through and collect data. Structured data has quantitative data such as age, contact, address, billing, expenses, credit card numbers, etc. Data that is stored in a relational database management system is an example of structured data.

- *Unstructured Data*: This refers to unorganized data such as video files, log files, audio files, and image files. Any data with unknown form or the structure is classified as unstructured data. Almost everything generated by a computer is unstructured data. It takes a lot of time and effort required to make unstructured data readable. Examples of unstructured data include Metadata, Twitter tweets, and other social media posts.

- *Semi-structured Data*: This falls somewhere between structured data and unstructured data, i.e., both forms of data are present. Semi-structured data can be inherited such as location, time, email address, or device ID stamp.

The different types of big data are depicted in Figure 5.4 [8]. Structured and unstructured data are generated in various types [9-11].

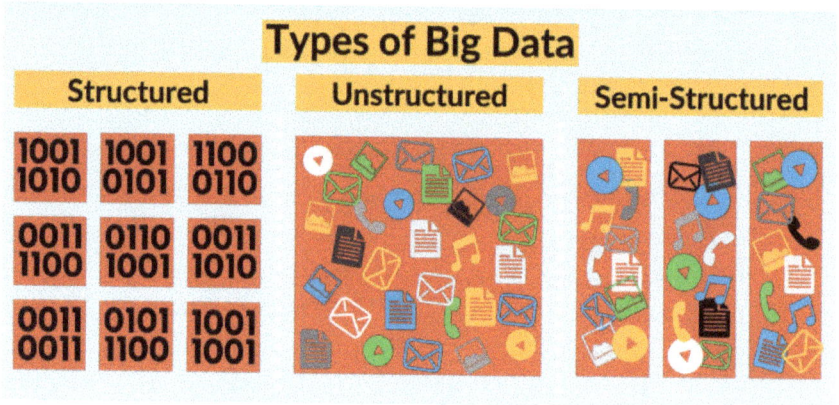

Figure 5.4 Types of big data [8].

The process of examining big data is often referred to big data analytics. It is an emerging field since massive computing capabilities have been made available by e-infrastructures [12]. Big data analytics is the application of advanced analytic techniques to large, heterogeneous data sets that comprise structured, semi-structured, and unstructured data from many sources with sizes ranging from terabytes to zettabytes.

Analytics include statistical models and other methods that are aimed at creating empirical predictions. Data-driven organizations use analytics to guide decisions at all levels. Several techniques have been proposed for analyzing big data. These include the HACE theorem, cloud computing, Hadoop, and MapReduce [13].

5.3 BIG DATA IN TELECOMMUNICATIONS INDUSTRY

Big data analytics is revolutionizing the telecommunication industry by enabling targeted marketing and enhancing customer behavior insights. This technology continues to be integral in shaping the future of telecom, providing innovative solutions. The telecommunications industry is making significant strides in technological advancements, and big data analytics (BDA) is playing a crucial role. Figure 5.5 shows the big data impacts on telecommunications industry [14], while Figure 5.6 illustrates big data analytics use cases in telecommunication industry [15]. Telecom startups and companies can take advantage of big data analytics in the following main areas [16,17]:

BIG DATA IMPACTS ON TELECOM INDUSTRY:

01 Predictive analysis
02 Customer churn prevention
03 Customer segmentation
04 Fraud detection

05 Lifetime value prediction
06 Recommendations engines
07 Price optimization
08 Network management

Figure 5.5 Big data impacts on telecommunications industry [14].

Big Data Analytics Use Cases in Telecom Industry

Network optimization

Price optimization

Targeted marketing

Product development

Performing preventive diagnostics

Predictive churn analysis

Attracting new subscribers

Preventing fraud

Product innovation

Recommendation engines

Figure 5.6 BDA use cases in telecommunication industry [15].

- *Customer Experience*: Big data analytics in the telecom industry can help companies improve customer experience. Maintaining a current customer relationship is considerably cheaper than acquiring a new one, and this improves the company's profitability in the long term. Processing big data can help with personalizing the customer experience. It also empowers telecoms to streamline their service portfolios, design, and implement new features, and provide the best customer support possible. For example, a telecom company can collect information from users regarding various service issues and then create an automated chatbot that will assist customers to resolve these issues immediately whenever possible. Figure 5.7 shows a typical Telco customer [18].

Figure 5.7 A typical Telco customer [18].

- *Network Optimization*: Network optimization stands as a cornerstone for telecom companies aiming to enhance service quality, maximize efficiency, and meet the ever-growing demands of users. It entails complex and quick evaluation of large volumes of data in real-time mode. Big data helps telecom operators in optimizing the quality of provided services by integrating network optimization. When combined, network telemetry, CDRs, data statistics, and equipment alerts enable communications service providers (CSPs) to set up and maintain effective network self-diagnostics and self-configuration tools. With big data analytics, telecom companies can monitor their network performance. For example, companies can record and gather issues raised by users from a particular area and look for solutions to resolve these issues, such as improving the connectivity.

- *Operational Analysis*: Companies can use big data for both analyzing and modifying operations as the need arises. Analysis can also be used to monitor the telecom's usage of resources and thereby prevent waste, which leads to savings of both resources and money. Real-time operational analysis also helps set the timetable for data updates and define other parameters so a company can best adapt the data analysis system to their unique business requirements.

- *Data Monetization*: Big data collected by telcos can be sold to or shared with third parties interested in monetizing it. Big data allows companies to gather a lot of user-related information, like demographics and location info, network and application usage, details about used devices, various preferences, and more. After processing, this data has value that extends beyond the companies that gathered them, opening a possibility for data monetization. Telecom companies can sell this data – without violating users' privacy – to companies from other industries like healthcare, financial services or advertising. For example, insurance companies, marketing agencies, banks, and other financial institutions may be interested in the behavior of a particular cohort of users, which will help them optimize their service offerings, and, thus, boost big data monetization in telecoms.

- *Fraud Detection*: Most fraud cases in the telecom industry are illegal access, fake profiles, authorization, cloning, or behavioral fraud. Each of these frauds affects the relationship established between the company and the customer directly. Therefore, fraud detection tools and techniques are needed. Big data analytics helps to monitor behaviors in real-time, thus preventing fraud. This technique has extremely high efficiency because it allows an almost real-time response to any suspicious activity. AI tools working on top of layers of accumulated and constantly updated relevant big data help telcos live up to high security standards and retain their customer base. Cybercriminals are raking millions of dollars by employing sophisticated scams across different geographies and vanishing even before the communication service provider knows. The revenue lost through Telco fraud amounts to billions of dollars each year.

- *Price Optimization*: The number of customers in the telecom industry customers is growing extremely fast. Therefore, pricing optimization becomes an important factor. The telecom industry is rife with cutthroat competition among different service providers, competing to have the largest subscriber market share. Product pricing is a key factor for operators competing to gain more subscribers. Telecoms use big data technologies to review several real-time metrics and settle on a particular product's price. For example, an operator may announce that users would get free minutes daily for calls made at a particular time frame under a particular voice bundle subscription. This sort of product offering comes about after analyzing data sources and then deriving actionable insights from them. The providers can set the optimal service prices to gain and retain customers.

- *Customer Churn Prevention*: Churn rate, also known as attrition rate, refers to the percentage of customers that stop using a particular service within a forecast period. In a recent study, the telecom industry has a churn rate of 21 percent, closely linked to poor customer service. Engaging new customers takes a lot of time and effort, and so does retaining customers. Companies have to analyze customers' behaviors and take corresponding actions to prevent customer churn. Telecom data analytics use cases give insights into this data, help disclose customers' feelings regarding services they receive, immediately address satisfaction issues, and prevent churn.

- *Product Development*: Developing a product is a complex process requiring proper control and management. It is a time-consuming. However, the integration of big data analytics ensures high-performing and quality products for the consumers, as per their needs and requirements. As a result of telecom data analysis, companies can develop data-driven products with internal feedback and marketing strategies. Big data analytics use cases in telecom companies can greatly assist with data-driven product development, internal feedback, and marketing intelligence.

5.4 BENEFITS

Big data can help the telecom industry in a myriad of ways. Big data is helpful for telecom operators in optimizing the quality of provided services by integrating network optimization. Companies can harness big data's potential by investing in custom data solutions that will help them with optimizing analytics to increase profitability. Big data opens up a sea of opportunities in the telecom industry, including improved customer experience, fraud detection, network optimization, risk mitigation, data monetization, and more. If done right, big data is the fast route to customer retention, growing subscriber base, and profitability. Other benefits include [19]:

- *Improved Customer Experience*: Competition within the telecom industry is fierce. Rival companies are always seeking opportunities to win over clients in ways besides decreasing prices or offering bonuses. And that is what makes big data so appealing; it opens new possibilities in improved customer experience, more personalized marketing, reducing churn rate, and generating new streams of revenue. Big data allows telecom companies to gather and categorize vast amounts of user information, enabling them to personalize customer experiences. By analyzing customer data, telecom companies can provide proactive assistance, resolve issues quickly, and offer tailored services.

- *Targeted Products*: Out of the customer micro-segments, you can tailor targeted and relevant product offerings that entice the customer. By leveraging customer behavior patterns, billing information, and issue resolution data, telecom companies can not only resolve customer problems and improve services but also target customers with relevant offerings. For example, a customer who makes frequent calls to a specific country can be targeted with a specific marketing campaign in real-time.

- *Predictive Capacity*: Big data can also help with developing predictive capacity models to predict network problems that may arise in the future. This includes predicting peak network loads and allocating adequate network resources to relieve congestion.

- *Personalized Offers*: Telecoms can use big data to segment customers into special categories based on their network usage data. This helps them present deeply personalized offers and services to the respective customer micro-segments, promoting customer retention and halting growing churn trends.

- *Targeted Marketing*: Under target marketing, the companies utilize big data network analytics in telecom to provide consumers with customized services on the basis of their purchase history, preferences, and feedback. Technology also helps companies identify customer behavior by evaluating their service usage.

- *Preventive Diagnostics*: Preventive diagnostics involve identifying the pattern of the service behavior to avoid system failures. Business analytics in telecom industry performs preventive diagnostics to analyze consumer intention

- *Enhanced Customer Experience*: The ultimate goal of telecommunication is to build a positive customer experience. By using data analytics systems, companies can use big data analytics system that uses comprehensive analysis to provide creative workflows using infographics. Besides, it also allows the industries to personalize the customer experience by sorting and separating the data into diverse categories.

- *Predictive Analysis*: The predictive analysis applied by telecom companies uses historical data to predict future behaviors and get valuable insights into customer data. With gathered insights, companies can become faster, more efficient, and better. It also helps with making data-driven decisions. For example, by analyzing customer preferences, companies can have a better understanding of each customer.

- *Customer Segmentation*: The content and strategy need to be tailored to the specific market. Therefore, telecom companies segment their customers and then target campaigns accordingly. Segmentation and targeting help with predicting customers' needs, preferences, and reactions to services and products.

- *Predicting Churn*: Churn refers to is a measure of the number of individuals or items moving out of a collective industry over a specific period making it a real issue of any business or industry. This can be due to several reasons like quality of service, network issues, social media trends, availability of other better options, sudden price hikes, unresolved queries. Understanding such scenarios with the data available can always be a preventive way of reducing churn.

- *Network Security*: Network security is of paramount importance in the telecom industry, given the sensitivity and value of the data transmitted over telecommunications networks. Big data analytics serves as a powerful tool for identifying and mitigating security threats, enhancing cybersecurity measures, and safeguarding network integrity and data confidentiality

- *Data Governance*: Data governance is very essential to protect the data and assets of telecom operators. It refers to the policies and procedures adopted in order to define how data assets could be accessed and manipulated and by whom in the organization. A common mistake that telecom operators makes is that they confuse data quality management, which comprises activities for the improvement of data quality, and data governance. This can be explained by the close connection between data governance and data quality management results from a data perspective as a company asset.

5.5 CHALLENGES

Like any other industry, the telecom industry is faced with many challenges. Competition in the telecommunications market has never been more vicious. The industry has every chance of beating these challenges. These challenges include the following:

- *Predicting Churn*: Churn, the number of customers leaving a service, poses a significant challenge for telecom companies. Big data analysis allows companies to understand the reasons behind churn, such as service quality, network issues, social media trends, price changes, and unresolved queries.

- *Detection of Fraud*: The most common types of fraud in the telecom business include unauthorized access, false profiles, authorization, duplication, behavioral fraud, and more. Fraud has a direct impact on the relationship that has been built between the organization and the user. As a result, big data analytics aids in real-time monitoring and fraud prevention. This technology is extremely efficient since it enables real-time response to any suspicious activity.

- *Talent Capability*: Talent capability in the context of analytics refers to the expertise of data analyst or scientists in executing tasks related to big data analytics. This capability is one of the defining components in creating and sustaining a competitive advantage. A close relationship between data scientists and other people within the organization can be very important. Figure 5.8 shows big data analytics talent capability pillar [20].

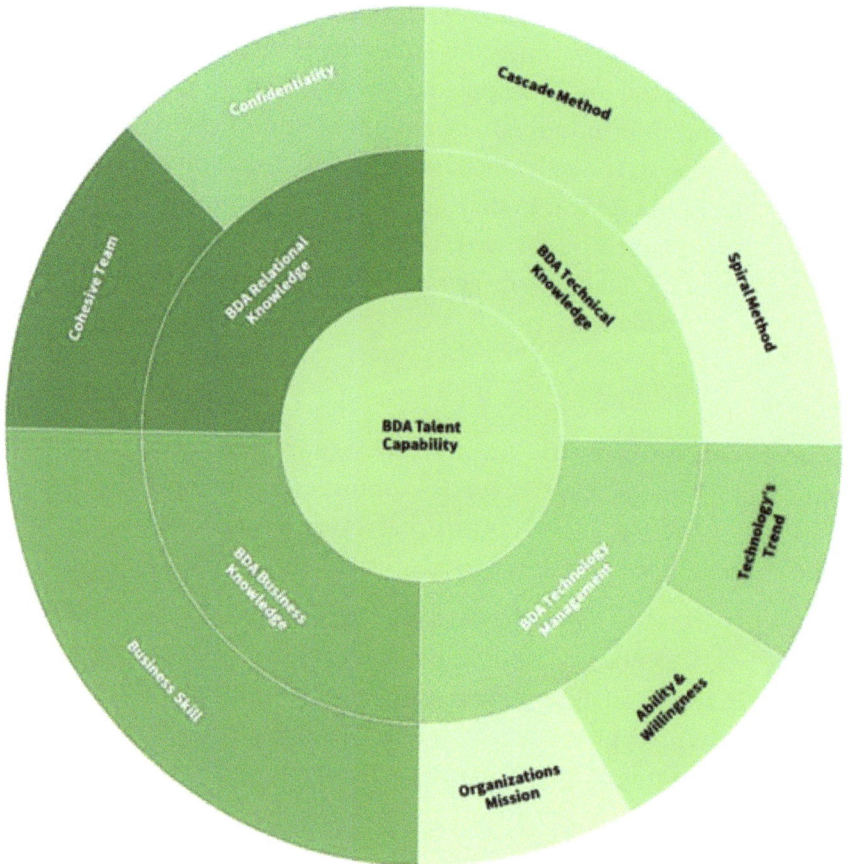

Figure 5.8 Big data analytics talent capability pillar [20].

- *Skills Shortage*: Lack of talented resources is a key challenge. The most challenging in BDA (big data analytics) projects is finding a qualified team. This can be explained by the fact that BDA is always considered as new technology compared to business intelligence, which most organizations have built over decades. Advanced analytics requires staff with deep knowledge in different domains, from data science to worldwide privacy laws, along with an understanding of the telecommunications business.

5.6 CONCLUSION

To cope with all the changes, companies have to stay alert to the newest trends in big data analytics in the telecom industry. Today, the application of big data in the telecom industry is multi-fold. Telcos can leverage big data technologies to turn vast amounts of raw data into actionable insights.

Big data analytics in the telecom industry refers to the process of analyzing large volumes of data generated by telecommunications networks and services to extract valuable insights. It is revolutionizing the telecommunication industry by enabling targeted marketing and enhancing customer behavior insights. The application of big data in telecom companies is crucial for success in the current and future telecom industry. The synergy between big data analytics and emerging technologies like artificial intelligence and machine learning continues to redefine the possibilities within the telecom sector, paving the way for innovation and growth. More information about big data in the telecommunications industry is available from the books in [21-23] and this related journal: *Journal of Big Data*.

REFERENCES

[1] R. Delgado, "The challenges of bringing BYOD to the military," https://socpub.com/articles/the-challenges-of-bringing-byod-to-the-military-11272

[2] M. Atherton, "Telecom infrastructure vulnerabilities: Assessing and enhancing resilience," January 2024,

https://www.linkedin.com/pulse/telecom-infrastructure-vulnerabilities-assessing-dr-marlon-atherton-c2rpe/

[3] A. Pareek, "Global examples of telecom companies using big data analytics," July 2022, https://customerthink.com/global-examples-of-telecom-companies-using-big-data-analytics/

[4] J. Moorthy et al., "Big data: Prospects and challenges," *The Journal for Decision Makers*, vol. 40, no. 1, 2015, pp. 74–96.

[5] M. N. O. Sadiku, P. A. Adekunte, and J. O. Sadiku, "Big data in telecommunications," *International Journal of Trend in Scientific Research and Development*, vol. 8, no. 6, November-December 2024, pp. 243-252.

[6] M. N.O. Sadiku, M. Tembely, and S.M. Musa, "Big data: An introduction for engineers," *Journal of Scientific and Engineering Research*, vol. 3, no. 2, 2016, pp. 106-108.

[7] "The complete overview of big data," https://intellipaat.com/blog/tutorial/hadoop-tutorial/big-data-overview/

[8] R. Allen, "Types of big data | Understanding & Interacting with key types (2024)," https://investguiding-com.custommapposter.com/article/types-of-big-data-understanding-amp-interacting-with-key-types

[9] A. K. Tiwari, H. Chaudhary, and S. Yadav, "A review on big data and its security," *Proceedings of IEEE Sponsored 2nd International Conference on Innovations in Information Embedded and Communication Systems*, 2015.

[10] M. B. Hoy, "Big data: An introduction for librarians," *Medical Reference Services Quarterly*, vol. 33, no 3. 2014, pp. 320-326.

[11] M. Viceconti, P. Hunter, and R. Hose, "Big data, big knowledge: Big data for personalized healthcare," *IEEE Journal of Medical and Health Informatics*, vol. 19, no. 4, July 2015, pp. 1209-1215.

[12] P. Baumann et al., "Big data analytics for earth sciences: the earthserver approach," *International Journal of Digital Earth*, vol. 19, no. 1, 2016, pp.3-29.

[13] X. Wu et al., "Knowledge engineering with big data," *IEEE Intelligent Systems*, September/October 2015, pp.46-55.

[14] K. Goworek, "The big impact of big data on the telecom industry," January 2021,
https://tasil.com/insights/big-data-in-telecoms/

[15] S. Srivastava, "How telecom companies use big data analytics – Top 10 use cases," August 2024,
https://appinventiv.com/blog/big-data-analytics-for-telecom-industry/

[16] "Big data in the telecom industry: A golden harvest on the digital fields," June 2024,
https://startups.epam.com/blog/big-data-analytics-for-telecommunications

[17] R. Makarchuk, "Big data in the telecom sector: Trends, use cases & case studies,"
https://intellias.com/big-data-telecom/

[18] "Big data analytics in telecom industry. Use cases," April 2024,
https://addepto.com/blog/the-role-of-big-data-in-the-telecom-industry/

[19] A. Kumar, "10 Use cases of data analytics in telecom industry," September 2024,
https://www.appventurez.com/blog/big-data-analytics-in-telecom-industry

[20] H. Keshavarz et al., "The value of big data analytics pillars in telecommunication industry," *Sustainability*, vol. 13, no. 13, June 2021.

[21] Y. Ouyang and M. Hu (eds.), *Big Data Applications in the Telecommunications Industry.* Information Science Reference, 2016.

[22] R. He and Z. Ding (eds.), *Applications of Machine Learning in Wireless Communications (Telecommunications).* The Institution of Engineering and Technology, 2019.

[23] A. K. Bashir et al. (eds.), *Implementing Data Analytics and Architectures for Next Generation Wireless Communications.* IGI Global, 2021.

CHAPTER 6

BIG DATA IN TRANSPORTATION

"Everybody is a genius, but if you judge a fish by its ability to climb a tree, it will live its whole life believing that it is stupid." – Albert Einstein

6.1 INTRODUCTION

Transportation, as a means for moving goods and people between different locations, is a vital element of modern society. The transportation industry ensures the efficient and safe transportation of people and goods from one place to another. In an era where technology continues to reshape our world, the transportation sector stands out as one of the most significantly impacted. In recent years, the transportation industry has been disrupted by multiple forces, including the COVID-19 pandemic, an ongoing road safety crisis, and a growing push for decarbonization. The transportation sector accounts for one-fifth of global CO_2 emissions and is one of the most challenging sectors to decarbonize due to its heavy reliance on fossil fuels. The planning of a city faces the transportation dilemma. On one hand, transportation is considered fundamental for the operation of the region. On another hand, it is considered one of the most important causes of environmental deterioration. Figure 6.1 shows a typical urban traffic [1].

Figure 6.1 A typical urban traffic [1].

Organizations have started to analyze and explore how to examine a vast array of information in innovative and new ways to derive the best possible business outcomes. We have seen significant benefits of big data in education, healthcare, telecommunications, media and entertainment, finance, and marketing. And the transportation industry is not outside of the race. From optimizing traffic flow to improving safety and reducing costs, big data analytics has radically transformed transportation management and operations. Organizations across various transportation and travel segments like airports, airlines, freight logistics, railways, hospitality, and others are enjoying the benefits of big data in managing a large amount of data that they handle. The era of big data generates massive volumes of transportation data daily, with storage exceeding petabytes and transmission rates reaching hundreds of terabytes per day [2].

Data is transformed into information helping us to understand buying trends, social behaviors, and various predictive analytics. Big data blends together the collection of large volumes of high-velocity, heterogeneous, evolving domain data and the use of advanced techniques and models to store, retrieve, manage, process, and analyze the captured information. Big data analytics has changed many sectors, including transportation. This technology helps us understand and predict transportation systems. It makes managing transportation data easier. In transportation, big data is able to exploit information and solve transportation problems at unprecedented scales [3].

In this chapter, we focus on the applications of big data and big data analytics in the transportation industry. The chapter begins with explaining what big data is all about. It discusses transportation data analytics. It provides some applications of big data in transportation. It highlights some benefits and challenges of big data in transportation. The last section concludes with comments.

6.2 WHAT IS BIG DATA?

Big data applies to data sets of extreme size (e.g. exabytes, zettabytes) which are beyond the capability of the commonly used software tools. It involves situation where very large data sets are big in volume, velocity, veracity, and variability [4]. The data is too big, too fast, or does not fit the regular database architecture. It may require different strategies and tools for profiling, measurement, assessment, and processing. Different components of big data are shown in Figure 6.2 [5]. The cloud word for big data is shown in Figure 6.3 [6].

Figure 6.2 Different components of big data [4].

Figure 6.3 The cloud word for big data [5].

Big Data is essentially classified into three types [7]:

- *Structured Data*: This is highly organized and is the easiest to work with. Any data that can be stored, accessed, and processed in the form of fixed format is known as a structured data. It may be stored in tabular format. Due to their nature, it is easy for programs to sort through and collect data. Structured data has quantitative data such as age, contact, address, billing, expenses, credit card numbers, etc. Data that is stored in a relational database management system is an example of structured data.

- *Unstructured Data*: This refers to unorganized data such as video files, log files, audio files, and image files. Any data with unknown form or the structure is classified as unstructured data. Almost everything generated by a computer is unstructured data. It takes a lot of time and effort required to make unstructured data readable. Examples of unstructured data include Metadata, Twitter tweets, and other social media posts.

- *Semi-structured Data*: This falls somewhere between structured data and unstructured data, i.e., both forms of data are present. Semi-structured data can be inherited such as location, time, email address, or device ID stamp.

The different types of big data are depicted in Figure 6.4 [8].

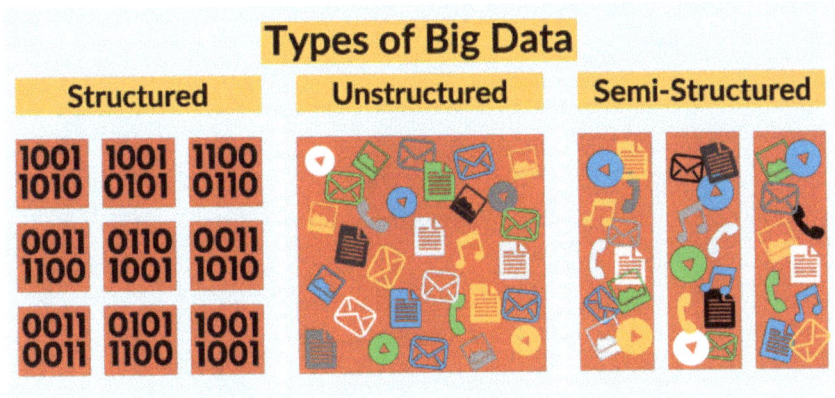

Figure 6.4 Types of big data [8].

The process of examining big data is often referred to big data analytics. It is an emerging field since massive computing capabilities have been made available by e-infrastructures [9]. Big data analytics is the application of advanced analytic techniques to large, heterogeneous data sets that comprise structured, semi-structured, and unstructured data from many sources with sizes ranging from terabytes to zettabytes.

It enables predictive analytics, which involves using historical data to forecast future outcomes. Analytics include statistical models and other methods that are aimed at creating empirical predictions. Data-driven organizations use analytics to guide decisions at all levels. Several techniques have been proposed for analyzing big data. These include the HACE theorem, cloud computing, Hadoop, and MapReduce [10].

6.3 TRANSPORTATION DATA ANALYTICS

Transportation data should be evaluated against an existing data set with confirmed accuracy. This is usually data from road sensors or counters. A powerful data set is not a one-size-fits-all solution to every question or problem that transportation planners and managers confront, but it is a versatile multi-tool in the transportation toolbox. Big data analytics has emerged as a powerful tool for businesses and organizations to gain insights and make informed decisions. It can potentially revolutionize the transportation industry. It provides valuable insights into customer behavior, traffic patterns, and operational efficiency. Big data analytics in transportation planning enables effective navigation through the complexities of urban mobility. Figure 6.5 shows big data in transportation [11].

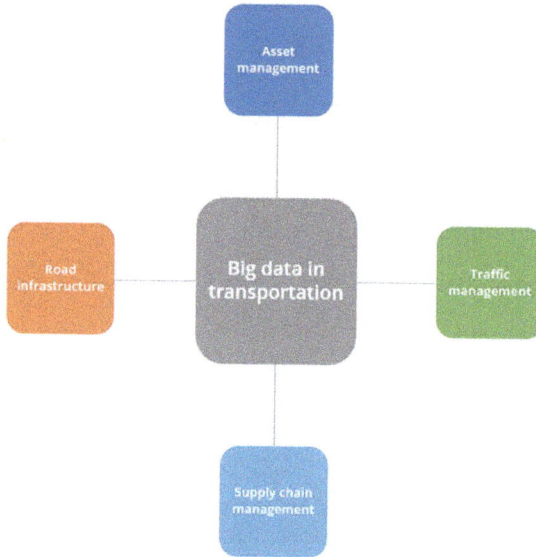

Figure 6.5 Big data in transportation [11].

Transportation big data analytics refers to the process of collecting, analyzing, and interpreting large, complex datasets related to transportation systems to gain insights and improve various aspects of transportation planning and management. This involves utilizing data from diverse sources like connected vehicles, IoT devices, and public transportation systems to understand travel patterns, predict future trends, and optimize transportation networks. Transportation data analytics increasingly power mobility information and insights – transforming transportation planning and operations by making it easier, faster, cheaper, and safer to collect and understand critical information. It can provide complete end-to-end trip information, including trip origins and destinations, routes, trip distances, travel time, and even real-time data on how vehicles are moving. Using transportation data analytics, transportation professionals can quickly access accurate data for every road in the country, every day of the year — even in real time. More and more cities, transit organizations, departments of transportation, and other localities are using transportation data analytics to solve problems, prioritize investments, and win stakeholder support [1]. Figure 6.6 is a representation of big data analytics in transportation [12].

Figure 6.6 A representation of big data analytics in transportation [12].

6.4 APPLICATIONS OF BIG DATA IN TRANSPORTATION

Some real-world applications of big data in transportation are depicted in Figure 6.7 [13]. Common areas of application of big data and big data analytics in transportation include the following [12,14,15]:

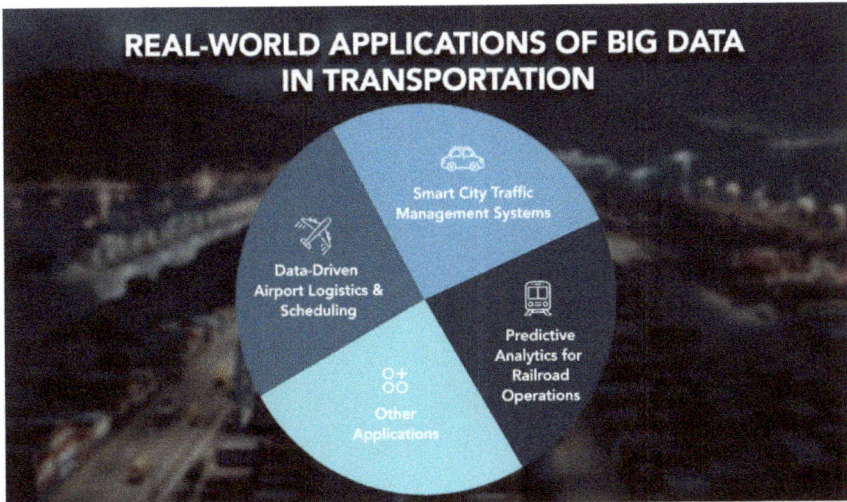

Figure 6.7 Some real-world applications of big data in transportation [13].

- *Smart Cities*: The term "smart city" denotes a city with the technology for instrumentation, interconnection, and smart systems. Instrumented means that the city is in the ability to capture and integrate data through the use of sensors, applications, personal devices, etc. Interconnected means that the data is on a computer platform that allows the communication of different sources of information for multiple services to the city. And the term smart means that analytics models, optimizations, and visualizations can be built as a result of complex decision-making applications. Every day, urban transport creates over 500 petabytes of data. This number grows with smart city tech. This rich data, from commuters, vehicles, and infrastructure, boosts transportation planning. Smart city transportation analytics inform sustainable urban development and transport policy-making. Cities must now use data-driven approaches to improve mobility, safety, and efficiency. For city dwellers, heavy traffic and a lack of parking are just part of urban living. But as cities get "smarter," both residents and commuters may reap benefits like less congestion and more readily identifiable parking spaces.

- *Smart Transportation*: Smart transportation refers to the integration of advanced technologies in transportation systems to improve efficiency, safety, and sustainability. It encompasses a wide range of applications, from traffic management and public transportation to logistics and freight operations. The core of smart transportation lies in real-time data collection and analysis, enabling better decision-making and improved service delivery. In the context of transportation, big data is generated from various sources, including GPS devices, traffic cameras, social media, and IoT sensors embedded in vehicles and infrastructure. The role of big data analytics and AI also plays a crucial role in predicting transportation demand.

- *Intelligent Transport Systems*: The systems that support transport in smart cities are called Intelligent Transport Systems (ITS). ITS are applications that use the synergy between technologies and engineering concepts to develop and improve multiple types of transportation systems. As far as urban population continuously grows, the need of ITS becomes more and more relevant to deal with transport needs for both people and cargo. Automated devices for data capture requires the implementation of analytics techniques in order to provide insights for actual decision-making and policy design. Intelligent transportation systems and machine learning for transportation data are changing how we move. In the near future, the big data paradigm is expected to become a core building block for ITS.

- *Traffic Management*: Traffic jams are the bane of many city dwellers and a locus of profound pressure for city managers. No city is completely free of traffic jams. Traffic management proves to be one of the most essential applications of big data analytics in transportation. It allows public transportation companies to monitor real-time patterns and optimize traffic flow. They can significantly reduce traffic congestion, improve travel times, and enhance safety. Big data analytics improves public transportation scheduling. It helps match bus or train times to when people need them. This makes travel better for everyone while cutting costs. By analyzing traffic flow and congestion patterns, transportation agencies can implement strategies to optimize traffic flow, reduce congestion, and improve overall travel times. By analyzing data from various sources, traffic management systems can optimize traffic flow, reduce congestion, and minimize travel times.

- *Transportation Planning*: We are at the brink of a major breakthrough in city design and connectivity. The use of big data analytics is key for advanced transportation infrastructure planning. As cities grow quickly, we face many new challenges. Data-driven planning has become essential because it builds a system where choices are guided by up-to-date data and forecasts. In a changing transportation landscape, it is more important than ever for planners to have access to detailed data and analytics. Given our increasingly complex transportation networks, planners must consider where to implement road diets, add EV charging infrastructure, establish tollways, expand access to multimodal transport, and so much more. Big data analytics offers tools to understand vast amounts of data from different sources. It helps make better decisions in transportation planning and optimization. Having access to detailed real-time and historical transportation data empowers planners and transportation departments to develop better strategies, reduce costs, prioritize initiatives, and measure the effectiveness of each change or improvement.

- *Predictive Analytics*: Predictive modeling considers various factors, like weather and events, to avoid traffic problems. Using predictive analytics enables smoother traffic flow across all transport modes. Predictive analytics are a game-changer for railways. They make trains more timely and safe. By predicting needs, railways can plan better and avoid. With predictive analytics, agencies can answer the question of "what's the best possible result?" instead of using prior history information.

- *Predictive Maintenance*: When it comes to maintenance prediction, big data analytics do a great job of monitoring vehicle health and forecasting necessary preservation. To achieve this, you have to use tools to collect data from sensors embedded in cars, maintenance logs, and historical data on vehicle performance. The data, later on, will be studied thoroughly. Employing data analytics will contribute to reducing downtime while strengthening safety and saving maintenance costs. Data from sensors and operational logs help predict equipment failures before they occur, minimizing downtime and repair costs.

- *Road Infrastructure*: Cities around the world have one problem in common: road infrastructure. Road repair and development is a frustrating, and probably one of the most delayed processes. To address this problem, many cities that have resorted to use big data to address road infrastructure by venturing into the development of a big data app. For example, Boston is one of the first users whose residents are experimenting with an app known as Street Bump. It enables residents to identify jolts and potholes on roads. The app uses signal data from a cell phone's accelerometer for the purpose of detection.

6.5 BENEFITS

Big data is revolutionizing the transportation industry by offering transformative benefits. The benefits of big data and analytics help the transportation companies to accurately optimize and model capacity, demand, pricing, revenue, customer sentiments, cost, and lot more. Transportation industry can make more informed decisions, improve safety, reduce costs, and gain positive customer feedback by leveraging the big data generated by sensors, cameras, and other devices. The new benefits that big data analytics brings to the table are speed and efficiency. Other benefits of big data in transportation include the following [16]:

- *Connectivity*: Connectivity is hugely important for transportation. As connected networks and technologies like 5G, IoT, and AI evolve, smart cities will get even smarter. In the city of the future, buses, trains, cars, and even roadways will be interconnected. This will enable digital systems to "talk" with one another, and help cities to move people more efficiently than ever.

- *Better Safety*: Big data and the IoT can help in mitigating faults of signals. Passengers and cargo are advantageous to big data analytics in ensuring they stay safe while traveling. You can reduce accidents, prevent theft, and enhance overall security.

- *Cost Savings*: A well-optimized logistics system reduces operational costs by minimizing unnecessary inventory holding, streamlining transportation and distribution, and optimizing routes. This leads to reduced warehousing expenses, lower transportation costs, and efficient use of resources, ultimately increasing profitability.

- *Enhanced Knowledge*: Big data and IoT are capable of making customers or users aware of the most efficient form of transport at any given time. There are several train operating companies that have already started using big data to process availability of seat data in real-time and also to inform the passengers waiting on platforms about the carriages having the most number of available seats. This benefit of big data not only enhances the experience of customers but also adds up to their knowledge.

- *Improved Customer Service*: One of the most significant benefits of big data is the fact that it has enhanced the experience of customers by improving their knowledge. Real-time data insights enable better tracking of shipments and more accurate delivery estimates, enhancing customer satisfaction. An effective logistics system ensures timely and accurate deliveries, leading to improved customer service. On-time deliveries, accurate order fulfillment, and real-time tracking capabilities enhance customer satisfaction, trust, and loyalty. Meeting or exceeding customer expectations is crucial for maintaining a competitive edge.

- *Competitive Advantage*: Big data empowers organizations to stay competitive, optimize their operations, and drive strategic decisions with confidence. Effective logistics systems enable businesses to respond quickly to market changes and customer demands. This agility provides a competitive advantage, allowing companies to adapt to evolving conditions, optimize inventory levels, and reduce lead times, ensuring they remain at the forefront of their industry.

- *Market Expansion*: Efficient logistics enable businesses to reach new markets and customers. With streamlined supply chain processes, companies can enter new regions or expand their customer base, unlocking growth opportunities and increasing market share.

- *Efficient Operation*: Big data can be used to eliminate errors and minimize unnecessary spending. It can be leveraged to identify the problems related to delays and downtimes for transport maintenance. Strukton rail in the Netherlands is a very good example of how the benefits of big data can make operations efficient.

Some of these benefits are displayed in Figure 6.8 [16].

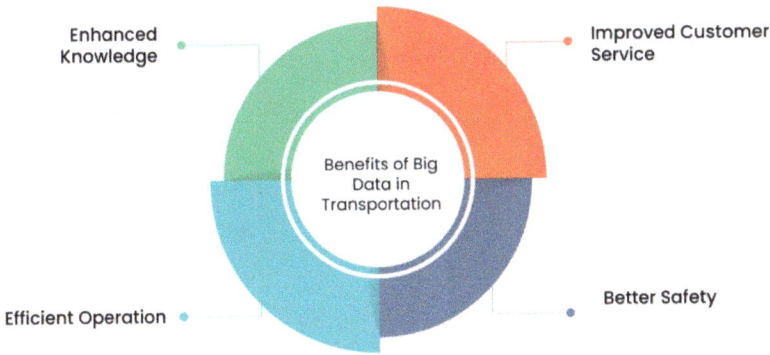

Figure 6.8 Some of the benefits of big data in transportation [16].

6.6 CHALLENGES

There are also significant challenges associated with transportation analytics. Extracting and processing transportation big data is complex. Capturing and mining video data requires a robust, low-latency data governance and management platform. There is a far more important question of personal data privacy. Various factors such as privacy, regulations, and confidentiality must be taken care of to use data 100% effectively to provide fruitful analysis. Other challenges include the following [12]:

- *Data Privacy and Security*: One of the main issues with data privacy and security is the potential for sensitive data to be accessed by unauthorized individuals or entities. As a matter of fact, data from a GPS device may contain information about the location and movements of individuals. And they could serve malicious purposes if it falls into the wrong hands. It is critical to control access to your data by permitting authorized individuals only. Others will be blocked right after entering the data system. Fortunately, best practices are emerging to ensure privacy protection.

- *Data Quality*: Data quality refers to the completeness, homogeneity, and trustworthiness of the data. With many forms of big data, quality and accuracy are less controllable, as large data volumes often make up for the lack of quality or accuracy. There exists a stereotype that analyzed data must be accurate, complete, and reliable. In the transportation industry, these requirements are considered big challenges due to the large volume of data generated from multiple sources. The main issue is the potential for errors or inconsistencies in the data. Governments or transportation service providers should take into account robust data quality control processes. They must check data validation for errors and inconsistencies and clean data to remove or correct inaccurate information.

- *Data Integration*: Integrating multiple data sources into a single, unified dataset has never been an easy task, particularly in the transportation industry. Data stored in different formats or structures prevents us from combining and analyzing them effectively. Data transformation techniques enable data scientists to convert data from different formats into a common one for practical analysis. Besides, they ought to implement data alignment to process multiple-source data together.

- *Data Cost*: Engineering and analyzing data cost organizations a lot of money. The larger volume of data you want to collect and store, the higher expense you have to spend. This also happens to processing and analyzing that data. It is necessary to provide clear and cost-effective data management strategies. This may involve implementing data archiving techniques to keep older data on less expensive storage media.

- *Data Storage*: Data storage and processing should take place in a secure data repository protected by multi-layered network security architecture, and supported by system audits and controls.

- *Transparency*: At a minimum, transportation data providers should be able to explain the modeling behind a transportation data algorithm, including the data sources, how the data is handled, and the algorithm's capabilities. Transparency is essential for assessing today's complicated data sets.

- *Sustainability*: Sustainability is a pressing concern for modern transportation systems. Big Data analytics can assess the environmental impact of various transportation modes, while

AI can suggest optimal routes for electric and hybrid vehicles, minimizing energy consumption. Together, these technologies can help cities achieve their sustainability goals, reducing carbon emissions and promoting greener alternatives.

6.7 CONCLUSION

Big data has remarkably impacted the transportation industry. Transportation data analytics are being used by an increasing number of cities, transit organizations, transportation departments, and other entities to solve problems, prioritize investments, and gain stakeholder support. It can give complete trip information from start to finish, including origins and destinations, routes, trip distances, and journey time. Transportation experts use analytics tools such as R, Python, and MATLAB to help analyze complex data effectively. Transportation professionals must make informed decisions based on current, reliable data, not on educated assumptions or the opinions of a few loud stakeholders. They may instantly obtain reliable data for every route in the country, every day of the year, using data analytics [17]. More information about big data in transportation can be found in the books in [18-24] and the following related journals:

- *Journal of Big Data*
- *Big Data and Cognitive Computing*
- *IET Intelligent Transport Systems*
- *Journal of Traffic and Transportation Engineering*

REFERENCES

[1] "What are big data analytics in transportation?" https://www.streetlightdata.com/what-transportation-big-data-analytics/

[2] Z. Luo et al., "Insights into transportation CO_2 emissions with big data and artificial intelligence," *Patterns*, vol. 6, no. 4, April 2025.

[3] M. N. O. Sadiku, P. A. Adekunte, and J. O. Sadiku, "Big data in transportation," *International Journal of Trend in Scientific Research and Development*, vol. 9, no. 4, July-August 2025, pp. 1049-1058.

[4] M. N. O. Sadiku, M. Tembely, and S.M. Musa, "Big data: An introduction for engineers," *Journal of Scientific and Engineering Research*, vol. 3, no. 2, 2016, pp. 106-108.

[5] "Big data: What it is and why it matters?" August 2024, https://www.inventateq.com/top-stories/big-data-what-it-is-and-why-it-matters/

[6] L. Rembert, "How accounting teams can leverage big data," https://tdwi.org/articles/2020/03/03/adv-all-how-accounting-teams-can-leverage-big-data.aspx

[7] "The complete overview of big data," https://intellipaat.com/blog/tutorial/hadoop-tutorial/big-data-overview/

[8] R. Allen, "Types of big data | Understanding & Interacting with key types (2024)," https://investguiding-com.custommapposter.com/article/types-of-big-data-understanding-amp-interacting-with-key-types

[9] P. Baumann et al., "Big data analytics for earth sciences: The earthserver approach," *International Journal of Digital Earth*, vol. 19, no. 1, 2016, pp.3-29.

[10] X. Wu et al., "Knowledge engineering with big data," *IEEE Intelligent Systems*, September/October 2015, pp.46-55.

[11] N. Joshi, "This is why big data in transportation is a big deal," September 2017 https://www.allerin.com/blog/this-is-why-big-data-in-transportation-is-a-big-deal

[12] T. Nguyen, "The potentials of big data analytics in transportation," https://www.neurond.com/blog/big-data-analytics-in-transportation

[13] V. Terekhov, "How to use big data analytics in transportation planning," May 2024, https://attractgroup.com/blog/big-data-analytics-in-transportation-planning/

[14] J. R. Montoya-Torres et al., "Big data analytics and intelligent transportation systems," *IFAC-PapersOnLine*, vol. 54, no. 2, 2021, pp. 216-220.

[15] N. Singh, "The role of big data analytics and AI in smart transportation," September 2024,

https://www.aeologic.com/blog/the-role-of-big-data-analytics-and-ai-in-smart-transportation/

[16] "Analyzing benefits of big data: The real application of big data in transportation," September 2024,
https://www.quantzig.com/blog/benefits-of-big-data-transportation/

[17] "What are big data analytics in transportation?"
https://www.streetlightdata.com/what-transportation-big-data-analytics/

[18] M. N. O. Sadiku, U. C. Chukwu, and P. O. Adebo, *Big Data and Its Applications*. Moldova, Europe: Lambert Academic Publishing, 2024.

[19] G. Zhao and G. Zhu, *Big Data Transportation Systems*. World Scientific Publishing Company, 2021.

[20] C. Yang and S. V. Ukkusuri (eds.), *Transportation Analytics in the Era of Big Data*. Springer, 2018.

[21] A. E. Hassanien et al. (eds.), *Big Data in Complex Systems: Challenges and Opportunities*. Springer, 2015.

[22] E. Simoudis, *The Big Data Opportunity in Our Driverless Future*. Corporate Innovators, 2017.

[23] E. L. Sanfilippo, *GPS Big Data and Mobility Analysis: A Practical Guide With 18 Real Case Studies To Effectively Understand and Use Big Data in Urban Planning, Transportation, And Traffic Models (Transport Big Data)*. Independently Published, 2024.

[24] S. Moridpour, A. T. Pour, and T. Saghapour, *Big Data Analytics in Traffic and Transportation Engineering: Emerging Research and Opportunities (Advances in Civil and Industrial Engineering)*. Engineering Science Reference, 2019.

CHAPTER 7

BIG DATA IN SUPPLY CHAIN

"Capitalism has its weaknesses. But it is capitalism that ended the stranglehold of the hereditary aristocracies, raised the standard of living for most of the world and enabled the emancipation of women." – Camille Paglia

7.1 INTRODUCTION

The supply chain involves a series of systematic processes in converting the raw material into finished products and transporting it to the distributor, which is then made available to the consumers. In a traditional business model, supply chains comprise a series of companies working together to deliver value by transforming raw material into a finished product. Each company adds value to the product or service to transform the raw materials in one location and deliver a finished product to the end customer through value creation and trade. Figure 7.1 illustrates supply chains [1].

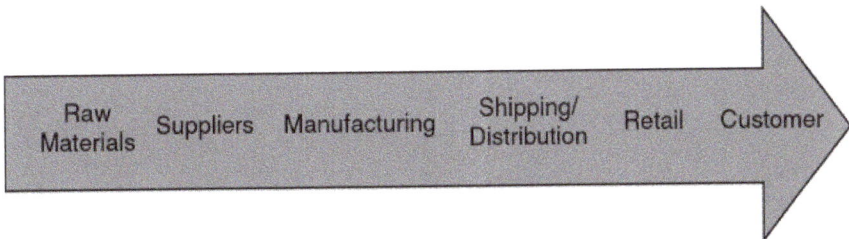

Raw Materials — Suppliers — Manufacturing — Shipping/Distribution — Retail — Customer

Figure 7.1 Supply chains [1].

Any enterprise supply chain directly produces a great amount of data. These volumes are too large for traditional data processing applications to handle. Modern organizations should consider this vast expanse of data an invaluable resource and implement best practices and tools that allow them to leverage it most effectively. Big data is altering how supply chain decision-makers make choices. The power of big data (speed, diversity, and volume) is changing supply chain decision-making. The role of big data in supply chain is pivotal in improving demand forecasting, inventory management, risk resilience, and personalized customer experiences. The use of big data in supply chain analysis and management projects is integral for optimized planning, operational efficiency, production, order fulfillment, and customer satisfaction.

An enormous amount of data is generated tremendously every second within supply chain industry all over the world. Big data is an extensive compilation of information that standard data-processing software finds challenging to manage. It refers to the vast amounts of data, structured and unstructured, that helps businesses to establish trends and patterns in human behavior and interactions. Big data has become a big business. Big data in supply chain refers to the vast amount of structured and unstructured data collected throughout various stages of a supply chain, which can be analyzed to improve operational efficiency, optimize inventory management, enhance demand forecasting, and make better data-driven decisions. The role of big data in supply chain is pivotal in improving demand forecasting, inventory management, risk resilience, and personalized customer experiences [2].

This chapter explores how big data is widely optimized and managed in the supply chain industry. It begins with explaining what big data is. It covers big data in supply chain, its examples and applications. It highlights the benefits and challenges of big data in the supply chain. The last section concludes with comments.

7.2 WHAT IS BIG DATA?

Big data applies to data sets of extreme size (e.g. exabytes, zettabytes) which are beyond the capability of the commonly used software tools. It involves situation where very large data sets are big in volume, velocity, veracity, and variability [3]. The data is too big, too fast, or does not fit the regular database architecture. It may require different strategies and tools for profiling, measurement, assessment, and processing. The cloud word for big data is shown in Figure 7.2 [4].

Figure 7.2 The cloud word for big data [4].

Big Data is essentially classified into three types [5]:

- *Structured Data*: This is highly organized and is the easiest to work with. Any data that can be stored, accessed, and processed in the form of fixed format is known as a structured data. It may be stored in tabular format. Due to their nature, it is easy for programs to sort through and collect data. Structured data has quantitative data such as age, contact, address, billing, expenses, credit card numbers, etc. Data that is stored in a relational database management system is an example of structured data.

- *Unstructured Data*: This refers to unorganized data such as video files, log files, audio files, and image files. Any data with unknown form or the structure is classified as unstructured data. Almost everything generated by a computer is unstructured data. It takes a lot of time and effort required to make unstructured data readable. Examples of unstructured data include Metadata, Twitter tweets, and other social media posts.

- *Semi-structured Data*: This falls somewhere between structured data and unstructured data, i.e., both forms of data are present. Semi-structured data can be inherited such as location, time, email address, or device ID stamp.

The different types of big data are depicted in Figure 7.3 [6]. Structured and unstructured data are generated in various types [7-10].

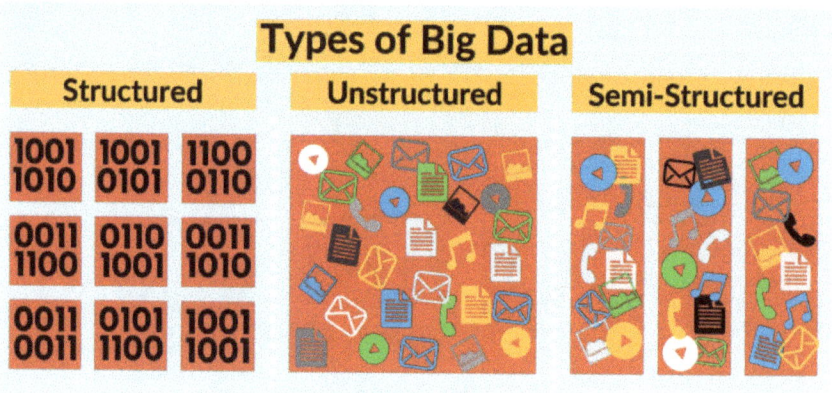

Figure 7.3 Types of big data [6].

The process of examining big data is often referred to big data analytics. It is an emerging field since massive computing capabilities have been made available by e-infrastructures [11]. Big data analytics is the application of advanced analytic techniques to large, heterogeneous data sets that comprise structured, semi-structured, and unstructured data from many sources with sizes ranging from terabytes to zettabytes.

Analytics include statistical models and other methods that are aimed at creating empirical predictions. Data-driven organizations use analytics to guide decisions at all levels. Several techniques have been proposed for analyzing big data. These include the HACE theorem, cloud computing, Hadoop, and MapReduce [12].

7.3 BIG DATA IN SUPPLY CHAIN

Like its name, big data refers to the entire amount of data collected during a process, including any form of structured, unstructured or semi-structured data. Big data in the supply chain refers to the structured and unstructured data gathered at various stages. It provides a comprehensive view that enhances process visibility, improves demand forecasting, and optimizes inventory management. Big data supply chain streamlines operations, reduces costs, and enhances customer satisfaction by enabling proactive responses to obstacles. In today's rapidly evolving world, the logistics and supply chain industry faces numerous challenges. Big data has become an invaluable asset in the logistics and supply chain industry. From globalization to customer demands for faster deliveries, companies need to continuously optimize their operations. Source examples of big data in supply chain include IoT devices, enterprise resource planning (ERP) systems, customer feedback, and external data about weather.

Supply chain analytics is the process by which companies and industries combine the available data from multiple systems to examine and analyze the various functions of the supply chain. It refers to the collection of data and information that provide insights into logistics performance, from inventory management to fulfilling and shipping orders. Supply chain analytics are guiding managers into the future with data-driven decision making. Advanced analytics is likely to become a decisive competitive asset in many industries and a core element in companies' efforts to improve performance. Figure 7.4 shows supply chain analytics [13].

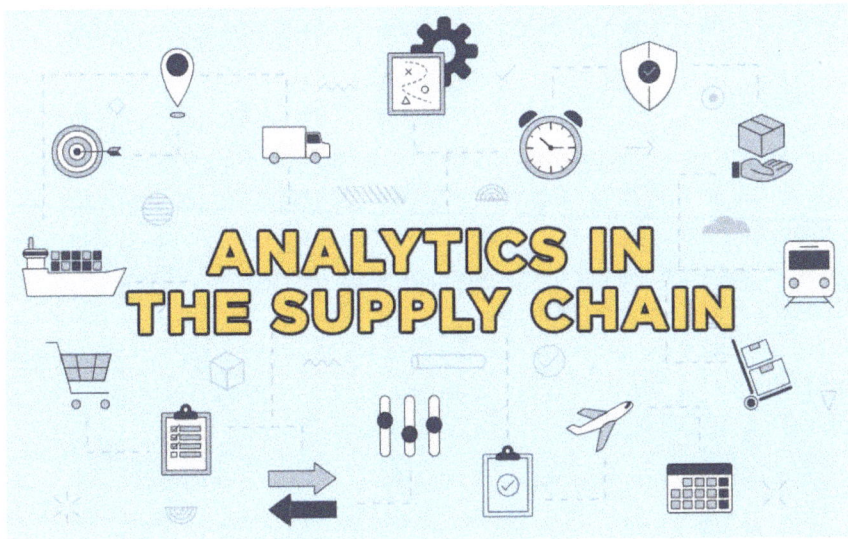

Figure 7.4 Supply chain analytics [13].

In an era defined by globalization, just-in-time manufacturing, and customer-centricity, supply chain management has become a critical component of business success. To thrive in this competitive landscape, organizations are turning to big data analytics as a powerful tool to optimize their supply chain operations.

Big data analytics leverages the vast volumes of data generated within and outside an organization's supply chain. Typical data sources in the supply chain include [14]:

- IoT in equipment, vehicles, and facilities tracks temperature, location, speed, and machine performance.

- Enterprise resource planning (ERP) systems capture essential internal data, including inventory levels, order statuses, procurement, and financials.

- Data from customer reviews and service interactions provide insights into product satisfaction, delivery times, and areas for improvement.

- Weather conditions and real-time traffic are crucial for managing disruptions and optimizing routes.

By leveraging data from real-time tracking systems, ERP systems, and social media, businesses can gain a holistic understanding of both internal operations and external influences on their supply chains.

7.4 BIG DATA SUPPLY CHAIN EXAMPLES

The ecommerce giants use big data to better meet customer demands. They utilize big data analytics in the supply chain to analyze their products or services, optimize the various supply chain operations, predict consumer behavior, and manage inventories. Successful big data in supply chain examples include Procter & Gamble, Amazon, General Electric, Siemens, DHL, Nestlé, Walmart, UPS, Coca-Cola, and Starbucks. Some of these companies are displayed in Figure 7.5 and explained as follows [14]:

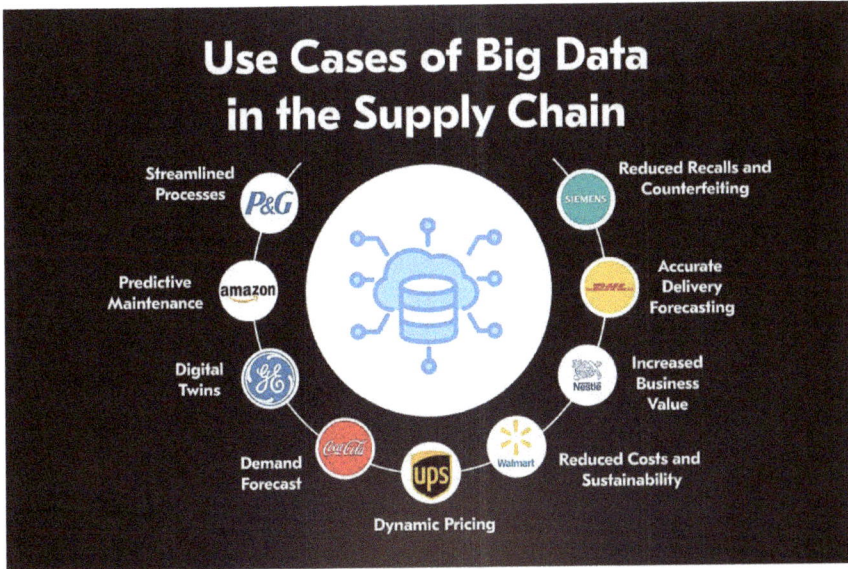

Figure 7.5 Companies using big data supply chain [14].

- *Procter & Gamble*: The collaboration between Procter & Gamble (P&G) and its retail partners is an excellent example of leveraging big data for vendor-managed inventory. By sharing real-time sales data and inventory levels, P&G and its partners can proactively manage stock replenishment, resulting in reduced out-of-stock situations and improved sales performance. Big data helps companies reduce unnecessary steps and integrate data-driven decisions. For example, in India, Procter & Gamble has achieved a 60% reduction in supply chain touchpoints compared to previous years. It led to faster operations, lower costs, and improved efficiency.

- *Amazon*: Amazon has a drive to deliver its orders to customers faster than its rivals. It uses data analytics to optimize its vast network of fulfillment centers, ensuring that products are strategically placed to minimize delivery times. Amazon deployed over 104,000 Amazon Monitron sensors to monitor 34,810 assets across 192 factories. Using big data for supply chain, the company achieved a 69% reduction in unplanned equipment downtime, saving approximately $37.83 million.

- *General Electric*: Digital twin technology enables real-time simulation and optimization of physical assets or processes. General Electric's Proficy CSense uses process digital twins to address challenges like demand fluctuations and workforce gaps, reducing product waste by 75%, quality complaints by 38%, and increasing throughput by 5%-20%.

- *Siemens*: 56% of food and beverage companies face at least one recall per year, incurring €9.5 million in direct costs and an additional €50-60 million in lost sales and reputational impacts. Siemens uses blockchain and IoT platform MindSphere to achieve full traceability and manage recalls and counterfeiting.

- *DHL*: DHL, a global logistics provider, uses big data analytics to optimize its freight operations. By analyzing historical shipping data and external factors such as weather patterns and port congestion, DHL can identify potential delays and take necessary actions to mitigate risks. DHL forecasts delivery volumes with 90-95% accuracy, optimizing courier routes based on real-time shipment data. AI-powered software from Wise Systems then fine-tunes the route in seconds, considering delivery priorities and time-sensitive requirements.

- *Nestle*: Deloitte and Nestlé USA collaborated to build a Microsoft Azure Data Lake, breaking data silos. The solution supported 400+ reports and integrated 15+ data sources, providing summarized reporting and insights for executives. Over four years, it has generated $200+ million in business value.

- *Walmart*: Walmart started using big data to track sales and inventory in 2003. It was able to reduce the time it takes to get products from its suppliers to its stores by 10% by using big data. Walmart employs data analytics to enhance inventory management and reduce stockouts, ultimately improving customer satisfaction. Walmart avoided 94 million pounds of CO_2 emissions, eliminated 30 million unnecessary miles, and optimized routes to bypass 110,000 inefficient paths, winning the 2023 Franz Edelman Award. Walmart utilizes big data analytics to monitor product sales and inventory levels, enabling them to proactively restock shelves. Figure 7.6 shows a typical Walmart store [15].

Figure 7.6 A typical Walmart store [15].

- *UPS*: UPS was able to reduce the average delivery time for its packages by 5% by using big data. UPS uses big data analytics in supply chain management through tools like Deal Manager. This system provides real-time pricing insights for small-to-medium business deals, achieving an 80% win rate. Currently, 95% of deals under $1 million utilize this tool. Every step of UPS's shipping process includes supply chain data analysis. Overall, UPS has saved 1.6 million gallons of gasoline in its trucks each year, greatly lowering delivery costs.

- *Coca-Cola*: By analyzing sales data and market trends, Coca-Cola forecasts demand with 90% accuracy, predicting consumer needs better and adjusting production schedules in real time. This improvement helps minimize excess inventory and associated costs while ensuring that high-demand products are available.

- *Starbucks*: With 90mn transactions made weekly across more than 25,000 stores, Starbucks is a renowned brand worldwide. The introduction of rewards apps via mobile devices has allowed the company an insight into its customers spending habits. Another way that Starbucks reaches customers is through targeted and personalized marketing.

7.5 APPLICATIONS OF BIG DATA IN SUPPLY CHAIN

At its core, big data is an extensive compilation of information that standard data-processing software finds challenging to manage. The promising applications of big data and how it might "revolutionize" the supply chain are hard to ignore. Common areas of applications of big data in supply chain include the following [14,15]:

- *Demand Forecasting*: The ability to foretell what lies on the horizon has long been something companies strive to have. Big data can help provide great insights into customers' and markets' behavior. For the supply chain, it enables in-depth and granular demand forecasting. Big data is used to create predictable patterns by analyzing historical data and market trends to predict customer behavior, highs, and lows of seasons, managing inventory and even how to provide a competitive edge using customized customer experiences. Companies could better anticipate potential demand and its changes through information like sales figures, social media, market trends, and weather forecasts. This helps optimize inventory levels, minimizes overstocking/stockouts, and enhances consumer satisfaction.

- *Warehouse Management*: Effective warehouse management is crucial for quick ordering fulfillment as well as inventory management. Big data analytics may give real-time insight into the warehouse's operations, which allows businesses to increase the efficiency of the level of inventory, monitor the movement of stock, and increase the overall efficiency of warehouses.

- *Optimum Facility Location*: Setting up a new facility is a massive capex expense for any company. Leveraging big data helps reduce the chances of error for such critical decisions. It helps businesses determine where to put brand-new warehouses and distribution centers. They can identify the ideal places for the lowest delivery times and expenses, combining information on customer locations, demand nodes, shipping times, and costs.

- *Supply Chain Risk Management*: Supply chain risk management is essential to your operational success. In the supply chain risk management process, big data can serve as a crucial asset. It allows companies to track and analyze large volumes of data that, when correctly processed, can reveal compelling insights. Supply chain risk management is all about identifying, assessing, and mitigating risks in your supply network. It involves careful planning and the use of tools, such as supply chain risk management software, to provide actionable insights. Big data analytics helps anticipate and determine supply chain risks in advance and help control them in time. Recognizing trends and patterns could help businesses prepare for disruption and take proactive actions. Big data can also help keep plan Bs ready and activate them immediately in case of an adverse supply chain event.

- *Supplier Performance*: Big data analytics helps businesses better measure and evaluate supplier performance. Continuous improvement metrics may be monitored and analyzed with big data, including delivery times, quality standards, and adherence. This provides improved insights into supplier performance, resulting in closer, much more cooperative relationships. Such step-by-step improvements unlock the power of a collaborative supply chain, leading to a more dependable and robust end-to-end supply chain.

- *Tracking*: Big data tracking allows supply chain managers to monitor the movement of goods, inventory levels, and production processes in real-time. It can significantly benefit supply chains by providing real-time visibility, predictive analytics, optimization capabilities, and improved decision-making. Big data tracking allows for overview, evaluation, and improvement of various supply chain processes, such as route planning, inventory management, and production scheduling.

Tracking also allows companies to track changes in their customers' behavior, such as shifts in buying habits, interests, and satisfaction levels. Through analysis of this data, companies can better tailor their output, including services and products, and strengthen customer satisfaction and loyalty. Platforms built on big data use technology to track each item by its unique product number and delivery address to ensure customers receive their correct orders on time. Figure 7.7 shows tracking systems in the supply chain [12].

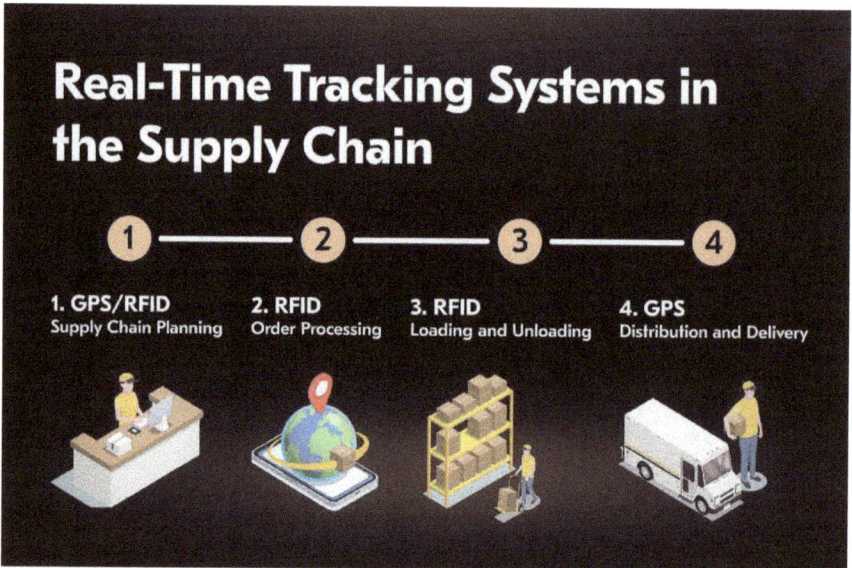

Figure 7.7 Tracking systems in the supply chain [12].

- *Real-time Visibility*: Big Data and IoT sensors provide real-time visibility into supply chain operations. This includes tracking the movement of goods, monitoring environmental conditions, and capturing data on production processes. This supply chain visibility plays a vital role in identifying blockages and inefficiencies in the chains, allowing companies to input corrective action swiftly.

- *Supply Chain Disruptions*: In today's interconnected global economy, supply chain disruptions can have severe consequences. Supply chain disruptions are a critical concern for businesses, as they can lead to significant operational challenges and financial losses. These disruptions can originate from a variety of sources, each with its own set of complications and required management strategies. Properly addressing these disruptions not only minimizes the immediate impacts on supply chain operations but also strengthens long-term resilience and reliability. Disruptions from natural disasters can cripple key infrastructure, leading to severe logistical setbacks. Market fluctuations can cause rapid changes in both supply and demand, disrupting established procurement and financial strategies. The data can help predict, respond to, and recover from supply network disruptions.

- *Predictive Analysis*: Predictive analytics, business analytics, big data analytics, and supply chain analytics are examples of quantitative and qualitative analyses. Big data analysis is highly effective when planning sales strategies and scaling your business. It may be utilized to boost market competitiveness while also improving data quality management and user experience. Big data allows you to explore consumer trends and better forecast demand. It helps to improve operational efficiency and reduce costs throughout the fulfillment process and entire supply chain. Big data is not biased. It is fact-based with numbers that show the broad picture of how your business is performing. With predictive analytics, logistic companies can spot patterns, anticipate fluctuations in demand and improve storage space usage.

- *Food Supply Chain*: The world's food supply is increasingly integrated. For example, maize from different regions of the world is traded in international markets and transported to most continents. The complexity of the network has led to data-driven systems being used to manage the supply chain. As the world becomes increasingly connected, the need for efficient and reliable food supply chains has never been greater. Big data is playing an increasingly important role in controlling food supply chains, from farm to table. It is being used to track consumer behavior. This information can be used by manufacturers and retailers to ensure that they are meeting consumer demand.

It can also be used to help identify new trends and develop marketing strategies. Figure 7.8 shows a food supply chain [18].

Figure 7.8 Food supply chain [18].

7.6 BENEFITS

Big data offers numerous benefits for supply chain management, such as enhancing visibility across the network, improving demand forecasting, and optimizing logistics. Smart business decisions are made by using data. Data analytics can aid in the smooth and effective operation of supply chains. It can assist supply chains in optimizing their routes and schedules, as well as tracking their success over time. Other benefits include the following [14,19]:

- *Enhanced Demand Forecasting*: Big data and supply chain enable more accurate demand forecasting by analyzing historical sales data, market trends, and real-time conditions. They adjust inventory in real time to avoid overstocking items unlikely to sell and ensure that popular items are available.

- *Better Visibility and Transparency*: One of the significant benefits of big data in logistics and supply chain management is improved visibility across the entire value chain. Big data consolidates information across all supply chain stages, from raw materials to warehousing and delivery. Also, you can analyze data from manufacturing and assembly lines to identify bottlenecks or inefficiencies.

- *Inventory Optimization*: By aligning stock levels with actual demand, you avoid overstocking, which ties up working capital and increases holding costs. Real-time data enables businesses to quickly restock fast-moving items and ensure products are available when customers want them.

- *Route Optimization*: Logistics companies deal with complex transportation networks and face challenges in finding the most efficient routes for deliveries. Big data analytics helps optimize routes by considering factors such as traffic conditions, weather patterns, and historical delivery data.

- *Efficiency*: Using big-time data in the various supply chain industries helps in figuring out the pros and cons, tackling future potential risks, and changing development strategies in the industry. It helps in minimizing the inefficiencies and enhancing productivity.

- *Optimization*: One of the key areas where big data has made a significant impact on supply chain management is in optimization. By analyzing vast amounts of data related to inventory levels, production schedules, transportation routes, and customer demand, companies can identify areas for improvement and make data-driven decisions to optimize their supply chain operations.

- *Risk Assessment*: Analytics can assess supply chain risks by analyzing historical data and external factors. By identifying potential risks and vulnerabilities, organizations can develop contingency plans and strategies to mitigate them.

- *Last-Mile Delivery*: The last-mile delivery, often the most expensive and challenging part of the supply chain, benefits from analytics. Data on customer locations, delivery preferences, and traffic conditions help companies optimize last-mile logistics.

- *Improved Logistics and Transportation*: Real-time data from GPS, traffic updates, and weather conditions allow companies to adjust delivery routes on the fly. By tracking vehicle performance and fuel usage and optimizing routes, you will reduce expenses and stay more sustainable.

- *Personalized Customer Experience*: Supply chain and big data enable supply chains to become more customer-centric by tailoring offerings and services. Providing timely, accurate, and personalized service builds trust and customer satisfaction, increasing long-term revenue potential.

- *Sustainability*: Big data analytics helps monitor and manage ethics and sustainability in supply chains. It can enable effective product trailing from procurement to delivery. Companies can track products' sourcing, production, and transport to meet environmental and social requirements. This lessens the carbon footprint, enhances the company's reputation due to ethical sourcing, and meets customer needs for environmentally and socially responsible business practices.

- *Integration*: For effective integration of big data into supply chain risk management, it is essential to ensure that the data is clean, relevant, and accurate. Clean data means that the information is free from errors and discrepancies. Ensuring relevance involves aligning the data collected with the specific risk management needs of the supply chain. Accuracy is critical as it enhances the reliability of the insights generated from the data analysis.

- *Collaboration*: Big data analytics facilitates collaboration among various stakeholders in the supply chain, including suppliers, manufacturers, distributors, and retailers. By sharing relevant data and insights, companies can improve coordination, synchronize production schedules, and optimize inventory levels.

- *Traceability*: Big data and analytics enable end-to-end traceability of products. This is crucial for product recalls, quality control, and compliance with regulatory requirements.

Some of these benefits are displayed in Figure 7.9 [14].

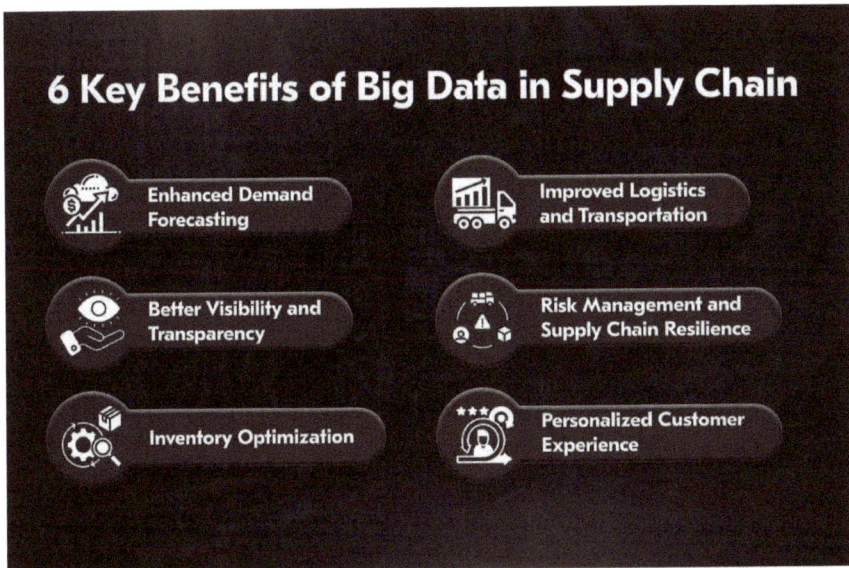

Figure 7.9 Some benefits of big data in supply chain [14].

7.7 CHALLENGES

In spite of the immense benefits of big data for supply chain management, many challenges prevent efficient use and implementation. Among the most pressing issues are data security and privacy concerns. One of the biggest challenges is the sheer volume of data generated through various sources. Another challenge is the quality of the data. Addressing these challenges is crucial for businesses looking to leverage big data. Other challenges include the following [14]:

- *Ethical Concern*: Within the big data industry, data is passed from one firm to the next within an information supply chain. All supply chains carry ethical issues both downstream and upstream. Software companies must ensure that their products are not eventually sold in Syria through a distribution center in Dubai. Data aggregators or data brokers may sell the information to researchers, government agencies or polling companies. Selling information increases the risk of secondary misuse of the data, with eventual harmful impacts on users. The harm resulting from the use of big data can also be identified by asking whether individuals' rights are being realized in the process of using the data.

- *Data Privacy*: Ensuring data privacy becomes increasingly complex in a regulatory environment that is both strict and varied across regions.

- *High Cost of Implementation*: Big data analytics in logistics and supply chain management often require significant upfront investment in infrastructure, technology, and training. Small and medium-sized enterprises may struggle with these expenses.

- *Data Quality and Integration*: Supply chains generate large volumes of data from diverse sources, and integrating them into a cohesive format for analysis is complex. Inconsistent or poor-quality data can lead to incorrect decisions and operational inefficiencies.

- *Lack of Skilled Workforce*: Data analysis is a growing job opportunity since every supply chain industry uses big data analytics to enhance efficiency. Data scientists, analysts, and IT specialists are in high demand, and small and medium-sized enterprises often struggle to recruit and retain talent. This can slow down the adoption and effective use of supply chain and big data analytics.

- *Change Management*: Employees may be reluctant to adopt new technologies, fearing job displacement or a steep learning curve. Introducing big data requires significant shifts in organizational processes, roles, and mindsets. Clearly communicate the pros of big data analytics for supply chain and how it will improve operations, not replace jobs. The goal is to foster a data-driven culture where the workforce is not only comfortable with big data tools but also sees them as invaluable assets in optimizing procurement outcomes.

- *Cybersecurity*: There is the challenge of data security. With the large volumes of data generated through various sources, there is a risk of data breaches and cyber-attacks. As the volume of data increases, so does the potential for breaches, which can jeopardize sensitive information and disrupt operations. The digitalization of supply chain processes has exposed businesses to increased risks of cyber-attacks. To effectively manage big data in supply chain management, businesses need to invest in cybersecurity measures that can protect their data from potential threats.

Some of these challenges are depicted in Figure 7.10 [14].

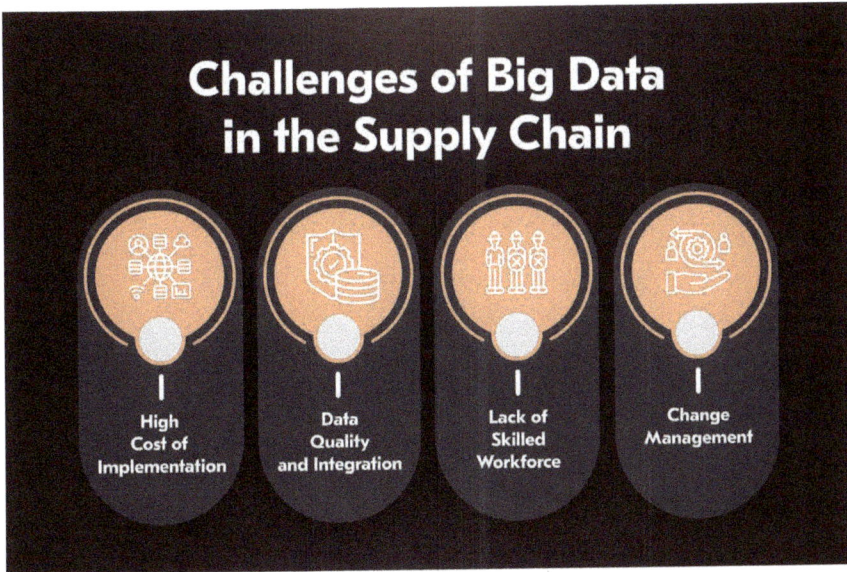

Figure 7.10 Some challenges of big data in supply chain [14].

7.8 CONCLUSION

Big data is a term used to describe a massive amount of data that is generated from various sources. This data can be used to track and analyze trends in order to better understand and manage supply chains. Big data analytics has emerged as a game-changer, enabling businesses to gather, analyze, and leverage massive amounts of data to make informed decisions and drive innovation. Big data applications in supply chain management enable companies to analyze vast datasets for critical insights, enhancing inventory optimization, demand forecasting, and risk management. The ever-increasing reliance on big data is altering the landscape of supply chains as we know it. The transition to data-driven decision making is reshaping the supply chain landscape and has far reaching implications for how businesses function. Big data is turning supply chain managers into "mind readers," allowing them to predict and react to buyer behaviors in new ways.

Big data analytics has emerged as an integral force in the supply chain. The role of big data in supply chain management has been rapidly evolving and growing in recent years. As big data evolves, so does its importance in supply chains. As we move towards a more data-driven and digital future, companies that harness the power of big data will be well-positioned to succeed in the ever-evolving business landscape. More information about big data in the supply chain industry can be found in the books in [20-24] and a related journal: *International Journal of Logistics Research and Applications*.

REFERENCES

[1] "The big data industry's supply chain," Unknown Source.
[2] M. N. O. Sadiku, P. A. Adekunte, and J. O. Sadiku, "Big data in supply chain," *International Journal of Trend in Scientific Research and Development*, vol. 9, no. 2, March-April 2025, pp. 128-139.
[3] M. N. O. Sadiku, M. Tembely, and S.M. Musa, "Big data: An introduction for engineers," *Journal of Scientific and Engineering Research*, vol. 3, no. 2, 2016, pp. 106-108.
[4] "Big data optimisation and management in supply chain management: a systematic literature review," *Open access*, vol. 56, June 2023, pp.253-284.
[5] "The complete overview of big data," https://intellipaat.com/blog/tutorial/hadoop-tutorial/big-data-overview/
[6] R. Allen, "Types of big data | Understanding & Interacting with key types (2024)," https://investguiding-com.custommapposter.com/article/types-of-big-data-understanding-amp-interacting-with-key-types
[7] J. Moorthy et al., "Big data: Prospects and challenges," *The Journal for Decision Makers*, vol. 40, no. 1, 2015, pp. 74–97. https://www.grandviewresearch.com/industry-analysis/industrial-wireless-sensor-networks-iwsn-market
[8] A. K. Tiwari, H. Chaudhary, and S. Yadav, "A review on big data and its security,"

Proceedings of IEEE Sponsored 2nd International Conference on Innovations in Information Embedded and Communication Systems, 2015.

[9] M. B. Hoy, "Big data: An introduction for librarians," *Medical Reference Services Quarterly,* vol. 33, no 3. 2014, pp. 320-327.

[10] M. Viceconti, P. Hunter, and R. Hose, "Big data, big knowledge: Big data for personalized healthcare," *IEEE Journal of Medical and Health Informatics,* vol. 19, no. 4, July 2015, pp. 1209-1215.

[11] P. Baumann et al., "Big data analytics for earth sciences: The earthserver approach," *International Journal of Digital Earth,* vol. 19, no. 1, 2016, pp.3-29.

[12] X. Wu et al., "Knowledge engineering with big data," *IEEE Intelligent Systems,* September/October 2015, pp.46-55.

[13] "Supply chain analytics: How it guides data-driven decision making (infographic)," https://usccg.com/blog/supply-chain-analytics-how-it-guides-data-driven-decision-making/

[14] "Big data in supply chain: Real-world use cases and success stories," November 2024, https://acropolium.com/blog/big-data-in-supply-chain-real-world-use-cases-and-success-stories/

[15] O. A. Gunes, "The role of big data in logistics and supply chain management," July 2023, https://www.threadinmotion.com/en/blog/the-role-of-big-data-in-logistics-and-supply-chain-management

[16] R. Fayolle, "5 Ways big data is transforming supply chains," January 2024, https://www.holocene.eu/blog-posts/5-ways-big-data-is-transforming-supply-chains

[17] "How is big data used to control food supply chains?" September 2022, https://www.aeologic.com/blog/how-is-big-data-used-to-control-food-supply-chains/

[18] I. Abbasi, "How is big data used to control food supply chains?" March 2022, https://www.azom.com/news.aspx?newsID=58688

[19] R. A. Vela, "Big data and analytics in supply chain operations," December 2023, https://www.azom.com/news.aspx?newsID=58688

[20] M. N. O. Sadiku, U. C. Chukwu, and P. O. Adebo, *Big Data and Its Applications*. Moldova, Europe: Lambert Academic Publishing, 2024.

[21] P. W. Robertson, *Supply Chain Analytics: Using Data to Optimise Supply Chain Processes*. Taylor & Francis, 2020.

[22] I. Rahimi et al. (eds.), *Big Data Analytics in Supply Chain Management: Theory and Applications*. Boca Raton, FL: CRC Press, 2020.

[23] H. K. Chan, N. Subramanian), and M. D. Abdulrahman (eds.), *Supply Chain Management in the Big Data Era (Advances in Logistics, Operations, and Management Science)*. Business Science Reference, 2017.

[24] N. R. Sanders, *Big Data Driven Supply Chain Management: A Framework for Implementing Analytics and Turning Information Into Intelligence*. Pearson Education, 2014.

CHAPTER 8

BIG DATA IN MEDIA AND
ENTERTAINMENT

"Education is the passport to the future, for tomorrow belongs to those who prepare for it today." – Malcolm X

8.1 INTRODUCTION

Today, the term "media" encompasses not only television, radio and print, but also phone calls, text messaging, social platforms, and video chatting — any channel through which information and entertainment is disseminated. The media and entertainment industry is all about art and employing big data in it. Publishers, broadcasters, news organizations, cable companies, and gaming companies in the media and entertainment industry are facing new business models for the way they create, market, and distribute their content. This is happening because today's consumers search and access content anywhere, at any time, and on any device. For the media and entertainment industry, their customers are the real kings and big data is helping them to treat their customers like a one. With millions of digital consumers, media and entertainment companies are in a unique position to leverage their big data assets for more profitable customer engagement [1].

The media and entertainment industries have frequently been at the forefront of adopting new technologies. The exploitation of data in the media industry has always played an important role, especially nowadays, when people interact with various sources of information and spend more time online, producing data through their devices (smartphones, tablets, laptops, etc). Media platforms use big data to track content performance across various platforms, such as social media, streaming services, and websites. This can help companies identify trends and optimize their content strategy. For example, media companies like Disney track the performance of their movies and TV shows across various platforms to understand audience engagement and optimize their content strategy.

We are living in the era of big data, which is huge amounts of data in digital form. From healthcare to finance, big data is being used to transform how industries function, enabling business enterprises to create new revenue streams, enhance customer experiences, and increase operational efficiency. Big data plays a crucial role in the media and entertainment industry by enabling companies to understand audience behavior, personalize content, and optimize marketing efforts. It significantly impacts the media and entertainment industry by enabling data-driven decision-making, improving user experiences, and streamlining operations. It is now the real hero for the media and entertainment industry [2].

This chapter presents an overview of the state of the art of big data in the media and entertainment industry. It begins with explaining what big data is all about. It describes big data in media and entertainment and provides some examples. It discusses some applications of big data in the media and entertainment industry. It highlights the benefits and challenges of big data in media and entertainment. The last section concludes with comments.

8.2 WHAT IS BIG DATA?

Big data applies to data sets of extreme size (e.g. exabytes, zettabytes) which are beyond the capability of the commonly used software tools. It involves situation where very large data sets are big in volume, velocity, veracity, and variability [3]. The data is too big, too fast, or does not fit the regular database architecture. It may require different strategies and tools for profiling, measurement, assessment, and processing. Different components of big data are shown in Figure 8.1 [4]. The cloud word for big data is shown in Figure 8.2 [5].

Figure 8.1 Different components of big data [4].

Figure 8.2 The cloud word for big data [5].

Big Data is essentially classified into three types [6]:

- *Structured Data*: This is highly organized and is the easiest to work with. Any data that can be stored, accessed, and processed in the form of fixed format is known as a structured data. It may be stored in tabular format. Due to their nature, it is easy for programs to sort through and collect data. Structured data has quantitative data such as age, contact, address, billing, expenses, credit card numbers, etc. Data that is stored in a relational database management system is an example of structured data.

- *Unstructured Data*: This refers to unorganized data such as video files, log files, audio files, and image files. Any data with unknown form or the structure is classified as unstructured data. Almost everything generated by a computer is unstructured data. It takes a lot of time and effort required to make unstructured data readable. Examples of unstructured data include Metadata, Twitter tweets, and other social media posts.

- *Semi-structured Data*: This falls somewhere between structured data and unstructured data, i.e., both forms of data are present. Semi-structured data can be inherited such as location, time, email address, or device ID stamp.

The different types of big data are depicted in Figure 8.3 [7]. Structured and unstructured data are generated in various types [8-11].

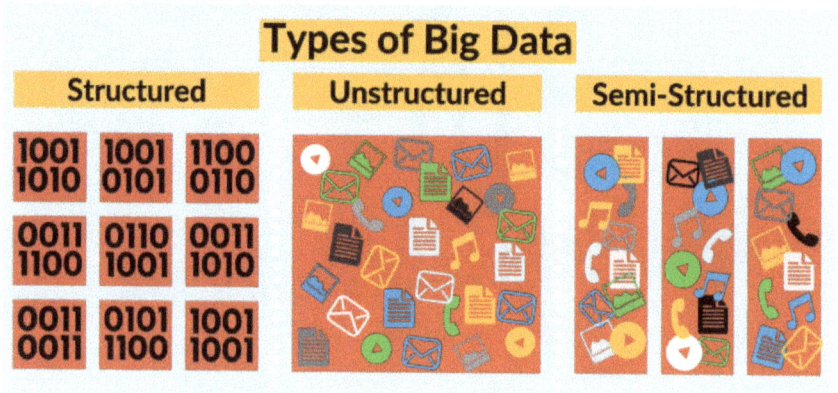

Types of Big Data

| Structured | Unstructured | Semi-Structured |

Figure 8.3 Types of big data [7].

The process of examining big data is often referred to big data analytics. It is an emerging field since massive computing capabilities have been made available by e-infrastructures [12]. Big data analytics is the application of advanced analytic techniques to large, heterogeneous data sets that comprise structured, semi-structured, and unstructured data from many sources with sizes ranging from terabytes to zettabytes.

Analytics include statistical models and other methods that are aimed at creating empirical predictions. Data-driven organizations use analytics to guide decisions at all levels. Several techniques have been proposed for analyzing big data. These include the HACE theorem, cloud computing, Hadoop, and MapReduce [13].

8.3 BIG DATA IN MEDIA AND ENTERTAINMENT

The media and entertainment industry is evolving constantly, and data analytics is emerging as a game-changer in shaping the landscape. It is evolving at an unprecedented rate, driven by the twin needs to reduce operating costs and simultaneously generate more revenue from increasingly competitive and uncertain markets. This transformational integration of big data and analytics is not just reshaping content creation and distribution but is also redefining the landscape of media and entertainment software development. The transformative impact of big data and analytics in the media and entertainment industry is enabling the industry to strategically use data analytics to reshape the industry in several key areas, drive innovation, and enhance user experiences. Figure 8.4 shows a representation of the media and entertainment industry [14].

Figure 8.4 A representation of the media and entertainment industry [14].

Over the past few years, big data has grown crucial in the media and entertainment industries. Entertainment businesses have obtained through insights into their clients, systems, and processes by embracing big data analytics. Big data in media and entertainment is not only assisting businesses to gain hidden insights into consumer behavior but is also helping the delivery of personalized content. Today, we can have access to our favorite shows and movies anytime, anywhere with the advancements of services by using big data analytics. We now have access to everything at our fingertips and big data has been the backbone of this amazing transformation. Because of this, technological development has become essential in bringing outside entertainment to consumers' homes.

8.4 EXAMPLES OF BIG DATA IN MEDIA AND ENTERTAINMENT

Big data in the media industry is a big deal. The most competitive media companies are adopting big data solutions to help manage their data, generate new insights, and improve their services. For example, the most pre-eminent players in the media and entertainment industry, such as Netflix, Amazon, Hulu, and Disney, have already been leveraging big data as part of their operations to enhance the customer experience. The following are examples of such companies [15]:

- *Spotify*: is a music streaming service using listening data to curate personalized experiences for its users. Spotify has more 80 million users, which translates to a ton of listening data. So much data, in fact, that Spotify has a blog that displays the different ways data is understood on the platform.

- *Instagram*: is a social platform that connects users through photos and videos. Acquired by Facebook in 2012, the widely used site has upwards of one billion users. That means it also has mountains of data. Instagram offers many kinds of profiles, including business profiles that offer users data insights about things like the reach of individual posts, past post comparisons, and the origins of audience impressions.

- *Ampersand*: is a digital advertising solution specializing in targeted TV ads. The company manages and analyzes large volumes of data to ensure effective targeting and campaign optimization. Ampersand works to equip advertisers with insights and solutions to help them make data-driven decisions that maximize the impact of their advertising campaigns.

- *NBCUniversal*: is a titan of media and entertainment that captivates audiences with shows and movies distributed through an array of network television, film studio, and streaming brands. Data plays an important role in NBCUniversal's business strategy. The company leverages analytics tools to access user insights that inform decision making — an approach that has led to increased viewership.

- *Hulu*: is a streaming service that provides access to a library of TV shows and movies, original content, and current seasons of television series airing on stations like FOX, ABC, and NBC. Accessible across devices, Hulu regularly adds content and recently expanded to offer a live TV service.

- *Netflix's*: leadership in the marketplace can be directly attributed to successfully harnessing the power of big data. Big data and a robust analytics program have been a competitive advantage for Netflix over the past decade. With over 200 million subscribers, Netflix leverages its wealth of audience data to deliver personalized content recommendations and platform experiences. As the world's most popular streaming platform, Netflix analyzes its financial data to forecast demand for content, estimate its financial impact, and invest dollars to bring audiences the content they want.

8.5 APPLICATIONS OF BIG DATA MEDIA AND ENTERTAINMENT

The integration of big data and analytics is foundational to the new era in the entertainment industry. Various areas where big data can be used in media and entertainment include consumer care, advertising, content monetization, and data journalism. Figure 8.5 shows some use cases of big data analytics in M&E industry [16]. Common applications of big data in the M&E industry include the following [17-19]:

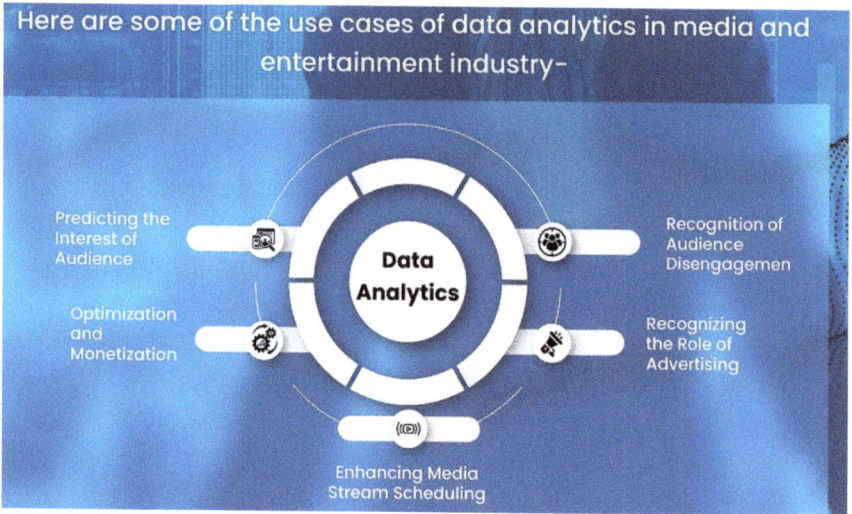

Figure 8.5 Some use cases of big data analytics in M&E industry [16].

- *Customer Care*: For a media and entertainment company, nobody is more important for them than its users and keeping its users happy is their toughest task. Companies need to ensure that they fulfill each of their customer's wishes. To attain the same, they must be aware of what their customers need. Big data analytics are used to recommend users shows or movies according to their preferences. Companies can even gain in-depth details about the other important things such as viewing history, ratings, reviews, data from social media, etc. Big data analytics is helping companies to connect with their customers in a much better way than they ever did.

- *Advertising*: Running a media and entertainment company without advertising is like winking at a person in the dark; you know what you are doing, but nobody else does. Advertising to media and entertainment companies is what food is to soul. A media company's success heavily depends on their advertising strategies. Big data helps media companies target advertisements more effectively by understanding consumer demographics, interests, and online behavior. Big data analysis helps companies to develop more personalized ads and provides insights about the best time to stream those ads to seek the attention of the maximum number of customers. As big data has made it possible for the media houses to understand their customer's exact preferences; it is quite easy for them to engross the customers.

- *Content Monetization*: Like all businesses, media companies aim to maximize revenue, minimize costs, and improve decision-making and business processes. As consumer interests shift from analog to digital media, there are substantial opportunities to monetize content and to identify new products and services. Entertainment and media companies can use big data to understand what content, products and features consumers want. Product updates have become more cost effective and time effective, thanks to the analysis of customer data. You will never know what features your consumers want or need you to release if you do not dive into the data; it could give you a competitive edge, increase revenue, and brand loyalty.

- *Data Analysis*: Media and entertainment companies generate and collect data from a variety of sources. They need to analyze data not only at the customer and product levels, but also at network and infrastructure levels. Audience data breaks down into three broad categories: personal data, demographic data, and behavioral data. Key technologies in the coming years will be descriptive analytics, more sophisticated customer relationship management solutions, and lastly data visualization solutions that are accessible to a wide range of users in the enterprise. It is only by "humanizing" these tools that big data will be able to deliver the benefits that data-driven businesses increasingly demand.

- *Data Journalism*: Journalism incorporated big data into its practices in a way that influenced the internal logic of the profession. In the last 30 years, digital technologies with the introduction of various tools have made journalistic work easier. However, they have also made journalist work more difficult, because they have overwhelmed journalists with more information than can be handled by their investigative toolboxes. Data journalism emerges as a result of these changes, and it is related to data-driven journalism. Specifically, the introduction of information and communications technology (ICT) and the availability big data have turned data journalism into its current form. Data journalism promotes open journalism and open data. The term open data is related to transparency, accountability, accessibility, and free, public, and recyclable use.

- *Audience Participation*: Although audience participation has always been part of the journalism practice, the diffusion of Web 2.0 tools along with the socio-economic circumstances have led to the proliferation of user-generated content and increased users' involvement in the news production process. Audience participation in news production can be enabled by data journalism projects as well. Thanks to the participation of victims and witnesses, a number of media organizations in Latin America have revealed situations involving huge breaches of human rights not identified in official records. Figure 8.6 shows an example of audience participation [20].

Figure 8.6 An example of audience participation [20].

- *Data Mining*: While it is clearly evident that there are multitudes of potential applications for big data in the media industry, the fact remains that these datasets are so large and complex that in practice they are particularly unwieldy. Data mining is defined as a logical procedure used in order to search through very big amounts of data, with the purpose of discovering new, non-trivial information, which can subsequently be used to arrive at previously unknown conclusions. By this definition, it is immediately obvious that data mining and big data go hand-in-hand when it comes to journalistic practices. As stated before, the nature of big data renders them inaccessible to being processed by humans, or even by simple software, because of various factors that make them hard to understand and compute.

8.6 BENEFITS

Integrating big data and analytics into the media and entertainment industry is laying the foundation of a new era. As these technologies continue to evolve, they are set to unlock more possibilities for creating engaging and innovative entertainment experiences. Big data in the media industry can yield three different types of insights: diagnostic, predictive, and prescriptive. By using big data analytics, entertainment companies have been able to gain detailed insights regarding not only their customers but also their systems and processes. Other benefits of big data in the M&E industry include the following [11,21]:

- *Personalized Content*: By analyzing viewer's viewing habits, preferences, and interactions, these technologies will enable entertainment platforms to design content that resonates with individual tastes.

- *Informed Decision-making*: Data analytics presents deep insights into viewer preferences, demographics, and behaviors, thereby equipping content creators and distributors with valuable insights for informed decision-making. This data is instrumental in shaping content strategies, scheduling releases, and guiding the creation of new content as per audience demands.

- *Predictive Analysis*: This helps anticipate future trends and viewer preferences, enabling the sector to stay ahead of the curve. By predicting potential successes, media and entertainment studios can make informed decisions about different projects, thus reducing the financial risks associated with content production.

- *Prescriptive Insights*: These are recommendations to make a business decision or take action in a certain way. Prescriptive insights are also the domain of artificial intelligence, requiring the AI application to translate its forecasts into actionable recommendations that support strategic business objectives. Media companies who leverage AI to analyze their big data can generate more accurate and higher-quality insights than those who stick to manual methods

- *Data Management*: Data management, including aggregation and normalization, is a time-consuming task for media companies who still depend on manual processes. Enterprise AI solutions with multi-platform integration features can streamline and automate the process of aggregating data from multiple sources into a centralized repository and normalizing the data to prepare it for analytics.

- *Targeted Marketing*: With detailed audience insights, organizations can create highly targeted marketing campaigns to resonate with specific viewer segments. This level of targeting will help enhance viewer engagement while ensuring a higher return on investment for marketing campaigns.

- *Advertising*: The primary factor determining a company's market worth and profitability is still advertising. Advertisements seem to be a natural component of any entertainment industry. This assists the businesses in acting as retargeting agents so that advertising will appear if people are watching a show or a movie with a connection to the items. Big data applications assist in analyzing user behavior and what they are likely to buy through targeted advertisements.

- *Content Optimization*: This is the ongoing practice of maximizing revenue from content distribution and licensing agreements. Enterprise AI solutions can help media companies forecast audience demand and assess the revenue potential of various types of content. As a result, media companies can make better strategic decisions about licensing or producing content and distribution teams can leverage insights to maximize licensing terms.

- *Revenue*: Another crucial aspect where big data has proven to be invaluable is revenue. It analyzes what customers want, what is in vogue in the market, the target audience's viewing history, etc. to offer recommendations about generating better sales, adapting marketing strategies, fine-tune the when and where of content delivery, etc. All these measures seek to ensure high customer engagement rates and thus, better revenue for the company. Media organizations realized that by studying content consumption data, they can extract useful information which may help in designing successful publishing strategies and lead to new revenue opportunities.

8.7 CHALLENGES

In spite of its benefits, integrating big data and analytics in entertainment software development comes with challenges, including data privacy concerns, managing vast data volumes, and ensuring data accuracy. Most media firms are already doing some big data analytics, but the technical challenges of efficiently pooling data from multiple sources and extracting insights may be preventing them from using their data to its full potential. Attracting and keeping customers engaged are the biggest challenges faced by media and entertainment companies across the world. Big data as a phenomena is still, by their very nature, hard to access and work. Other challenges of big data in the M&E industry include the following [21]:

- *Siloed Data*: Big data in the media industry may be collected from subscribers, generated internally and stored in a database, provided by distribution partners, or sourced from a third-party organization. These multiple sources of data live in separate systems (data silos), and this segmentation means they cannot easily be integrated for analytics applications.

- *Non-standardized Formats*: Big data in the entertainment industry comes from multiple sources and may be in a variety of different formats. A media firm that licenses content to ten different distributors might receive ten different profit-sharing reports, each with their own fields and format. The lack of a standardized format means that this data must be normalized before it can be analyzed effectively.

- *Manual Data Processes*: While some media companies are using complex algorithms to process big data, others are still dependent on manual processes for data aggregation, normalization, analytics, and reporting. But as big data continues to grow, manual processes become more time-consuming, insights are delayed, and the overall impact and value of big data diminishes.

- *Ethical Considerations*: It is crucial for media companies to use big data responsibly and ethically, ensuring that data is used to benefit users and not exploit them.

- *Infrastructure*: While start-ups and SMEs can operate efficiently with open source and cloud infrastructure, for larger, older players, updating legacy IT infrastructure is a challenge. Legacy products and standards still need to be supported in the transition to big data ways of thinking and working. Failure to transform the culture and skillset of staff could impact companies who are profitable today but cannot adapt to data-driven business models.

- *Consumer Awareness*: There is increased consumer awareness and concern about how personal data is being used. There is regulatory uncertainty for European businesses that handle personal data, which potentially puts them at a disadvantage compared to, say, US companies who operate within a much more relaxed legal landscape.

8.8 CONCLUSION

Media and entertainment industry is advancing at an unprecedented, governed by dual requirements to minimize costs while at the same time generating more revenues from a highly competitive and uncertain market. The media and entertainment sector is in many respects an early adopter of big data technologies, but much more evolution has to happen for the full potential to be realized. The sector is experiencing a significant transformation with the integration of big data and analytics. Big data and analytics are key drivers for industry growth, extending beyond content personalization to strategic decision-making and significantly influencing the entertainment sector's overall success.

With the influence of big data and analytics in media and entertainment on the rise, it is becoming evident that these technologies are pivotal to the industry's future trajectory. The future of entertainment is here, and it is decidedly data-driven. More information about big data in the media and entertainment industry can be found in the books in [22-24] and the following related journal: *Journal of Big Data*

REFERENCES

[1] "Big data in media and entertainment,"
https://www.qubole.com/big-data-in-media-and-entertainment
[2] M. N. O. Sadiku, P. A. Adekunte, and J. O. Sadiku, "Big data in media and entertainment," *International Journal of Trend in Scientific Research and Development*, vol. 9, no. 3, May-June 2025, pp. 875-884.
[3] M. N. O. Sadiku, M. Tembely, and S.M. Musa, "Big data: An introduction for engineers," *Journal of Scientific and Engineering Research*, vol. 3, no. 2, 2016, pp. 106-108.
[4] A. Slamecka, "Big data explosion," April 2022,
https://blogs.cisco.com/financialservices/big-data-explosion
[5] "Passion points: Analytics in the sports, media & entertainment industries," February 2017,
https://gradblog.schulich.yorku.ca/event/passion-points-analytics-in-the-sports-media-entertainment-industries/
[6] "The complete overview of big data,"
https://intellipaat.com/blog/tutorial/hadoop-tutorial/big-data-overview/
[7] R. Allen, "Types of big data | Understanding & Interacting with key types (2024),"
https://investguiding-com.custommapposter.com/article/types-of-big-data-understanding-amp-interacting-with-key-types
[8] J. Moorthy et al., "Big data: Prospects and challenges," *The Journal for Decision Makers*, vol. 40, no. 1, 2015, pp. 74–96.
https://www.grandviewresearch.com/industry-analysis/industrial-wireless-sensor-networks-iwsn-market
[9] A. K. Tiwari, H. Chaudhary, and S. Yadav, "A review on big data and its security,"

Proceedings of IEEE Sponsored 2nd International Conference on Innovations in Information Embedded and Communication Systems, 2018.

[10] M. B. Hoy, "Big data: An introduction for librarians," *Medical Reference Services Quarterly*, vol. 33, no 3. 2014, pp. 320-326.

[11] M. Viceconti, P. Hunter, and R. Hose, "Big data, big knowledge: Big data for personalized healthcare," *IEEE Journal of Medical and Health Informatics*, vol. 19, no. 4, July 2015, pp. 1209-1218.

[12] P. Baumann et al., "Big data analytics for earth sciences: The earthserver approach," *International Journal of Digital Earth*, vol. 19, no. 1, 2016, pp.3-29.

[13] X. Wu et al., "Knowledge engineering with big data," *IEEE Intelligent Systems*, September/October 2015, pp.46-58.

[14] R. Williamson, "Media and entertainment: How this industry is impacted by big data," January 2021, https://www.datasciencecentral.com/media-and-entertainment-how-this-industry-is-impacted-by-big-data/

[15] A. Schroer, "Big data in media & entertainment: 15 examples to know," August 2024, https://builtin.com/articles/big-data-media

[16] "Data analytics in media and entertainment (M&E) industry," https://www.sganalytics.com/blog/data-analytics-in-media-and-entertainment-industry/

[17] "Big data in media and entertainment – The new hero in industry," https://data-flair.training/blogs/big-data-in-media-and-entertainment/

[18] "5 Ways big data plays a major role in the media and entertainment industry," July 2018, https://www.maropost.com/blog/5-ways-big-data-plays-a-major-role-in-the-media-and-entertainment-industry/

[19] A. Veglis et al., "Applications of big data in media organizations," *Social Sciences*, vol. 11, no. 9. 2022.

[20] "Data-driven decisions: How big data and analytics are shaping the future of media & entertainment," April 2024, https://www.sprinterra.com/data-driven-decisions-how-big-data-and-analytics-are-shaping-the-future-of-media-entertainment/

[21] "5 AI-Driven use cases for big data in media & entertainment," October 2022, https://www.symphonyai.com/resources/blog/media/5-ai-driven-use-cases-for-big-data-in-media-entertainment/

[22] M. N. O. Sadiku, U. C. Chukwu, and P. O. Adebo, *Big Data and Its Applications*. Moldova, Europe: Lambert Academic Publishing, 2024.

[23] P. C. K. Hung, *Big Data Applications and Use Cases (International Series on Computer, Entertainment and Media Technology)*. Springer, 2016.

[24] T. Hennig-Thurau and M. B. Houston, *Entertainment Science: Data Analytics and Practical Theory for Movies, Games, Books, and Music*. Springer, 2018.

CHAPTER 9

∾

BIG DATA IN OIL AND GAS

"We make a living by what we get. We make a life by what we give." – Sir Winston Churchill

9.1 INTRODUCTION

The world has seen a digital revolution where more and more work is being conducted online. Storing this activity has led to the concept of big data, i.e., large datasets that are otherwise difficult to manage. Because of these characteristics, big data requires new technologies and techniques to capture, store, and analyze. The cloud word for big data is shown in Figure 9.1 [1]. Typical sources of big data are shown in Figure 9.2 [2]. Big data is of great interest to oil and gas production and operation. With the advent of new technologies, there has been a massive increase in the amount of data generated within oil and gas sector.

Figure 9.1 The cloud word for big data [1].

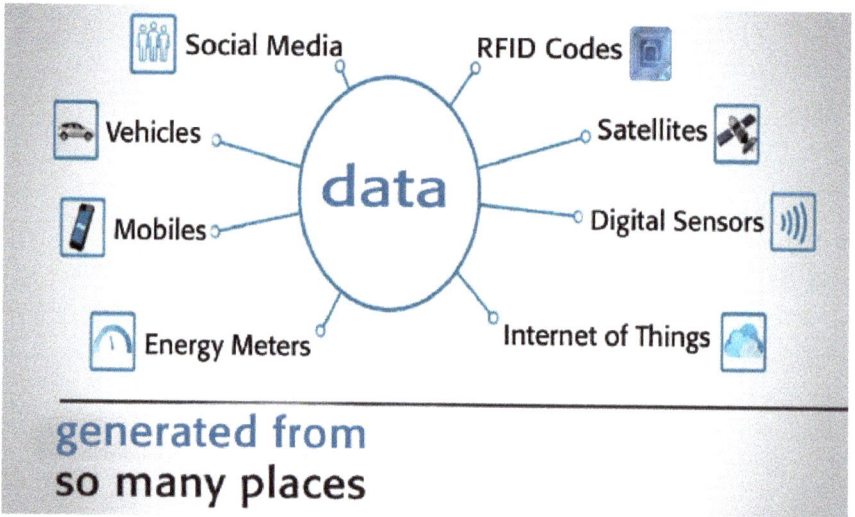

Figure 9.2 Typical sources of big data [2].

The oil and gas sector is one of the largest and most complex industries in the world, involving the exploration, extraction, refining, and distribution of hydrocarbon resources. The complexity of the O&G operation is illustrated in Figure 9.3 [3]. With the recent advent of data recording sensors in exploration, drilling and production operations, oil and gas industry has become a massive data intensive industry. There are ample opportunities for oil and gas companies to use big data to get more oil and gas out of hydrocarbon reservoirs, reduce capital and operational expenses, increase the speed and accuracy of investment decisions, and improve health and safety while mitigating environmental risks. Big data can be used to improve decision-making and operational efficiency by analyzing the data to uncover patterns and correlations. Other new technologies such as deep learning, cognitive computing, and augmented and virtual reality can be used to extract useful information enormously reducing the data processing time.

Figure 9.3 The complexity of the O&G operation [3].

With the recent introduction of data recording sensors in exploration, drilling, and production processes, the oil and gas industry has transformed into a massively data-intensive industry. These data can come from sensors, data recording devices, spatial and GPS coordinates, weather services, and seismic data. Since the data recording devices and sensors are different in types, the generated data can be in different sizes and formats. The vast quantity of data is challenging to be handled due to storage, sustainability, and analysis issues. The main application of big data is to provide processing and analysis tools for the increasing amounts of data. Big data analyzes huge data sets to reveal the underlying trends and help the engineers forecast the potential issues [4].

This chapter reviews the utilization of big data and data analytics in the oil and gas industry. It begins with explaining what big data is all about. It describes the oil and gas industry and big data in the industry. It covers big data in oil and gas. It presents some applications of big data in oil and gas. It highlights the benefits and challenges of big data in oil and gas. The last section concludes with comments.

9.2 WHAT IS BIG DATA?

Big data applies to data sets of extreme size (e.g. exabytes, zettabytes) which are beyond the capability of the commonly used software tools. It involves situation where very large data sets are big in volume, velocity, veracity, and variability [5]. The data is too big, too fast, or does not fit the regular database architecture. It may require different strategies and tools for profiling, measurement, assessment, and processing.

Big Data is essentially classified into three types [6]:

- *Structured Data*: This is highly organized and is the easiest to work with. Any data that can be stored, accessed, and processed in the form of fixed format is known as a structured data. It may be stored in tabular format. Due to their nature, it is easy for programs to sort through and collect data. Structured data has quantitative data such as age, contact, address, billing, expenses, credit card numbers, etc. Data that is stored in a relational database management system is an example of structured data.

- *Unstructured Data*: This refers to unorganized data such as video files, log files, audio files, and image files. Any data with unknown form or the structure is classified as unstructured data. Almost everything generated by a computer is unstructured data. It takes a lot of time and effort required to make unstructured data readable. Examples of unstructured data include Metadata, Twitter tweets, and other social media posts.

- *Semi-structured Data*: This falls somewhere between structured data and unstructured data, i.e., both forms of data are present. Semi-structured data can be inherited such as location, time, email address, or device ID stamp.

The different types of big data are depicted in Figure 9.4 [7]. Structured and unstructured data are generated in various types [8-10].

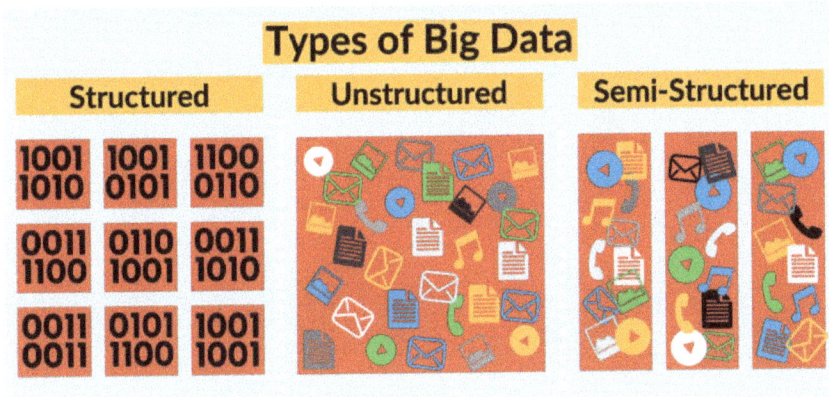

Figure 9.4 Types of big data [7].

The process of examining big data is often referred to big data analytics. It is an emerging field since massive computing capabilities have been made available by e-infrastructures [11]. Analytics include statistical models and other methods that are aimed at creating empirical predictions. Data-driven organizations use analytics to guide decisions at all levels. Several techniques have been proposed for analyzing big data. These include the HACE theorem, cloud computing, Hadoop, and MapReduce [12].

9.3 OIL AND GAS INDUSTRY

Oil is difficult to locate. The oil reservoirs are typically found 5,000 to 35,000 feet below the earth's surface, making them hard to find. Oil is an expensive commodity, and a lot of science, engineering, and workforce are required to produce oil. Given the cost, quantity, and availability of oil, the companies involved in this industry must identify methods to stay profitable. Big data analytics has benefited the oil and gas industry in many ways.

The oil industry divides into upstream, midstream, and downstream, as shown in Figure 9.5 [13] and explained as follows:

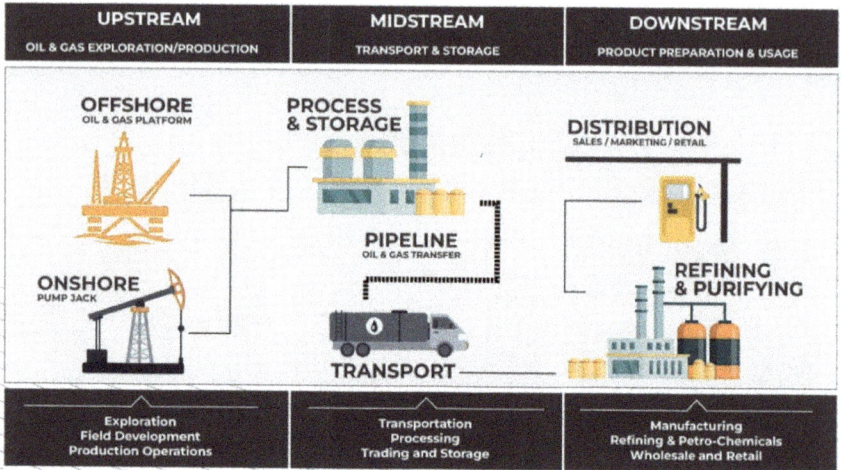

Figure 9.5 The oil industry divides into upstream, midstream, and downstream [13].

- *Upstream Sector:* The upstream process in oil and gas operations refers to the discovery and production of oil and gas . Many activities are done in the upstream area, wherein big data analytics plays a crucial role. Among all business segments upstream segment is the most dominant segment owing to increasing use of big data analytics for the discovery of non-conventional shale gas. Upstream analytics begins with the collection of seismic data with sensors across a potential area of interest looking for petroleum sources. Then the data is aggregated, cleaned, processed, and analyzed to choose the best location for drilling. Figure 9.6 show the upstream operation [14].

Figure 9.6 Upstream operation [14].

- *Midstream Sector*: The midstream activities in the oil and gas industry refer mainly to the transportation of oil and gas, i.e., logistics. Big data analytics is used to enhance shipping performance. For example, to improve the performance of ships and reduce greenhouse emissions, big data analytics helps by predicting the propulsion power. Big data analytics is essential for planning pipelines and infrastructure to transport oil from sources to refineries and pumping stations. Its significance in logistics makes it a critical tool for oil and gas companies, given the highly flammable nature of the transported material.

- *Downstream Sector*: The downstream is responsible for refining petroleum products and delivering them to end-users. It mainly involves refining and selling oil and gas. It is expected to be the second largest segment due to increasing use of product analytics solution which assist refineries to standard chemical composition of the finished products. The downstream oil and gas industry is undergoing a significant transformation due to the integration of dig data technologies. The sector is leveraging big data in numerous ways to enhance efficiency and sustainability.

Plenty of raw information is available for analysis in the oil and gas industry. Whether you are involved upstream, midstream, downstream, administration, or the commodities market, you are surrounded by data.

9.4 BIG DATA IN OIL AND GAS

Big data in oil and gas (O&G) is one of the prominent technologies that are now disrupting the industry with innovative methods. It gives businesses and business owners a huge potential to move forward and grow. More industry executives believe that big data is the solution to boost their business operations. For example, major O&G companies like ExxonMobil, BP, and Shell heavily invest in big data and AI solutions. The companies that embrace and implement new technologies are positioning themselves as frontrunners in shaping the industry's future landscape. To make high profits, these companies must make an environment-friendly commitment and apply IoT for price and asset monitoring.

9.5 APPLICATIONS OF BIG DATA IN OIL AND GAS

The oil and gas industry is no stranger to data. For decades, it has generated massive volumes of information from exploration, production, and distribution operations. The recent technological improvements have resulted in daily generation of massive datasets in oil and gas exploration and production industries. Big data in the oil and gas industry is the massive amount of data generated by various processes and transactions in the sector. The advent of modern sensing technologies, such as the Internet of things (IoT), and remote satellite monitoring, has created an explosion in data generation throughout the sector. Figure 9.7 shows data analytics in oil and gas sector [13], while Figure 9.8 shows the key components of big data analytics in oil and gas industry [15]. Here are some ways big data is used in the oil and gas industry [16,17]:

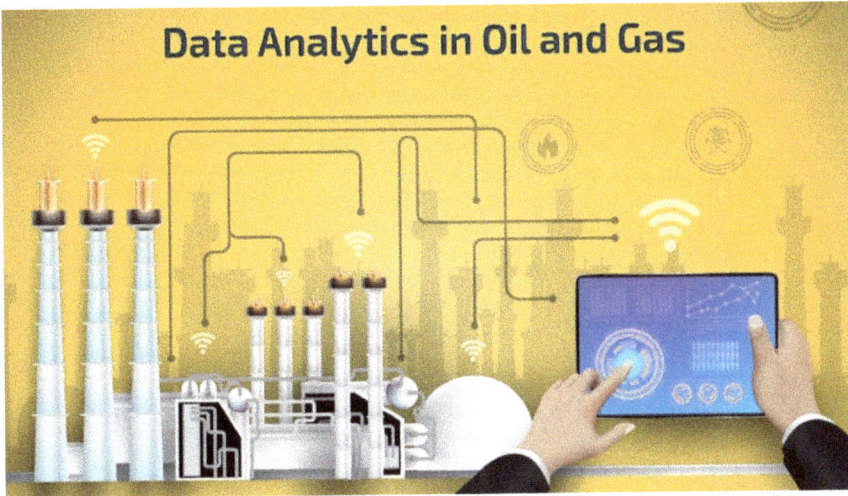

Figure 9.7 Data analytics in oil and gas sector [13].

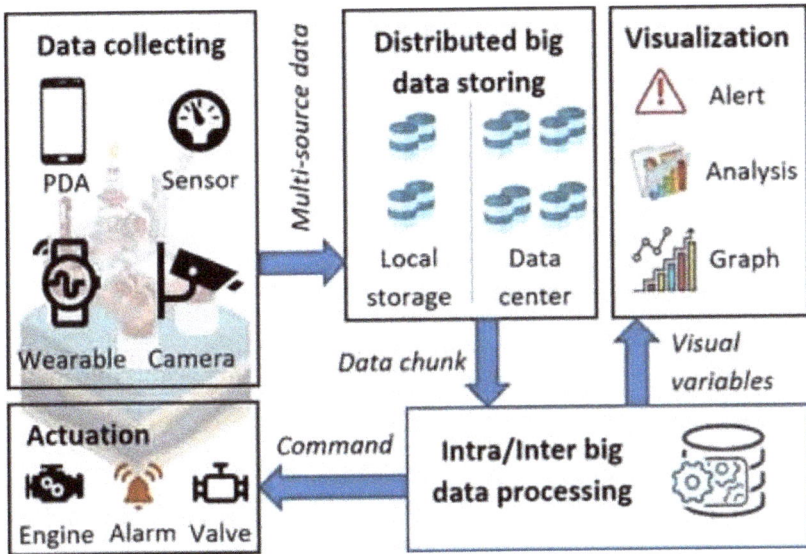

Figure 9.8 Key components of big data analytics in oil and gas industry [15].

- *Supply Chain Optimization*: One key area of application is supply chain optimization. By optimizing logistics, tracking inventory levels, and improving distribution efficiency, downstream companies reduce operational costs while minimizing waste-- thus ensuring that products reach customers in a timely manner.

Big data can help optimize supply chains by analyzing data on inventory, transportation, demand, and market trends. Data-driven demand forecasting models help companies manage their inventories, optimize logistics, and make informed decisions for both upstream and downstream operations.

- *Assessing New Prospects*: Competitive intelligence is created using analytics applied to geospatial data, oil and gas reports and other syndicated feeds in order to bid for new prospects.

- *Enhanced Oil Recovery*: Enhancing oil recovery from existing wells is a key objective for oil and gas companies. Analytics applied to a variety of big data at once (seismic, drilling, and production data) could help reservoir engineers map changes in the reservoir over time and provide decision support to production engineers for making changes in lifting methods. This type of approach could also be used to guide fracking in shale gas plays.

- *Real-time Production Optimization*: Real-time SCADA and process control systems combined with analytics tools help O&G producer to optimize resource allocation and prices by using scalable compute technologies to determine optimum commodity pricing. They also, help to make more real time decisions with fewer engineers. Big data can be used to monitor and analyze production processes in real time, which can help identify bottlenecks and predict equipment failures.

- *Prevent Cyber-Terror Acts*: Oil companies need to identify events or patterns that could indicate an impending security threat or cyber-terrorist act in order to keep their personnel, property and equipment safe. Predictive analytics is central part of identifying patterns that can help detect these threats beforehand.

- *Data Crunching*: From wells, digs, and extraction to transportation and refining, there are ample opportunities to collect data on every single aspect of your business operations. Investing in machine learning will help a company absorb petabytes of sensor data from drills faster than a whole fleet of workers on the actual job site. This frees up the people to make better, more informed decisions.

- *Predictive Analysis*: Algorithms can use historical data and experience to make better and more enlightened predictions about future operations. Companies in possession of this level of enhanced analysis can use it to make very educated guesses about future trends, prices, production, and actions in the market. The more you understand what could happen with your industry, the better prepared you will be for any contingency.

- *Decision-Making*: Data plays a critical role in the decisions that create value. Today, data analytics is being leveraged throughout the oil and gas value chain to optimize decision-making and improve overall performance. Operators make decisions every day in the field, typically with limited involvement by central functions or subject matter experts. With predictive analysis, you can make faster decisions, supported by faster delivery of decision support information, to identify possible threats. You can make the move from educated guesses to confirmed, real-time decisions with ease and confidence. In essence, data analytics does not remove the human element from making decisions. It helps humans make better decisions.

- *Predictive Maintenance*: Big Data analytics enable predictive maintenance through IoT devices and sensors deployed in downstream facilities. Predictive maintenance models based on data analysis can proactively identify areas requiring maintenance and reduce equipment failures, leading to optimized operational efficiency and reduced costs. Everyday operations in the oil and gas industry depend upon a substantial amount of machinery. Thus, it is essential for a business to keep tabs on the condition and fitness of its equipment so it can address problems before a shutdown occurs. Advanced analytics can compare the age of a given machine with its rate of past and future usage to determine when it is most likely to need maintenance and replacing.

- *Data Mining*: This is the extraction of relevant information and insights from large datasets using statistical and computational methods. Data mining is an integral part of big data analytics, which entails processing, analyzing, and interpreting large and complex datasets to discover patterns, trends, and insights that can assist organizations in making informed decisions. Data cleansing, data validation, data normalization, and data transformation are some of the methods used by data mining and analytics practitioners to reduce the likelihood of these errors.

9.6 BENEFITS

Big data is used to identify conditions or anomalies that would impact on drilling operations. Big data solutions can provide companies in the oil and gas industry with insights into exploration, drilling, and production processes to ensure their optimization, reduce environmental risks, streamline equipment maintenance planning, enhance oil recovery, and more. Big data also has other benefits for the oil and gas industry, including the following [18]:

- *Safety*: The responsibility for the health and safety of the individuals working in the oil and gas industry is with the companies that employ them. Big data can be used to monitor for safety hazards and environmental risks, such as leaks, air quality, and pipeline integrity. Big data analytics helps prevent accidents by predicting and detecting anomalies and issues, such as stress corrosion and fatigue cracks in pipes and trucks, along with early detection of seismic movements.

- *Cost-Effectiveness*: The effectiveness of big data analytics in the oil and gas industry has been widely acknowledged as it has evolved into a crucial instrument for enhancing operational efficiency and lowering costs. When you have access to game-changing information about your operations, it becomes easier to increase the efficiency and efficacy of your projects. This increase in productivity can be experienced at every level of the oil and gas industry. This streamlined supply chain not only enhances cost-effectiveness but also contributes to a more sustainable operation by reducing the environmental footprint associated with transportation and storage.

- *Manage Seismic Data*: Drilling for oil in deep water can cost over $100 million, and it is crucial that you find the right location. In fact, to avoid any risks and save time and money, Shell uses fiber optic cables and the data is then transferred to its private servers.

- *Optimize Drilling Process*: Today's oil drilling platforms have about 80,000 sensors, which are expected to generate 15 petabytes of data during the lifetime of a platform. The large amount of data gathered by these sensors allows for predictive maintenance of equipment and timely replacements in order to reduce downtime and increase efficiency.

- *Improve Reservoir Engineering*: Big data solutions help oil and gas companies to collect, process, and analyze data that is essential for making reservoir production more effective. They help to collect and process data that O&G companies need to make reservoir production more effective. This data is collected using a number of downhole sensors (temperature sensors, acoustic sensors, pressure sensors, and others). To make energy more affordable and sustainable, we use big data tools to understand the earth's subsurface better.

- *Improve Logistics*: The oil and gas industry faces the problem of safely transporting petroleum. The major problem that concerns logistics in the oil and gas industry is transporting petroleum while reducing risks as much as possible. To ensure that gas and oil are transported safely, companies use sensors and predictive maintenance. Sensors, predictive maintenance, and other technologies help detect any faults in pipelines or tankers. This allows for safe logistics of petroleum products.

- *Quality*: Just as with petroleum data analytics, the use of big data analytics can be instrumental in maintaining consistent product quality. By monitoring and controlling the refining process in real time, companies can ensure that their products meet stringent specifications and safety standards. This proactive approach also enhances customer trust and brand reputation.

- *Workforce Management*: Data-driven insights help employers optimize their workforce strategy and develop training programs tailored to specific job roles and skillsets.

- *Prescriptive Analytics*: By incorporating human expertise and external data sources into AI models, companies can generate detailed recommendations for specific actions and their potential outcomes.

- *Data Integration*: The oil and gas industry has focused on data integration, i.e., how do we get all the data in one place and make it available to the geo-scientists and engineers working to find and produce hydrocarbons. Proper data integration grows more crucial as oil fields mature because operators must understand changing field conditions. Managers know more than anyone that they must maximize hydrocarbon production while reducing drilling costs.

9.7 CHALLENGES

The sheer volume, complexity, and speed of data generation in the O&G industry have created both significant challenges and opportunities. Leveraging big data in the oil and gas sector poses challenges, such as data integration from diverse sources, data quality assurance, data privacy, and security concerns, and the need for skilled team to understand and analyze the data. Implementing big data in the oil and gas industry presents challenges related to data transfer, collection frequency, and data quality. They include [18,19]:

- *Legacy Systems*: Many oil and gas firms still rely on legacy systems and outdated technologies, which can hinder the integration and effective utilization of modern data analytics platforms.

- *Historical Data*: The oil and gas industry faces the challenge of handling vast amounts of historical data accumulated over decades. This historical data, often in various formats and from different sources, needs to be integrated and made compatible with modern operations. Accumulated and analyzed historical data of various injury-causing accidents help identify patterns and trends to mitigate the risk of working in this field.

Overcoming this challenge requires robust data management strategies and investments in data infrastructure to facilitate seamless data transfer.

- *Data Integration*: Merging data from disparate sources and systems can be a complex and resource-intensive task. The establishment of a unified data model (or data lake) is crucial for successful analytics implementation.

- *Data Quality*: The data available in the oil and gas industry is unique and peculiar. Data quality and accuracy issues are among serious problems that are present in the industry. Ensuring data accuracy, reliability, and timeliness is critical for analytics success, otherwise, the insights drawn might be misleading or even detrimental. Stringent data governance mechanisms and maintaining the data integrity should be prioritized.

- *Scalability*: Oil and gas companies should have scalable analytics infrastructure and agile analytics platforms that can evolve and handle massive amounts of data while adapting to the ever-changing industry landscape.

- *Talent and Skills*: The oil and gas industry has traditionally been an engineering-driven domain, but success in the big-data era requires diverse talents and expertise to navigate the multi-disciplinary landscape of analytics. In addition to that, you need a thorough understanding of the physics of the problem.

- *High Cost*: One of the major challenges of big data's application in any industry including oil and gas industry is the cost associated with managing the data recording, storage, and analysis. There is a high financial cost associated with dealing with data. This includes various data management activities such as data recording, storage, maintenance, and analysis. A huge investment is involved in the infrastructure of energy pipelines; hence its integrity is a must for reliable operations.

9.8 CONCLUSION

Big data is the idea that some aspect of your business operations generates large amounts of information, and you need to figure out what to do with it. No matter how entrenched in the "old ways" a company might be, now is the time for the entire oil and gas industry to embrace the benefits of big data analytics. Since O&G companies create lots of information, it makes sense to find new and improved ways to put that information to the best possible use.

The integration of advanced analytics and the increasing reliance on big data are driving the oil and gas sector toward a future where fully autonomous control systems for complex processing facilities become a reality. The future of big data in the oil and gas industry is promising, with the potential to drive efficiency, safety, and sustainability. However, realizing these benefits requires careful planning, investment, and a commitment to addressing challenges such as data security and integration. More information about big data in O&G operations can be found in the books in [20-28] and the following related journals:

- *Petroleum*
- *Energy Reports*
- *Oil & Gas Journal*

REFERENCES

[1] R. Delgado, "The challenges of bringing BYOD to the military," https://socpub.com/articles/the-challenges-of-bringing-byod-to-the-military-11272

[2] J. Moorthy et al., "Big data: Prospects and challenges," *The Journal for Decision Makers*, vol. 40, no. 1, 2015, pp. 74–96.

[3] "Repsol launches big data, AI project at Tarragona refinery," June 2018, https://www.ogj.com/refining-processing/refining/operations/article/17296578/repsol-launches-big-data-ai-project-at-tarragona-refinery

[4] M. N. O. Sadiku, C. M. M. Kotteti, and J. O. Sadiku, "Big data in oil & gas industry," *International Journal of Science, Engineering and Technology*, vol. 12, no. 5, 2024, pp. 1-10.

[5] M. N.O. Sadiku, M. Tembely, and S.M. Musa, "Big data: An introduction for engineers," *Journal of Scientific and Engineering Research*, vol. 3, no. 2, 2016, pp. 106-108.

[6] "The complete overview of big data," https://intellipaat.com/blog/tutorial/hadoop-tutorial/big-data-overview/

[7] R. Allen, "Types of big data | Understanding & Interacting with key types (2024)," https://investguiding-com.custommapposter.com/article/types-of-big-data-understanding-amp-interacting-with-key-types

[8] A. K. Tiwari, H. Chaudhary, and S. Yadav, "A review on big data and its security," *Proceedings of IEEE Sponsored 2nd International Conference on Innovations in Information Embedded and Communication Systems,* 2015.

[9] M. B. Hoy, "Big data: An introduction for librarians," *Medical Reference Services Quarterly,* vol. 33, no 9. 2014, pp. 320-326.

[10] M. Viceconti, P. Hunter, and R. Hose, "Big data, big knowledge: Big data for personalized healthcare," *IEEE Journal of Medical and Health Informatics,* vol. 19, no. 4, July 2015, pp. 1209-1215.

[11] P. Baumann et al., "Big data analytics for earth sciences: the earthserver approach," *International Journal of Digital Earth,* vol. 19, no. 1, 2016, pp.3-29.

[12] X. Wu et al., "Knowledge engineering with big data," *IEEE Intelligent Systems,* September/October 2015, pp.46-55.

[13] "Oil-gas industry and big data analytics: How data analytics is impacting oil & gas industry," February 2024, https://www.analytixlabs.co.in/blog/data-analytics-in-oil-and-gas/

[14] "Hype aside: Real-world use cases of artificial intelligence in the oil and gas industry," https://medium.com/instinctools/hype-aside-real-world-use-cases-of-artificial-intelligence-in-the-oil-and-gas-industry-a8c6f12fd10d

[15] S. Srivastava, "Big data analytics in the oil and gas industry – Benefits, use cases, examples, challenges," September 2024, https://appinventiv.com/blog/big-data-analytics-in-oil-and-gas/

[16] E. Brancaccio, "Big data in oil and gas industry," https://www.oil-gasportal.com/big-data-in-oil-and-gas-industry/?print=pdf

[17] "Using big data analytics for oil & gas," https://eaginc.com/big-data-analytics-oil-gas-industry/

[18] "Benefit from big data analytics in the oil and gas industry," September 2023,
https://wezom.com/blog/benefit-from-big-data-analytics-in-the-oil-and-gas-industry

[19] M. Jensen, "The big data boom - How data analytics is revolutionizing the oil & gas industry," January 2024,
https://www.linkedin.com/pulse/big-data-boom-how-analytics-revolutionizing-oil-gas-matthew-jensen-vuipc

[20] M. N. O. Sadiku, U. C. Chukwu, and P. O. Adebo, *Big Data and Its Applications*. Moldova, Europe: Lambert Academic Publishing, 2024.

[21] K. R. Holdaway, *Harness Oil and Gas Big Data with Analytics: Optimize Exploration and Production with Data Driven Models*. John Wiley & Sons, 2014.

[22] J. Gohil and M. Shah, *Application of Big Data in Petroleum Streams*. Boca Raton, FL: CRC Press, 2022.

[23] K. Srivastava et al. (eds.), *Understanding Data Analytics and Predictive Modelling in the Oil and Gas Industry*. Boca Raton, FL: CRC Press, 2029.

[24] K. R. Holdaway and D. H. B. Irving, *Enhance Oil and Gas Exploration with Data-Driven Geophysical and Petrophysical Models*. Wiley, 2017.

[25] A. S. Al-Harrasieh, *Exploring the Factors Impacting the Adoption of Big Data Analytics: Oil and Gas Industry in Oman*. Sultan Qaboos University, 2012.

[26] A. Baaziz, *How to Use Big Data Technologies to Optimize Operations in Upstream Petroleum Industry*. SSRN, 2015.

[27] F. Aminzadeh, L. A. Zadeh, and M. Nikravesh (eds.), *Soft Computing and Intelligent Data Analysis in Oil Exploration. Volume 51*. Elsevier Science, 2009.

[28] S. Mishra, and A. Datta-Gupta, *Applied Statistical Modeling and Data Analytics: A Practical Guide for the Petroleum Geosciences*. Elsevier Science, 2017.

CHAPTER 10

BIG DATA IN SPACE EXPLORATION

"The man who does not read has no advantage over the man who cannot read." – Mark Twain

10.1 INTRODUCTION

The world has seen a digital revolution where more and more work is being conducted online. Storing this activity has led to the concept of big data, i.e., large datasets that are otherwise difficult to manage. Because of these characteristics, big data requires new technologies and techniques to capture, store, and analyze. The cloud word for big data is shown in Figure 10.1 [1]. Typical sources of big data are shown in Figure 10.2 [2]. Big data plays a central role in space exploration, where satellites, telescopes, rovers, and space probes collect and analyze colossal volumes of data from space and celestial bodies. It empowers the transformation of raw data into transformative knowledge. It meticulously sifts through terabytes of information, uncovering patterns, predicting celestial events, and optimizing missions. It is about pushing the boundaries of human understanding and propelling us further into the cosmic abyss [3].

Figure 10.1 The cloud word for big data [1].

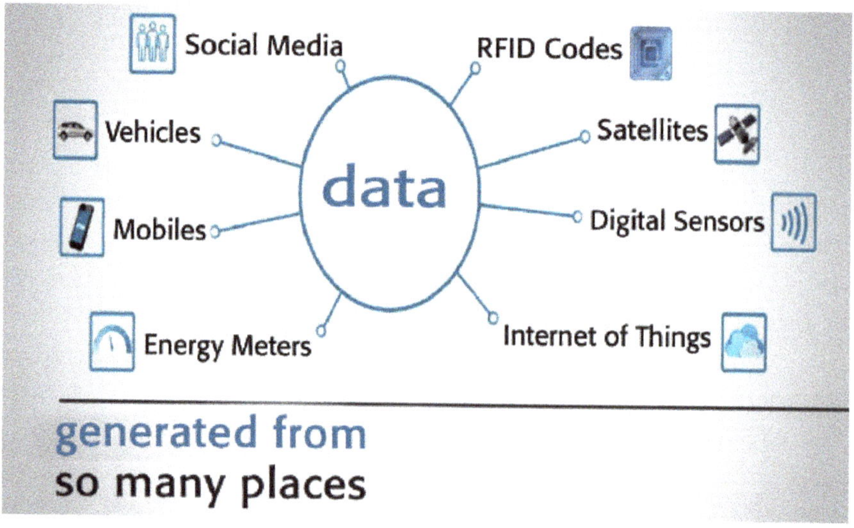

Figure 10.2 Typical sources of big data [2].

Space exploration has always been a primary goal for humanity, pushing the boundaries of our understanding and opening up new frontiers. Space exploration, once guided primarily by telescopes and human curiosity, now relies heavily on data analytics to decipher the secrets of the cosmos. Figure 10.3 depicts the journey through the history of space data [4]. Data analytics is important in contemporary space missions, encompassing data collection, processing, analysis, and interpretation. It plays a fundamental role in spacecraft design and trajectory optimization by employing mathematical models, simulations, and optimization techniques. It supports communication, navigation, and lunar exploration through techniques like error correction codes, encryption, and machine learning. It is essential for tasks such as filtering, noise reduction, and anomaly detection, ensuring data integrity, and instrument reliability during processing.

Journey Through the History of Space Data

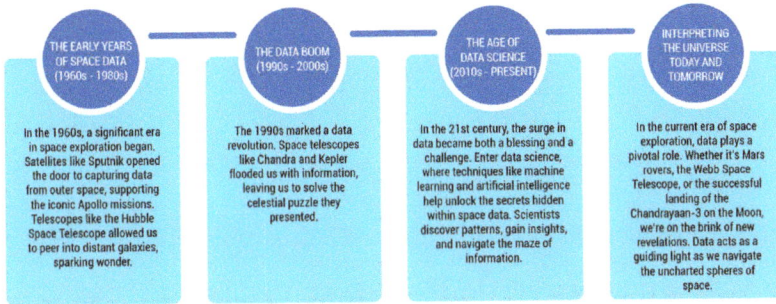

Figure 10.3 Journey through the history of space data [4].

Big data plays a crucial role in space exploration by enabling scientists to analyze vast amounts of data collected from telescopes, satellites, and space probes. The role of big data in space exploration is undeniable, revolutionizing the way we observe, analyze, and understand the universe. Big data analysis influences space exploration by enabling us to better understand space data, and unlock the mysteries of the universe. Big data analytics has become an indispensable tool for space agencies and researchers worldwide. Utilizing big data analytics techniques, astronomers are now able to process immense datasets and uncover patterns and trends that would otherwise remain hidden [5].

In this chapter, we will delve into the fascinating role of big data in space exploration. The chapter begins with explaining what big data is all about. It describes big data space exploration. It covers some applications of big data in space exploration. It highlights the benefits and challenges of big data in space exploration. The last section concludes with comments.

10.2 WHAT IS BIG DATA?

Big data applies to data sets of extreme size (e.g. exabytes, zettabytes) which are beyond the capability of the commonly used software tools. It involves situation where very large data sets are big in volume, velocity, veracity, and variability [6]. The data is too big, too fast, or does not fit the regular database architecture. It may require different strategies and tools for profiling, measurement, assessment, and processing.

Big Data is essentially classified into three types [7]:

- *Structured Data*: This is highly organized and is the easiest to work with. Any data that can be stored, accessed, and processed in the form of fixed format is known as a structured data. It may be stored in tabular format. Due to their nature, it is easy for programs to sort through and collect data. Structured data has quantitative data such as age, contact, address, billing, expenses, credit card numbers, etc. Data that is stored in a relational database management system is an example of structured data.

- *Unstructured Data*: This refers to unorganized data such as video files, log files, audio files, and image files. Any data with unknown form or the structure is classified as unstructured data. Almost everything generated by a computer is unstructured data. It takes a lot of time and effort required to make unstructured data readable. Examples of unstructured data include Metadata, Twitter tweets, and other social media posts.

- *Semi-structured Data*: This falls somewhere between structured data and unstructured data, i.e., both forms of data are present. Semi-structured data can be inherited such as location, time, email address, or device ID stamp.

The different types of big data are depicted in Figure 10.4 [8]. Structured and unstructured data are generated in various types [9-11].

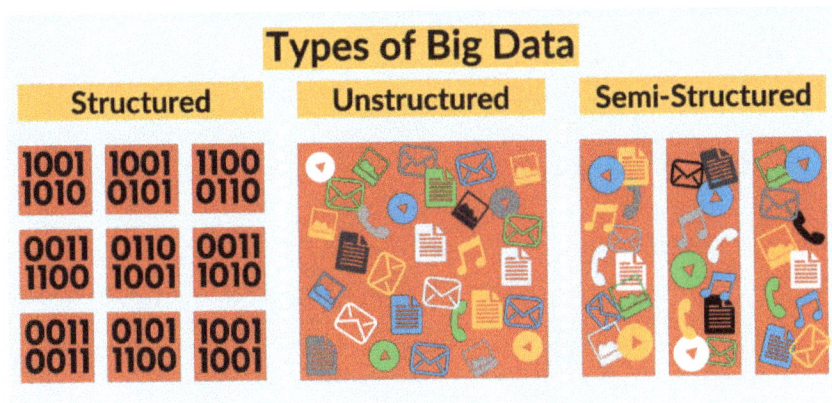

Figure 10.4 Types of big data [8].

The process of examining big data is often referred to big data analytics. It is an emerging field since massive computing capabilities have been made available by e-infrastructures [12]. Analytics include statistical models and other methods that are aimed at creating empirical predictions. Data-driven organizations use analytics to guide decisions at all levels. Several techniques have been proposed for analyzing big data. These include the HACE theorem, cloud computing, Hadoop, and MapReduce [13].

10.3 BIG DATA SPACE EXPLORATION

Space exploration has always been a realm of discovery, pushing the boundaries of human knowledge and technology. It has always been at the forefront of human ambition, pushing the boundaries of our understanding and opening up new frontiers. The vast unknown of space has captivated humanity for millennia, but unlocking its secrets demands more than celestial gazing.

The sheer volume of data has presented a new challenge for astronomers. How to process and analyze this massive amount of information effectively is not an easy task. Processing and making sense of big data from space is a monumental task. This is where big data comes into play. Big data analysis plays a crucial role in the study of dark matter and dark energy, which together constitute around 95% of the universe. Analyzing big data from space has transformed the field of astronomy, enabling scientists to unlock the secrets of the universe.

Today, data analytics in space industry plays a pivotal role, acting as the bridge between raw information and profound knowledge. Data is the backbone of space exploration, and with advancements in technology, we are now generating an unprecedented amount of data. From analyzing planetary formation data to predicting space weather patterns, big data plays a crucial role in virtually every aspect of space exploration. Data analytics has become a pivotal tool, transforming how we explore, understand, and utilize the cosmos. It enables continuous monitoring of astronaut health, analyzing biometric data to detect potential health issues, optimize life support systems, and ensure astronaut safety. It enhances deep space communication, optimizing data transmission and reducing communication delays. Data analytics in space exploration is illustrated in Figure 10.5 [14].

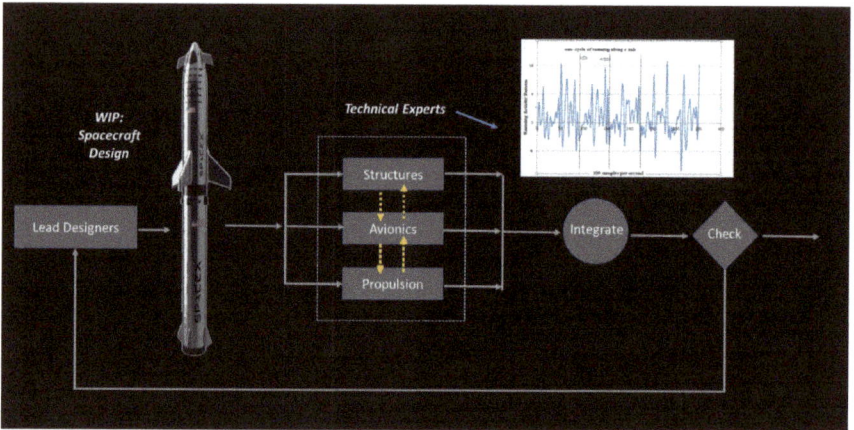

Figure 10.5 Data analytics in space exploration [14].

More than 50 years ago, space exploration was a race to the moon between the US and the former Soviet Union. In 1998, the International Space Station launch marked a highlight for international cooperation in space between the U.S., Russia, Japan, Canada and Europe. Today, more countries like as India and China are pursuing their own goals in space, which could challenge the US as a world leader. Americans continue to see an essential role for the United States as a leader in space exploration. Most Americans agree that it is essential for US to be a leader in space exploration.

NASA is engaged in a wide range of activities in space, including exploration and applied and basic research. Since its creation in 1958, NASA has achieved some pretty impressive feats of science. When NASA was created, it had to invent the technology to get where we needed to go, and we will continue to push the boundaries of technology into the future. New emerging technologies that open opportunities for research and exploration with minimal investments include NASA's satellites, such as typically shown in Figure 10.6 [15].

Figure 10.6 Satellites for exploration [15].

There is far less public urgency for NASA to send humans to the moon or Mars and to search for other planets that could support life. Americans by and large view NASA as critical to space exploration [19]. NASA collects, stores, processes, and analyzes data. It uses a system called the Mission Data Processing and Control System (MPCS) to manage and process data. The application for the NASA's Mars Curiosity rover uses production data and creates an easy way for engineers to monitor instruments and measurements faster and more efficiently. Elasticsearch permits handling large amounts of data from Curiosity's sensors, such as the temperature on the Martian surface. Figure 10.7 shows the artist's concept of NASA's X-57 'Maxwell' aircraft [17], while Figure 10.8 displays NASA's gateway in lunar orbit [17]. The X-57 will be the first all-electric X-plane and will be flown to demonstrate the benefits that electric propulsion may yield for the future of aviation. NASA will continue to be a global leader in scientific discovery. It has continued to push the boundaries of knowledge to deliver on the promise of American ingenuity and leadership in space. Its future will continue to be a story of human exploration, technology, and science.

Figure 10.7 The artist's concept of NASA's X-57 'Maxwell' aircraft [17].

Figure 10.8 NASA's gateway in lunar orbit [17].

10.4 APPLICATIONS OF BIG DATA SPACE EXPLORATION

Big data analytics in space exploration unlocks patterns within volumes of observations to advance astrophysics, guide future missions, and reveal our universe's deepest mysteries. The cosmos may be vast, but through data, it becomes knowable. Scientists and engineers use big data for everything from predicting weather on earth to monitoring ice caps on Mars to searching for distant galaxies. Here are some ways that big data is used in space exploration [18]:

- *Astronomy*: Astronomy has always been a data-intensive science. Data science has significantly transformed the field of space exploration, particularly in the realm of astronomy. By leveraging data science techniques, researchers are able to tackle complex astrophysical problems, uncovering hidden patterns and shedding light on the universe's origin, evolution, and large-scale structure. Data science techniques can help researchers understand the universe's origin, evolution, and structure. For example, machine learning algorithms can classify galaxies and their mergers, while image recognition algorithms can identify celestial objects.

- *Predicting Space Weather*: Space weather can impact satellites, spacecraft, and even power grids on earth. Big data analysis plays a crucial role in predicting space weather patterns by analyzing vast amounts of data from satellites, ground-based observatories, and space weather models. The predictions enable space agencies and operators to take proactive measures to protect spacecraft and astronauts and mitigate the effects of space weather on critical infrastructure. Space exploration models predict space weather events that could severely impact satellites and astronauts in space. Crucial data-driven analytics will forecast perilous space weather to ensure mission success.

- *Astronauts' Health*: Radiation exposure poses significant risks to astronauts' health during space missions, especially during long-duration flights beyond Earth's protective magnetosphere. Big data analysis of radiation monitoring data collected from spacecraft, space stations, and dosimeters worn by astronauts helps scientists assess exposure levels and mitigate health risks. This data-driven approach enables space agencies to optimize mission planning, crew scheduling, and spacecraft design to ensure the safety and well-being of astronauts.

- *Earth Observation*: Data analytics plays a crucial role in interpreting satellite data for earth observation. The Sun's activity, characterized by phenomena such as solar flares, coronal mass ejections, and sunspot cycles, influences space weather conditions in the solar system. Satellites play a crucial role in monitoring and studying earth's environment, climate, and natural resources from space. Big data analysis of satellite imagery and remote sensing data provides valuable insights into changes and trends in earth's surface, atmosphere, and oceans. By analyzing multi-spectral imagery, radar data, and other earth observation datasets, scientists can track deforestation, urbanization, pollution, and other environmental changes over time. Information derived from this analysis supports decision-making in areas such as land use planning, disaster response, and natural resource management. Big data analysis of cosmic ray data collected by ground-based detectors and space-based observatories helps scientists study the origins, propagation, and interactions of cosmic rays. Free earth-observation datasets from the European Space Agency, NASA and the US Geological

Survey have helped organizations around the world develop object-detection platforms.

- *Space Telescope Data*: Modern telescopes equipped with sophisticated sensors and cameras capture detailed images of celestial objects. They generate an astronomical amount of data. Space telescopes equipped with advanced instrumentation enable astronomers to search for signs of extraterrestrial life beyond our solar system. For example, the Hubble Space Telescope has collected over 150 terabytes of data throughout its mission. Analyzing this vast amount of data manually would be an impossible task. Big data analysis of space telescope data, including spectroscopic observations and transit surveys, helps scientists identify potentially habitable exoplanets and study their atmospheres for biosignatures.

10.5 BENEFITS

Many analysis tools offer fast analysis and visualization of data, and have proven to be very valuable. They help space probes make faster and better decisions, reduce failure, and improve life on planet earth. Big data analysis of data collected from space probes, telescopes, and simulations allows researchers to identify patterns and trends that reveal the underlying mechanisms of planetary formation. Data analytics enhances deep space communication, optimizing data transmission, and reducing communication delays. As space missions grow more complex, data scientists play a vital role in ensuring success. One of the significant advantages of data science in astronomical research is the ability to unveil the secrets of the universe. Other benefits include [18]:

- *Decision Making*: From mission design to resource allocation, data science in space industry, empowers informed decision-making throughout exploration endeavors, maximizing efficiency, minimizing risks, and paving the way for future discoveries. Space agencies are using big data tools to rapidly analyze their data and make time-efficient decisions. Data science helps make informed decisions throughout space exploration, from mission design to resource allocation. The ability to tell stories with data is paramount for inspiring decision makers.

- *Farming*: The Climate Corporation uses their satellite data to enable farmers all around the globe to find more sustainable ways to grow substantially more food. Farmers can use image data to better understand what factors affect the growth of crops. There are factors that can be detected from space, such as weather patterns, exposure to sunlight, air quality or pest activity.

- *Monitoring*: Spacecraft monitor everything from our home planet to faraway galaxies, beaming back images and information to earth. Spacecraft operates in extreme conditions, making health monitoring a critical aspect of space missions. Wearable sensors and advanced analytics are transforming how astronaut health is monitored during space missions. By continually tracking vital signs, biometrics, and even microbial flora in the body, subtle shifts can trigger earlier medical alerts than relying on scheduled tests or self-reported issues alone.

- *Autonomous Systems*: Data science is instrumental in developing autonomous systems for space exploration. Autonomous robots and spacecraft rely on data analysis to make informed decisions and adapt to dynamic environments. By integrating data science techniques with robotics, scientists can develop intelligent systems capable of exploring distant planets.

- *Simulation*: Data science helps in simulating and modeling complex astronomical scenarios, allowing astronomers to test theories and hypotheses. These simulations aid in understanding celestial processes and predicting the behavior of astronomical objects under different conditions.

- *Communication*: Data analytics improves communication reliability and data quality by analyzing signal patterns, noise, and interference. Releasing public domain images of a lonely blue planet or footage of astronauts on spacewalks elegantly communicate their accomplishments to the public while inspiring future engineers and scientists.

- *Mission Planning*: Predicting celestial events becomes more accurate through the use of data analytics. Data analytics helps optimize mission trajectories and improve spacecraft design by analyzing past mission data, current space weather conditions, and predictive models.

- *Data Processing*: Data analytics transforms raw data from onboard instruments into meaningful information using signal and image processing, data mining, and pattern recognition. Data analytics in space exploration is pivotal for processing the enormous volumes of data transmitted back to earth by space probes, satellites, and telescopes. Big data analytics techniques are essential for managing, processing, and extracting meaningful information from this data deluge.

- *Data Quality*: Astronomy heavily relies on observational data to study celestial objects. By applying data analytics techniques, filtering out noise and extracting relevant information enhances the quality of data. Data science improves the precision and accuracy of observational data collection.

- *Improved Efficiency*: By automating data analysis processes, astronomers can focus more on the interpretation of results and the formulation of new theories. This leads to a significant increase in efficiency and productivity.

- *Space Photography*: Photographs are universal means of communication. Over time, photography techniques grew from pointing a camera out of a window to using powerful mirrors and telescopes to capture impossibly distant subjects. To share these images with the world, NASA needed to solve photographic and data challenges. The space photography is crucial to communicating the mission of NASA. From the beginning, NASA understood that space photography played a vital role in its missions. The data from satellites and cameras is captured and stored locally.

- *Space Tourism*: Most adults in US expect that people will routinely travel in space as tourists in the next 50 years. More than half expect space tourism to become routine. However, Americans are not enthusiastic about traveling to space themselves.

10.6 CHALLENGES

Data captured via space satellites pose significant challenges and risks, such as data quality and reliability, data security and privacy, data ownership and access, data ethics and fairness, and data regulation and compliance. Data transmission in space is still a challenge and finding a way to ease that process would be beneficial for many space missions. Some challenges associated with data analytics in space exploration include data accuracy, privacy, ethical use of AI, and making ai algorithms compatible with harsh space environments. Space missions generate enormous volumes of data, presenting significant challenges in data storage, processing, and analysis. Other challenges include [18,20]:

- *Space Debris*: As Americans look to the future of space, a large share expect problems with human-made debris. There will be a major problem with debris in space from rockets, satellites, and other human-made objects. Ratings are more mixed when it comes to the job private companies are doing to limit debris from objects like rockets and satellites. Figure 10.9 shows some space debris [21].

Figure 10.9 Space debris [21].

- *Safety*: Space debris poses a growing threat to spacecraft and satellites in orbit. Big data analysis of space debris tracking data helps space agencies and operators predict debris trajectories and assess collision risks.

- *Communication*: Communicating from the ground station to a spacecraft is a complex challenge, largely due to the extreme distances involved. When data are transmitted and received across thousands or millions of miles, the delay and potential for disruption or data loss is significant. Transferring data also becomes more challenging because the signal gets weaker due to distances involved. Advanced communication technologies are required to enhance deep space exploration for both robotic and human missions. Optical communications technologies can dramatically improve communications between spacecraft and earth far better than radio communications.

- *International Collaboration*: Space exploration and scientific research are inherently collaborative endeavors that require cooperation among nations and space agencies worldwide. Big data analysis of space data often involves international collaboration, with researchers sharing data, resources, and expertise to address complex scientific questions and challenges. International collaborations enable scientists to tackle fundamental questions in astronomy, planetary science, and space physics more effectively.

- *Risk*: Whenever an astronaut steps out of a space vehicle, it is an incredible, high-level-risk activity. We need to critically think about the risk to human life and the value return for assigning humans to do activities. Smart autonomous systems have the capability to improve the efficiency and speed while minimizing the risk and cost involved with planetary missions.

- *Data Quality*: How can we ensure that the data collected in space are accurate, dependable, and consistent? How can we deal with the noise, interference, and distortion that may affect the data transmission? How can we validate, verify, and correct the data?

- *Data Security*: How can we protect the data from unauthorized access, modification, or deletion? How can we prevent cyberattacks, hacking, or sabotage that may compromise the data or the spacecraft? How can we encrypt, authenticate, and backup the data?

- *Data Availability*: How can we ensure that the data are accessible and usable by the intended users? How can we overcome the limitations of bandwidth, latency, and storage that may affect the data transfer? How can we manage the data lifecycle, from collection to disposal?

- *Data Usability*: How can we make the data understandable and meaningful for the users? How can we standardize, harmonize, and integrate the data from various sources, formats, and systems? How can we analyze, visualize, and share the data?

10.7 CONCLUSION

Space data is about to get big. Big data has revolutionized the field of space technology, enabling us to explore the universe with unprecedented precision and efficiency. The integration of big data analytics has revolutionized the way we explore and understand the cosmos. It will play an increasingly vital role in shaping the future of space exploration. As technology evolves, the future holds even greater opportunities for data analytics in revolutionizing our understanding of the cosmos. By combining powerful data analytics techniques with increasingly vast amounts of data, astronomers are revolutionizing the way they conduct research, analyze celestial objects, and make groundbreaking discoveries.

Data analytics is not just transforming space exploration; it is redefining our understanding of the universe. This versatile tool has been a cornerstone of space missions, ensuring efficiency and success in the exploration of space and celestial bodies.

It provides astronomers with the tools and techniques necessary to analyze the massive volumes of data generated by telescopes and satellites. Data-driven intelligence provides the analytical foundation needed to realize humanity's boldest visions. As we continue to push the frontiers of space exploration, there is no doubt that big data will remain a cornerstone of astronomical research. More information about big data in space can be found in the books in [22-24].

REFERENCES

[1] R. Delgado, "The challenges of bringing BYOD to the military," https://socpub.com/articles/the-challenges-of-bringing-byod-to-the-military-11272

[2] J. Moorthy et al., "Big data: Prospects and challenges," *The Journal for Decision Makers*, vol. 40, no. 1, 2015, pp. 74–96.

[3] "10 Uses of data science in space exploration," March 2024, https://medium.com/@analyticsemergingindia/10-uses-of-data-science-in-space-exploration-d958045213c2

[4] "Navigating uncharted space: Harnessing data analytics in space exploration," October 2023, https://www.dasca.org/world-of-data-science/article/navigating-uncharted-space-harnessing-data-analytics-in-space-exploration

[5] M. N. O. Sadiku, U. C. Chukwu, and J. O. Sadiku, "Big data in space exploration," *Innovative Mult-disciplinary Journal of Applied Technology*, vol. 2, no. 10, 2024, pp. 227-239.

[6] M. N. O. Sadiku, M. Tembely, and S.M. Musa, "Big data: An introduction for engineers," *Journal of Scientific and Engineering Research*, vol. 3, no. 2, 2016, pp. 106-108.

[7] "The complete overview of big data," *https://intellipaat.com/blog/tutorial/hadoop-tutorial/big-data-overview/*

[8] R. Allen, "Types of big data | Understanding & Interacting with key types (2024)," https://investguiding-com.custommapposter.com/article/types-of-big-data-understanding-amp-interacting-with-key-types

[9] A. K. Tiwari, H. Chaudhary, and S. Yadav, "A review on big data and its security," *Proceedings of IEEE Sponsored 2ⁿᵈ International Conference on Innovations in Information Embedded and Communication Systems*, 20110.

[10] M. B. Hoy, "Big data: An introduction for librarians," *Medical Reference Services Quarterly*, vol. 33, no 3. 2014, pp. 320-326.

[11] M. Viceconti, P. Hunter, and R. Hose, "Big data, big knowledge: Big data for personalized healthcare," *IEEE Journal of Medical and Health Informatics*, vol. 19, no. 4, July 2015, pp. 1209-12110.

[12] P. Baumann et al., "Big data analytics for earth sciences: the earthserver approach," *International Journal of Digital Earth*, vol. 19, no. 1, 2016, pp.3-29.

[13] X. Wu et al., "Knowledge engineering with big data," *IEEE Intelligent Systems*, September/October 2015, pp.46-510.

[14] T. Ebrahimi, " Dispatches from deep space: Imaging data and space photography," July 2022,
https://blog.westerndigital.com/space-photography/

[15] D. Kekare, "Data analytics in space exploration: Beyond earth's boundaries," March 2024,
https://www.linkedin.com/pulse/data-analytics-space-exploration-beyond-earths-durgesh-kekare-v5iwf#:~:text=Data%20analytics%20enhances%20deep%20space,mission%20control%20and%20-scientific%20research.

[16] "Americans' views of space: U.S. role, NASA priorities and impact of private companies," July 2023,
https://www.pewresearch.org/science/2023/07/20/americans-views-of-space-u-s-role-nasa-priorities-and-impact-of-private-companies/

[17] "60 Years and counting - The future,"
https://www.nasa.gov/specials/60counting/future.html

[18] "Exploring the role of big data in space exploration," March 20
https://1ansah.in/blog/exploring-the-role-of-big-data-in-space-exploration/#:~:text=The%20role%20of%20big%20data%20in%20space%20exploration%20is%20undeniable,space%20agencies%20and%20researchers%20worldwide.24,

[19] D. Werner, "Big data, advanced algorithms and new approaches for space missions," October 2024,
https://spacenews.com/big-data-advanced-algorithms-and-new-approaches-for-space-missions/

[20] "Data governance in space — Key challenges and opportunities,"
https://www.cdomagazine.tech/opinion-analysis/data-governance-in-space-key-challenges-and-opportunities

[21] "Space debris: A threat just beyond the horizon," July 2022,
https://www.rfa.space/space-debris-a-threat-just-beyond-the-horizon/

[22] M. N. O. Sadiku, U. C. Chukwu, and P. O. Adebo, *Big Data and Its Applications*. Moldova, Europe: Lambert Academic Publishing, 2024.

[23] A. Agarwal, *Interplanetary Data Governance: Navigating the New Digital Frontier in Space*. Kindle Edition, 2024.

[24] F. Adam and P. Skoda (eds.), *Knowledge Discovery in Big Data from Astronomy and Earth Observation: Astrogeoinformatics*. Elsevier Science, 2020.

CHAPTER 11

BIG DATA IN MARITIME INDUSTRY

"Love is the highest act of selfishness, the best gift you can give to yourself."
– Bernard Werber

11.1 INTRODUCTION

Global trade has been the backbone of human civilizations since time immemorial. The maritime industry is one of the largest and most important industries in the world, responsible for keeping global trade alive. It is the backbone of international trade and transportation, connecting countries, economies, and people. It is one of the oldest and traditional industries to still rely more on intuition than on data. The industry is involved in three-quarters of all worldwide trade. In spite of this, studies on the synthesis of big data application in maritime are rare, which has created a gap in the academic literature due to the importance of big data and AI in maritime operations. The applications of big data in the maritime industry are considerable.

Big data refers to large datasets analyzed computationally to reveal patterns, trends, and associations. In the maritime sector, this implies a vast and deep sea of facts, figures, and statistics from weather conditions to logistics, all crucial for operational performance and informed decision-making. Imagine harnessing large amounts of data to steer ships more efficiently, predict maintenance, and optimize routes. Big data analytics is transforming the maritime industry, enabling fuel optimization, vessel performance monitoring, regulatory compliance, and predictive maintenance. Big data in the maritime sector is derived from key sources such as [1]:

- Ship sensors provide real-time information on vessel performance and condition.

- Weather reports give updates on conditions that could impact sailing routes.

- Port information includes data about cargo, berthing schedules, and more.

This data optimizes shipping routes when harnessed effectively, resulting in significant fuel savings and timely deliveries.

Big data analytics is revolutionizing the maritime industry, enabling better decision-making, improved efficiency, and enhanced safety through the analysis of vast amounts of data generated by vessels and ports. Big data has become a game-changer in the maritime industry. The industry heavily relies on data analytics and has embraced big data to optimize operations, improve efficiency, and enhance safety [2].

This chapter explores big data as a tech trend that is shaping the maritime industry. It begins with explaining what big data is all about. It describes maritime big data and provides some of its examples and applications. It highlights the benefits and challenges of maritime big data. The section concludes with comments.

11.2 WHAT IS BIG DATA?

Big data applies to data sets of extreme size (e.g. exabytes, zettabytes) which are beyond the capability of the commonly used software tools. It involves situation where very large data sets are big in volume, velocity, veracity, and variability [3]. The data is too big, too fast, or does not fit the regular database architecture. It may require different strategies and tools for profiling, measurement, assessment, and processing. Different components of big data are shown in Figure 11.1 [4]. The cloud word for big data is shown in Figure 11.2 [5].

Figure 11.1 Different components of big data [4].

Figure 11.2 The cloud word for big data [4].

Big Data is essentially classified into three types [6]:

- *Structured Data*: This is highly organized and is the easiest to work with. Any data that can be stored, accessed, and processed in the form of fixed format is known as a structured data. It may be stored in tabular format. Due to their nature, it is easy for programs to sort through and collect data. Structured data has quantitative data such as age, contact, address, billing, expenses, credit card numbers, etc. Data that is stored in a relational database management system is an example of structured data.

- *Unstructured Data*: This refers to unorganized data such as video files, log files, audio files, and image files. Any data with unknown form or the structure is classified as unstructured data. Almost everything generated by a computer is unstructured data. It takes a lot of time and effort required to make unstructured data readable. Examples of unstructured data include Metadata, Twitter tweets, and other social media posts.

- *Semi-structured Data*: This falls somewhere between structured data and unstructured data, i.e., both forms of data are present. Semi-structured data can be inherited such as location, time, email address, or device ID stamp.

The different types of big data are depicted in Figure 11.3 [7].

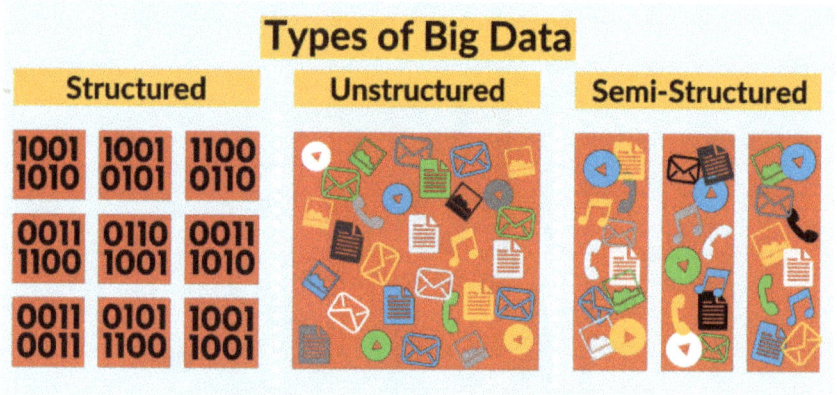

Figure 11.3 Types of big data [7].

The process of examining big data is often referred to big data analytics. It is an emerging field since massive computing capabilities have been made available by e-infrastructures [8]. Big data analytics is the application of advanced analytic techniques to large, heterogeneous data sets that comprise structured, semi-structured, and unstructured data from many sources with sizes ranging from terabytes to zettabytes.

Analytics include statistical models and other methods that are aimed at creating empirical predictions. Data-driven organizations use analytics to guide decisions at all levels. Several techniques have been proposed for analyzing big data. These include the HACE theorem, cloud computing, Hadoop, and MapReduce [9].

11.3 MARITIME BIG DATA

Maritime big data encompasses the extensive information collected from sources such as satellites, aerial remote sensing, observation stations, ships, and buoys, which are employed across a range of marine-related applications. The principal types of maritime big data employed in this field encompass ship navigation data, meteorological data, marine environment data, channel and port data, accident and emergency data, and ship inspection and management data. These datasets provide crucial support for comprehensive maritime safety assessments [10]. Figure 11.4 shows a symbol for maritime big data [11].

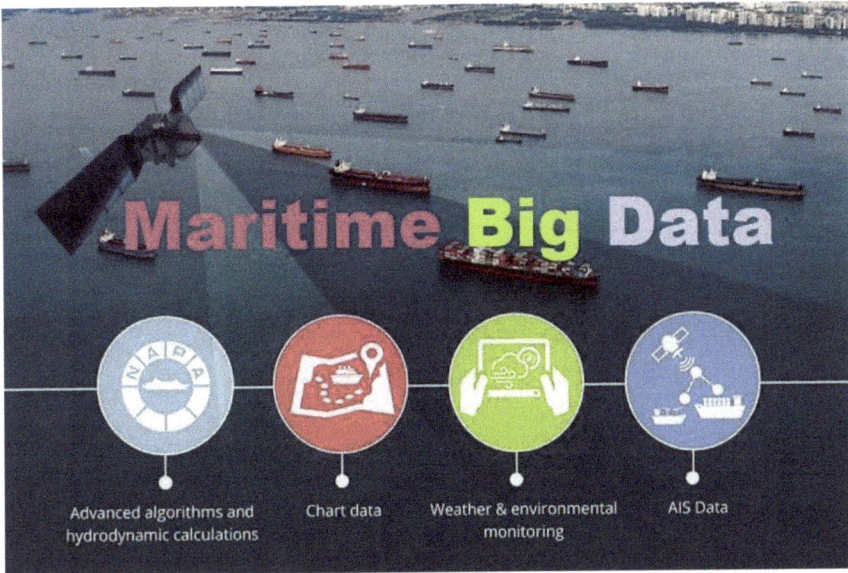

Figure 11.4 A symbol for maritime big data [11].

Big data analytics has become a powerful tool for extracting valuable insights from large and complex data sets. With the help of advanced analytics techniques and big data tools, companies can now analyze vast amounts of data to uncover hidden patterns, trends, and correlations.

Big data in the maritime industry is not just about the volume of data but the valuable insights and actionable intelligence you derive from it. Big data in shipping refers to the vast amount of information generated within the maritime sector and the use of data systems to process and analyze this information. By harnessing shipping data, companies can gain valuable insights that help improve operational efficiency. With the vast amount of data generated by vessels, ports, and logistics systems, maritime companies can now analyze and interpret this information to make informed decisions and drive innovation. In the maritime industry, leveraging big data has led to better route planning, improved cargo tracking, and enhanced supply chain management. Figure 11.5 shows data transmission between ships [12].

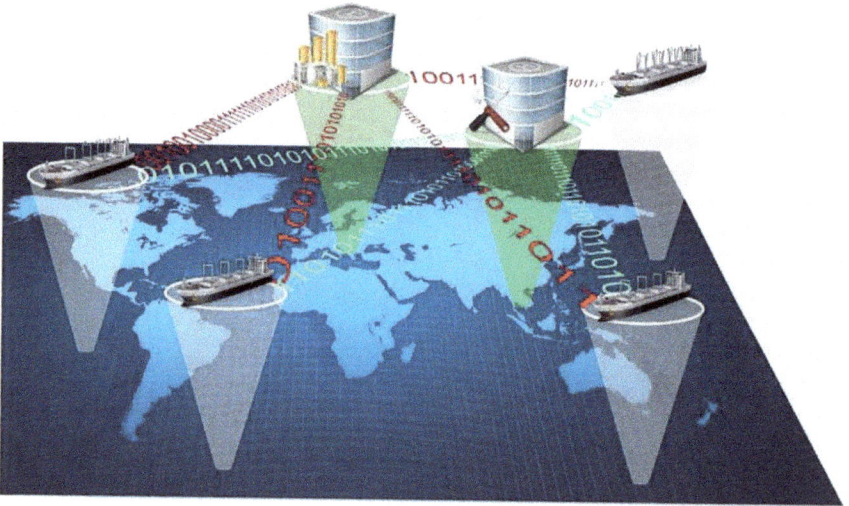

Figure 11.5 Data transmission between ships [12].

11.4 EXAMPLES OF MARITIME BIG DATA

Marine big data can be described as a large amount of data collected through remote aerial sensing, ships, stations, buoys, and satellites. Big data is a large set of data that is structured and unstructured to enable the industry to make accurate, informed decisions. By analyzing vast amounts of data, companies like Transmetrics, CoVadem, LogComex, and HiLo are revolutionizing the shipping and logistics industry, with their innovative use of big data. These companies are at the forefront of leveraging big data to drive innovation and efficiency in the shipping industry. We briefly discuss these examples of companies leveraging maritime big data [13]:

- *Transmetrics*: uses predictive analytics to optimize freight capacity utilization and reduce inefficiencies in the supply chain. By analyzing historical data and using machine learning algorithms, they can accurately forecast demand and suggest optimal cargo allocation.

- *CoVadem*: leverages big data to provide real-time water depth information, enabling ships to navigate more efficiently and safely.

- *LogComex*: utilizes big data to streamline customs processes and improve trade compliance. Their platform integrates multiple data sources to provide customs brokers with accurate and up-to-date information.

- *HiLo*: analyses data from many different sources by using advanced algorithms and machine learning. It analyzes big data to identify and mitigate safety risks in the shipping industry, helping to prevent accidents and improve overall safety standards. HiLo's risk management platform provides data and insights that help shipping companies to proactively prevent incidents, protecting crew, ships, and cargo.

11.5 APPLICATIONS OF MARITIME BIG DATA

Key uses of big data in maritime sector include analytics for shipowners, data engineering, vessel performance, and fleet situational management. Big data is used to manage ship sensors and for predictive analysis, which is needed to prevent delays and improve the overall operational efficiency of the industry. Common areas of application of maritime big data include the following [1,13-16]:

- *Shipbuilding*: The shipbuilding industry will be one of the prime beneficiaries of the advent of big data. Big data can play an important role in shipbuilding. Basically, this will be possible by analyzing the results obtained from the sensors of previously used vessels. Data collected and analyzed over the life of the vessel will be useful for future improvements in ship design.

Previous datasets could help in testing the proposed ship design without physically developing it. That is a big win-win situation for the shipping industry.

- *Route Optimization*: Shipping companies harness vast amounts of data to determine the most efficient paths for their vessels. By analyzing historical and real-time information, such as weather patterns, ocean currents, and vessel speeds, big data algorithms predict the optimal route for a ship. This involves a complex calculation considering fuel consumption, time efficiency, and safety.

- *Predictive Analytics*: Predictive analytics is a key component of big data. It allows companies to forecast demand and optimize storage and transportation. This helps reduce costs and minimize delays in the supply chain. Predictive analytics and artificial intelligence in the maritime industry employ advanced techniques to monitor and analyze information from sources such as sensors on ship equipment, maintenance logs, and environmental conditions. By aggregating and analyzing data, predictive models identify patterns and anomalies that signal potential equipment failures. Big data analytics can also help identify potential risks and predict disruptions in the shipping process. Predictive analytics, powered by maritime analytics and shipping data, provide valuable insights into direction of asset prices and demand patterns over time. Figure 11.6 shows predictive analytics in shipping [17].

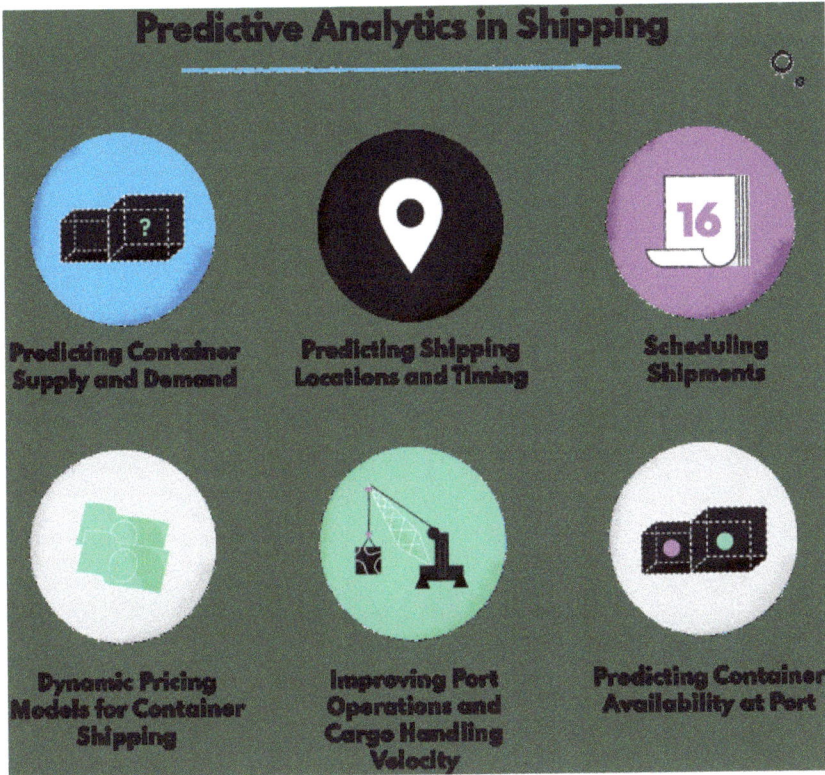

Figure 11.6 Predictive analytics in shipping [17].

- *Chartering*: Vessel owners and operators try to ensure that their fleets are acceptable for use by charterers. A key function of charterers is to find the right ship for cargo at the most economical price. The task is highly dependent on information provided to them by known brokers and ship owners. Big data analytics can provide charters with readily available, accurate, and actionable information to improve decision-making. Charters can find all available alternatives as well as the freight forecast. This can give charterers and ship owners access to more options thus improving transparency and competitiveness.

- *Fleet Management*: Big data analytics in the shipping industry can also support fleet management through predictive analytics and maintenance. By predicting equipment anomalies and failures, shipping carriers can schedule preventative maintenance initiatives to reduce downtime, increase productivity and extend the working life of equipment. Analysis of container shipping data and marine statistics can be performed by shipping companies to assess the performance of individual vessels, identify areas for improvement, and make informed decisions about fleet composition and deployment. For example, shipping companies can use big data to analyze fuel consumption patterns, monitor equipment performance, and track maintenance history.

11.6 BENEFITS

The benefits of big data analytics in the maritime industry range from operational efficiency and cost savings to enhanced safety measures and environmental sustainability. Big data analysis helps identify optimal routes, speeds, and engine settings to minimize fuel consumption, a significant cost in shipping. Big data for the shipping industry can be used to make decisions in the future to predict and avoid costly problems, and to create more reliable cargo delivery options. Other benefits of maritime big data include [1]:

- *Improved Safety*: The most important benefit of big data analytics in maritime industry is improved safety. Shipping is a high-risk industry, and accidents can have serious consequences. By analyzing data on vessel performance, maintenance records, and crew behavior, shipping companies can identify and address potential safety risks before they lead to accidents. By analyzing the data points collected every day by shipping companies, it is possible to identify the red flags pointing to future incidents, reducing the risk of human injury and damage to ships and cargo. The knowledge gained from marine accidents serves as the cornerstone for the development of modern marine safety management practices. The automatic identification system (AIS) is a system for enhancing the safety and efficiency of navigation. It is designed to automatically provide information about a ship to other ships and to coastal authorities.

- *Enhancing Security*: Maritime companies detect and mitigate potential security threats by collecting and analyzing data from ship sensors, navigation systems, and communication networks. For example, anomaly detection systems powered by big data analytics identify unusual patterns in ship-to-shore communications, indicating a cyberattack or system vulnerability.

- *Time-saving*: The implementation of big data analytics in the maritime industry significantly streamlines communication and email management. This way, critical information is easily accessible, reducing the time staff spends sifting through their inboxes. This is particularly beneficial in managing the high volume of emails typical in shipping operations. Data analytics can be used to identify areas where processes can be streamlined, reducing costs and increasing productivity.

- *Maintenance*: Decisions regarding vessel maintenance, including hull cleaning and propeller polishing, are taken based on intuition or a schedule rather than on actual vessel performance. Fuel consumption data can also be used for cost-benefit analysis of vessel maintenance. Data analytics can make it easier for operators to decide the timing and the benefits of performing maintenance.

- *Marine Engineering*: In the maritime business, big data is transforming the field of marine engineering. By analyzing vast amounts of data, engineers can optimize the design and performance of container ships, making them more efficient and environmentally friendly.

- *Maritime Efficiency*: In an industry where conditions change rapidly, real-time data processing is critical. Scholars have used big data and AI to achieve better energy efficiency in maritime transport from different perspectives. For better energy efficiency of vessels, liner companies usually consider slow steaming as the best practice.

11.7 CHALLENGES

While big data offers unparalleled insights for optimizing operations, its implementation is not without challenges. The shipping industry has been facing numerous disturbances and challenges such as market fluctuations, over supply, margin pressures, and labor shortages. Players are uncertain about implementing big data as it is a relatively new technology in the industry. These challenges are expected to impact the industry's profitability. There is a lack of cross-enterprise processes. Companies are concentrating on automating processes within functional silos instead of taking a holistic view of the enterprise. This prevents the true potential of big data from being realized. Other challenges of maritime big data include the following [1,14]:

- *Cost of Infrastructure*: Implementing big data systems and analytics can be costly, and shipping companies may be hesitant to invest in these technologies if they are not convinced of the potential benefits. Setting up a robust big data system entails significant investment, primarily in high-powered computing resources, sophisticated software for data analysis, and secure data storage solutions to handle the vast quantities generated daily. This setup includes data collection, processing hardware, advanced analytics, and visualization software. Maritime companies, especially smaller ones, frequently face budget constraints, making it crucial to find cost-effective solutions.

- *Complexity*: The maritime industry has always been complex, involving numerous stakeholders such as charterers, shipowners, and operators. It is a complex network of people, countries, agencies and authorities. This complexity makes operational efficiency critical. Due to the complexity and large size of ships, implementing autonomous control has proven to be a very challenging undertaking. Dealing with data volume and complexity in the maritime industry involves the enormous amount of information generated from various operations, such as vessel tracking, cargo handling, and crew management. There are numerous formats and types of data sources, like ship sensor data, port transaction records, and weather tracking systems. Navigating the complexities of communication flow, particularly while integrating big data in the maritime industry, requires the right technology solution. The complexity of the maritime industry is typically shown in Figure 11.7 [18].

Figure 11.7 The complexity of the maritime industry [18].

- *Real-time Processing*: Making timely decisions based on current maritime data is crucial in scenarios like navigating treacherous weather or managing fleet logistics. The difficulty lies in rapidly processing and analyzing all the data continuously generated by sources such as GPS systems, weather stations, and onboard sensors. The shipping company needs to process this data in real-time to optimize routes and ensure safety.

- *Integration with Legacy Systems*: Another significant challenge is the integration of big data technologies with existing systems. Many shipping companies operate with legacy systems that are not readily compatible with modern big data solutions. Many maritime operations rely on older technology not designed to integrate today's advanced data processing tools. This mismatch leads to significant hurdles in data utilization and operational continuity. Merging these disparate systems requires custom solutions, like developing middleware for effective data processing.

- *Data Quality*: Ensuring the quality and accuracy of the data being analyzed is critical for reliable insights and decision-making. In the maritime industry, data may be generated from a variety of sources, including vessel sensors, cargo tracking systems, and manual record-keeping. Ensuring the consistency and integrity of this data can be a huge challenge.

- *Data Security*: Ensuring data security and privacy is a twofold challenge: protecting sensitive information from external breaches and managing internal privacy concerns. The maritime industry handles sensitive information, such as vessel and cargo tracking data, and ensuring the security of this data is essential. Implementing big data systems and analytics can introduce new security risks, and shipping companies must have robust security measures in place to protect against these threats. Marine IT and telecommunication infrastructures are at high risk of penetration from cyber criminals, terrorists or other malevolent interests. A breach leads to severe financial and reputational damage for companies and, in some cases, even poses national security risks. Maritime companies address security issues by implementing advanced encryption methods to protect data in transit and at rest. Cybersecurity is becoming a greater concern as the level of digitalization increases, and obsolete methods of obtaining and storing data will need to be updated to guard against potential dangers.

- *Regulatory Compliance*: In the dynamic realm of the shipping industry, adherence to international regulations and standards is not just a legal obligation but a cornerstone of operational integrity. The complexity of maritime regulations, such as the International Maritime Organization (IMO) standards, SOLAS (Safety of Life at Sea), and MARPOL (Marine Pollution) conventions, demands meticulous monitoring and reporting. Big data analytics plays a crucial role here, enabling companies to efficiently track and manage compliance-related data. Stricter environmental regulations, like the IMO 2023 targets, require accurate tracking and reporting of emissions, which big data analytics facilitates. Moreover, big data facilitates streamlined reporting and documentation processes, a critical aspect of regulatory compliance.

- *Safety Compliance*: This is another area where big data proves indispensable. Advanced analytics can predict potential safety hazards by assessing historical incident data and real-time inputs from onboard sensors. This proactive approach to safety management not only aligns with regulatory standards but significantly enhances the safety of crew and cargo.

- *Labor Shortage*: Ensuring enough quantity and quality of human resources is essential for developing the use of big data solutions for maritime. There is a shortage of highly trained data scientists. Despite the massive amount of data generated by shipping companies, extracting meaningful insights becomes challenging when you lack the necessary skilled personnel and analytical expertise. Maritime education plays a vital role in equipping industry professionals with the necessary skills and knowledge to navigate the ever-changing landscape.

11.8 CONCLUSION

Big data has already taken the maritime industry by storm globally. As the maritime industry continues to embrace big data, the evolution of data analysis and the rise of big data tools have become instrumental in optimizing operations and improving decision-making processes. With the advent of advanced data processing techniques and the utilization of artificial intelligence, the maritime industry is now able to analyze massive amounts of data in real-time. By leveraging big data, the industry can improve route optimization, enhance supply chain management, increase overall efficiency, and improve operations and better decision-making processes. Moreover, big data enables maritime companies to personalize their services, offer more targeted advertising and marketing campaigns, and improve customer satisfaction.

Big data analytics can provide valuable insights into various aspects of maritime trade, including vessel performance, route optimization, cargo tracking, and port operations. The future of big data in maritime trade holds immense potential for enhancing operational efficiency and reducing risks. More information about big data in the maritime industry can be found in the books in [19-22] and the following related journals:

- *Journal of Big Data*
- *Maritime Policy & Management*
- *Marine Policy*
- *Ocean Engineering*
- *Journal of Marine Science and Engineering*
- *Journal of Navigation*

REFERENCES

[1] "Big data in the maritime industry: Use cases and challenges," https://sedna.com/resources/big-data-in-the-maritime-industry-use-cases-and-challenges

[2] M. N. O. Sadiku, P. A. Adekunte, and J. O. Sadiku, "Big data in maritime industry," *International Journal of Trend in Scientific Research and Development*, vol. 9, no. 3, May-June 2025, pp. 1195-1204.

[3] M. N. O. Sadiku, M. Tembely, and S.M. Musa, "Big data: An introduction for engineers," *Journal of Scientific and Engineering Research*, vol. 3, no. 2, 2016, pp. 106-108.

[4] A. Slamecka, "Big data explosion," April 2022, https://blogs.cisco.com/financialservices/big-data-explosion

[5] "Passion points: Analytics in the sports, media & entertainment industries," February 2017, https://gradblog.schulich.yorku.ca/event/passion-points-analytics-in-the-sports-media-entertainment-industries/

[6] "The complete overview of big data," https://intellipaat.com/blog/tutorial/hadoop-tutorial/big-data-overview/

[7] R. Allen, "Types of big data | Understanding & Interacting with key types (2024)," https://investguiding-com.custommapposter.com/article/types-of-big-data-understanding-amp-interacting-with-key-types

[8] P. Baumann et al., "Big data analytics for earth sciences: The earthserver approach," *International Journal of Digital Earth*, vol. 19, no. 1, 2016, pp.3-29.

[9] X. Wu et al., "Knowledge engineering with big data," *IEEE Intelligent Systems*, September/October 2015, pp.46-511.

[10] X. Zhou et al., "The integrated application of big data and geospatial analysis in maritime transportation safety management: A comprehensive review," *International Journal of Applied Earth Observation and Geoinformation*, vol. 138, April 20211.

[11] "Marine big data market global trends, market share, industry size, growth, opportunities and market forecast – 2021 to 2027," May 2021, https://www.openpr.com/news/2288479/marine-big-data-market-global-trends-market-share-industry

[12] H. Segercrantz, "Big data & big savings for maritime ops," February 2016, https://www.marinelink.com/news/maritime-savings-data405723

[13] "Big data in the shipping industry: It's changing everything," November 2023, https://valtran.com/blog/big-data-in-the-shipping-industry-its-changing-everything/

[14] "Maritime technology: Big data," https://teqplay.com/blog/maritime-technology-big-data/

[15] "Big data in maritime: How a shipping company can effectively use data," https://marine-digital.com/article_bigdata_in_maritime

[16] Z. H. Munim, "Big data and artificial intelligence in the maritime industry: A bibliometric review and future research directions," *Maritime Policy & Management*, vol. 47, no. 5, 2020, pp. 577-597.

[17] D. Owczarek, "Navigating the ocean of big data in maritime and shipping industry," April 2025, https://nexocode.com/blog/posts/big-data-in-maritime/

[18] "Maritime technology: Big data," https://teqplay.com/blog/maritime-technology-big-data/

[19] M. N. O. Sadiku, U. C. Chukwu, and P. O. Adebo, *Big Data and Its Applications*. Moldova, Europe: Lambert Academic Publishing, 2024.

[20] C. Ducruet (ed.), *Advances in Shipping Data Analysis and Modeling: Tracking and Mapping Maritime Flows in the Age of Big Data (Routledge Studies in Transport Analysis)*. Routledge, 2019.

[21] A. E. Hassanien et al. (eds.), *Big Data in Complex Systems: Challenges and Opportunities*. Springer, 20111.

[22] B. Ko and D. Song (eds.), *New Maritime Business: Uncertainty, Sustainability, Technology and Big Data*. Springer, 2021.

CHAPTER 12

BIG DATA IN THE MILITARY

"Injustice anywhere is a threat to justice everywhere." – Martin Luther King Jr

12.1 INTRODUCTION

There is no doubt that information is the most precious commodity for any business. Data is information in raw format, while information represents data after processing and analysis. There is data everywhere. It has invaded all aspects of our life. Data comes from a variety of sources such as sensors, social media sites, smart phones, Internet, emails, ecommerce transactions, weather data, medical records, insurance records, RFID devices, video sharing, etc. This huge amount of data is collectively called big data. The cloud word for big data is shown in Figure 12.1 [1].

Figure 12.1 The cloud word for big data [1].

As its name implies, big data is a structured, semi-structured, and unstructured data, which is very big, fast, and comes in many forms. Big data may be regarded as a phenomenon since we can observe its effects like growing volume and variety. It has become the fuel that every industry needs today to flourish. Data is constantly generated in the modern era by everything. Vast amounts of data are generated by various sources like satellites, drones, social media, and sensors. Typical sources of big data are shown in Figure 12.2 [2].

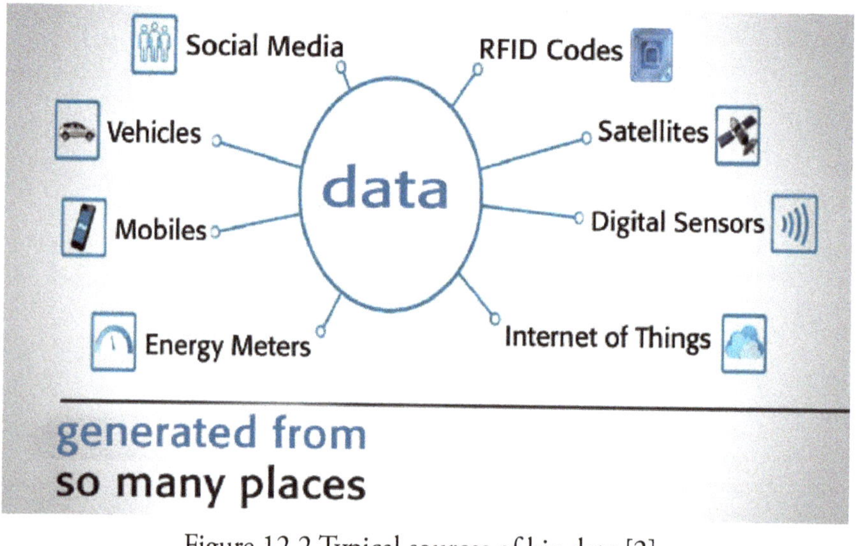

Figure 12.2 Typical sources of big data [2].

Large volumes of data, managed properly, are a boon for many industries, including the military. The US military is currently witnessing a significant shift in warfare, predominantly propelled by advancements in technology. At the heart of this paradigm shift lies the capacity to effectively gather, analyze, and rapidly and securely distribute essential information to military units. The foundational principles governing battlefield dynamics, encompassing observation, engagement, mobility, communication, protection, and logistical support, are undergoing notable transformations. Although the prospect of big data in revolutionizing the battlefield is promising, its effective integration into defense intelligence analysis poses a series of challenges and opportunities [3]. Big data will play a key role in how the Army operates and wins its future combats.

Big data refers to massive volumes of structured and unstructured data that cannot be processed using traditional methods and is characterized by high volume, velocity, variety, veracity, and value. Data has become a crucial asset in various domains, including the military. The potential of big data to revolutionize battlefield dynamics has attracted considerable attention within military and intelligence circles. Big data has become a vital weapon system in modern warfare. It will determine the results of current and future conflicts [4].

In this chapter, we will delve into the role of big data in military operations and explore the realm of possibilities in military data analytics. The chapter begins with explaining what big data is all about. It discusses military data and provides some of its applications. It addresses military big data around the world. It highlights the benefits and challenges of military big data. It concludes with comments.

12.2 WHAT IS BIG DATA?

Big data applies to data sets of extreme size (e.g. exabytes, zettabytes) which are beyond the capability of the commonly used software tools. It involves situation where very large data sets are big in volume, velocity, veracity, and variability [5]. The data is too big, too fast, or does not fit the regular database architecture. It may require different strategies and tools for profiling, measurement, assessment, and processing.

Big Data is essentially classified into three types [6]:

- *Structured Data*: This is highly organized and is the easiest to work with. Any data that can be stored, accessed, and processed in the form of fixed format is known as a structured data. It may be stored in tabular format. Due to their nature, it is easy for programs to sort through and collect data. Structured data has quantitative data such as age, contact, address, billing, expenses, credit card numbers, etc. Data that is stored in a relational database management system is an example of structured data.

- *Unstructured Data*: This refers to unorganized data such as video files, log files, audio files, and image files. Any data with unknown form or the structure is classified as unstructured data. Almost everything generated by a computer is unstructured data. It takes a lot of time and effort required to make unstructured data readable. Examples of unstructured data include Metadata, Twitter tweets, and other social media posts.

- *Semi-structured Data*: This falls somewhere between structured data and unstructured data, i.e., both forms of data are present. Semi-structured data can be inherited such as location, time, email address, or device ID stamp.

The different types of big data are depicted in Figure 12.3 [7]. Structured and unstructured data are generated in various types [8-10].

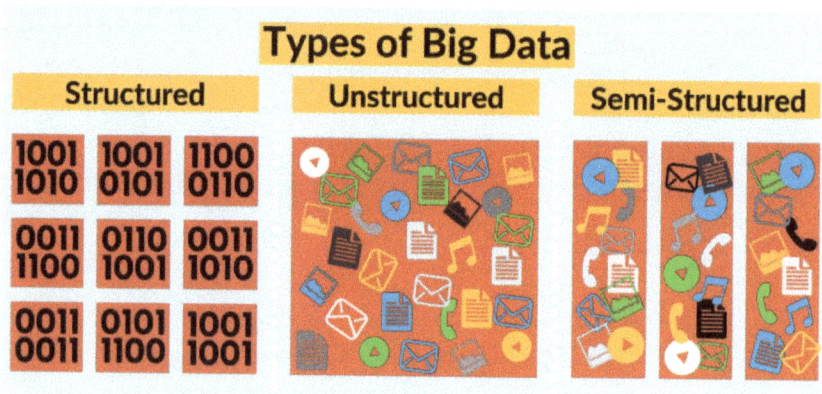

Figure 12.3 Types of big data [7].

One of the major strengths of big data is its flexibility and universal applicability to so many industries. Big data is used in several areas such as education, business, finance, government, healthcare, engineering, manufacturing, agriculture, social media, tourism, industry, entertainment, sports, construction, transportation, defense, etc. Increasingly, big data is regarded as the most strategic resource of the 21st century, similar in importance to gold and oil. It may also be regarded as the new form of currency [11].

The process of examining big data is often referred to big data analytics. It is an emerging field since massive computing capabilities have been made available by e-infrastructures. Analytics include statistical models and other methods that are aimed at creating empirical predictions. Data-driven organizations use analytics to guide decisions at all levels. Several techniques have been proposed for analyzing big data. These include the HACE theorem, cloud computing, Hadoop, and MapReduce [12].

12.3 MILITARY BIG DATA

Big data represents a paradigm shift in data management, requiring innovative approaches to harness the potential value hidden within vast and complex data repositories. The advent of big data has revolutionized how armed forces conduct operations, enhancing their capabilities and effectiveness. By leveraging advanced analytics techniques, such as machine learning and artificial intelligence, militaries can extract actionable insights from vast datasets, enabling them to gain a competitive edge on the battlefield. Although the essence of war remains constant, its manifestations evolve over time. These evolving manifestations necessitate the adaptation of military methodologies. Figure 12.4 shows that using data is critical to the success on the battlefield [13].

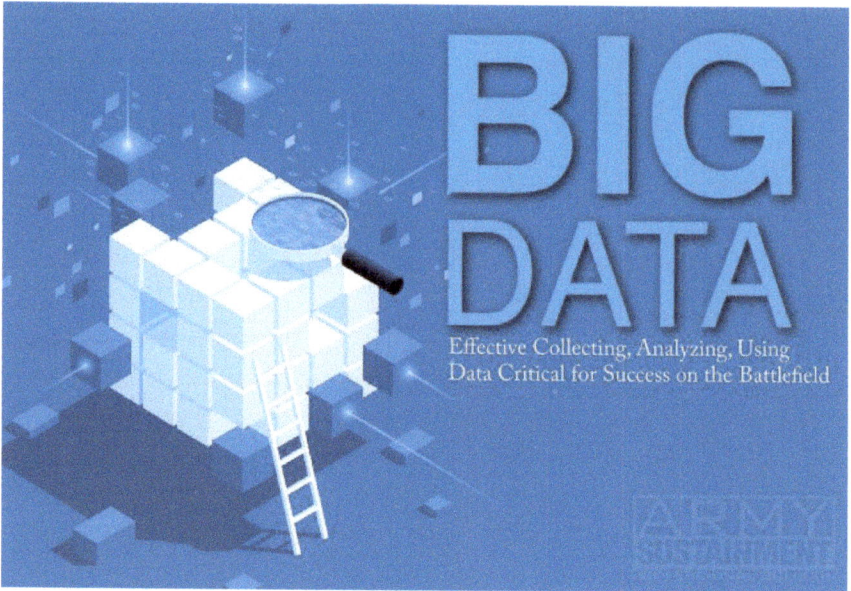

Figure 12.4 Using data is critical to the success on the battlefield [13].

Defense and security have often been at the forefront of new technologies, but has lagged other industries with respect to data analytics. Militaries, in the current environment, use big data for surveillance, processing of intelligence, prioritizing of targets, engagement, post-strike damage assessment. Big data enables military planners to identify trends, patterns, and anomalies. It enhances situational awareness on the battlefield. In military war planning, big data analytics plays a vital role in converting raw data into actionable intelligence. Imagine soldiers equipped with real-time insights on enemy movements, logistics officers predicting supply chain bottlenecks before they occur. This is not science fiction; it is the power of data analytics in defense, as displayed in Figure 12.5 [14].

Figure 12.5 Soldiers equipped with real-time insights on enemy movements [14].

12.4 APPLICATIONS OF MILITARY BIG DATA

Big data offers diverse applications in military operations, including intelligence gathering, predictive maintenance, strategic decision-making, predictive analysis, situational awareness enhancement, threat assessment, decision-support mechanisms, surveillance, leadership, and optimization of logistical operations. Big data is being used in the military in the following specific ways [13,15]:

1. *Intelligence Gathering*: Intelligence is at the heart of all defense planning and implementation. One of the most critical aspects of military operations is intelligence gathering, which can now be augmented and improved using big data. Traditional intelligence gathering in the field includes teams splitting up, gathering information, returning to base, and writing reports, and then the different teams may or may not learn of what the other teams discovered. This is quickly becoming an outdated way to collect information. By analyzing massive datasets, big data can help identify patterns and trends in enemy behavior, troop movement, and communication networks. These patterns can provide valuable insights into enemy strategies, weaknesses, and potential threats. Big data analytics can also process and analyze satellite images and geographic data to provide an accurate and updated overview of the

terrain, infrastructure, and resources in a conflict zone. This geospatial intelligence aids in planning and executing military operations with greater precision. In today's interconnected world, social media has become a goldmine of information. By using big data analytics, military forces can monitor and analyze the chatter on social media platforms to gather intelligence on public sentiment, enemy propaganda, and potential security threats. Figure 12.6 indicates that the future of defense is big data and military intelligence [15].

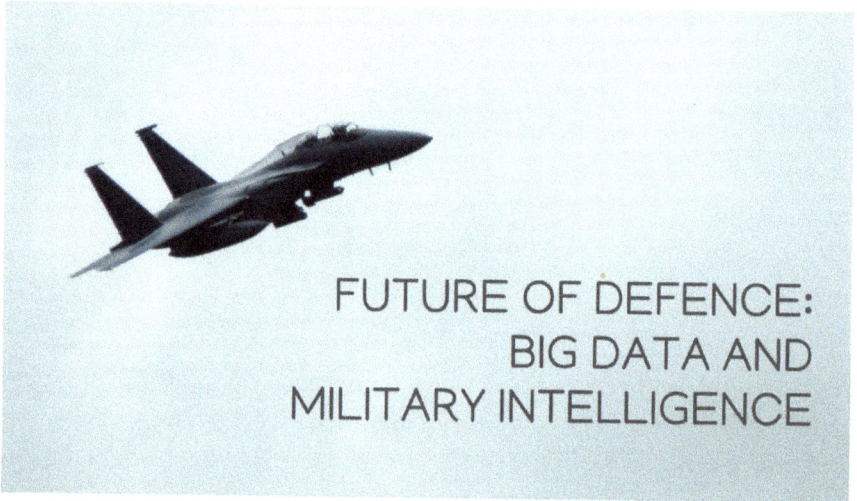

Figure 12.6 The future of defense is big data and military intelligence [15].

2. *Predictive Maintenance*: The maintenance and upkeep of military assets like vehicles, aircraft, and weaponry are essential for ensuring the operational readiness of armed forces. Big data analytics can help in predictive maintenance and resource optimization in many ways. First, by analyzing data from sensors and other monitoring devices, big data can identify early signs of wear and tear, potential system failures, and other maintenance issues in military equipment. This early warning system enables armed forces to address issues proactively, ensuring optimal performance and reducing the risk of unexpected breakdowns during operations. Second, big data analytics can help military forces optimize their resources by identifying inefficiencies and redundancies in their supply chains and logistics networks. By streamlining processes and allocating resources more effectively, armed forces can reduce costs, improve response times, and enhance their overall operational efficiency.

Third, beyond equipment maintenance, big data can also be used to monitor the health and well-being of military personnel. By analyzing factors such as physical fitness, stress levels, and cognitive performance, big data can identify potential risks to soldiers' health and recommend preventative measures to maintain peak performance.

3. *Strategic Decision-Making*: The emergence of big data has prompted decision-makers and commanders to acknowledge its importance in shaping strategic insights and intelligence analysis. It marks the commencement of a new stage in data-centric decision-making. Big data has a transformative impact on strategic decision-making in military operations. By providing real-time insights and predictive analysis, it can help military leaders make informed decisions and improve the overall effectiveness of their strategies. Big data analytics can integrate data from multiple sources, including satellite imagery, surveillance feeds, and intelligence reports, to provide a comprehensive and real-time understanding of the operational environment. This enhanced situational awareness can help military commanders make better-informed decisions and adapt their strategies to changing circumstances. Big data can be used to create sophisticated war-gaming scenarios and simulations that allow military leaders to test and refine their strategies in a controlled environment. By analyzing the results of these simulations, military planners can identify potential weaknesses, anticipate enemy responses, and develop more effective strategies for real-world operations. Big data can also be integrated into decision support systems that use artificial intelligence (AI) and machine learning algorithms to analyze and process information, providing military leaders with data-driven recommendations. These systems can help identify the most effective course of action, taking into account multiple factors such as mission objectives, available resources, and potential risks.

4. *Data-driven Leadership*: Leaders at all levels must understand data, data collection, data analysis, and what it means to the future of the Army. Giving leaders at all levels the understanding and tools necessary to navigate the data-centric environment allows for a more effective decision-making process. All leaders within the officer, warrant officer, and noncommissioned officer cohorts must develop valuable training for their formations if the Army is to be successful and take full advantage of the tools at its disposal. When leaders take the big data movement

and apply artificial intelligence, they can discover trends, break through a typical bureaucratic structure, and make quick decisions with the right information. Predictive analytics plays a crucial role in cultivating data-driven leadership. Utilizing advanced analytical techniques to examine historical sustainment patterns with increased efficiency at the grassroots level offers significant advantages for future strategic planning efforts. This proactive approach assists leaders in better preparing their units to address a range of potential scenarios. Equipping leaders with suitable analytical instruments reveals opportunities to identify areas where resources are either underutilized or overstretched, such as in inventory stockpiles and maintenance facilities. Armed with this understanding, leaders can deploy resources more prudently, ensuring their distribution corresponds with operational demands. The impact of big data is particularly evident in addressing questions pertaining to who, what, where, and when, primarily with structured data. This underscores the crucial role of expert leadership and analysts in navigating intricate defense intelligence challenges. Figure 12.7 shows President Obama holding a meeting with military leadership [16].

Figure 12.7 President Obama holding a meeting with military leadership [16].

5. *Data Collection and Analysis*: This is integral to modern military operations. Data are emerging as a key component of military operations, both on and off the battlefield. The utilization of big data and advanced analytics provides militaries with unprecedented capabilities in war planning. By harnessing the power of data, military leaders can enhance situational awareness, predict enemy behavior, optimize logistics, and support decision-making processes. As the defense industry grapples with exponential increases in mission, data must be collected, managed, and analyzed. The promise of artificial intelligence (AI) to harness the power of big data and drive strategic decision-making represents an unprecedented shift in the industry. The collection and use of large data sets in weapons systems and for other purposes raise significant questions about data acquisition, retention, and privacy as well as bias. Data analytics can assist the Army in optimizing the allocation of limited resources. By giving leaders the proper tools, they can identify areas where resources are underutilized or overextended. Automated data collation and analytics would both save analyst effort and enable powerful new capabilities.

6. *Surveillance*: The fundamental role of big data in defense intelligence analysis revolves around the realm of military operations and surveillance. In the field of surveillance, it would be essential to know the areas to focus and the likelihood of attaining the best results with devices. Today, surveillance includes a plethora of devices. These are satellites, unmanned aerial vehicles, aerostats, Airborne Warning and Control System (AWACS), reconnaissance helicopters and aircraft, ground-based electronic devices, and human intelligence. Big data is used to develop sophisticated surveillance systems that enable real-time monitoring, threat detection, and early warning capabilities. For example, the United States ARGUS ground surveillance system mounted on a UAV collects more than 40 gigabytes of information per second. The data collected is massive. The information gathered through military operations can be put to varied use. Another prime example would be the US Air Force E-8 Joint STARS (Surveillance Target Attack Radar System) which conducts airborne ground surveillance; collects data on enemy positions, vehicles, and aircraft, collects imagery, and relays tactical pictures to ground and air theater commanders.

12.5 MILITARY BIG DATA AROUND THE WORLD

Military organizations around the world are often huge producers and consumers of big data. They stand to gain from the many benefits associated with data analytics. Worldwide, the amount of data gathered by the military grows, as does the desire and need by the military to extract and use this data to form actionable intelligence. Successful gathering, processing, and analyzing will effectively change warfare as it is understood today. We consider how the following nations are employing big data in their military operations.

- *United States*: The US is the top country for big data roles in the military industry. In the United States today, all aircraft already emit their locations through a system called automatic dependent surveillance–broadcast, and most ships do the same through the automatic identification system. US warfighters operate in a more technologically augmented arena since September 11, 2001, where sensors, wearable computers, Internet of things (IoT)-enabled devices, and artificial intelligence (AI) systems all contribute to mission success. Today's warfighter often operates in remote, environmentally hostile, and actively contested regions. Their operations are increasingly dependent on analyzing data quickly to make critical decisions and respond to potential threats. Year after year, the US military faces increased operational commitments and budget constraints, thereby forcing it to do more with fewer resources. The National Security Agency (NSA) typically gathers SIGINT (Signals Intelligence) on terrorists, organizations, and persons with international or foreign associations using various methods. SIGINT is information about the actions, objectives, and capabilities of a foreign target acquired through the interception of signals and transmissions. A potential use of SIGINT technology is to take on a more active defensive role.

- *Europe*: Europe is seeing a hiring boom in military industry big data roles. The European Defense Agency has made numerous recommendations about how the data is to be analyzed and thereafter fed to each combatant. The Europeans have included Modelling and Simulation (M&S) applications over the Cloud and the utilization of predictive analysis data in the development of M & S models.

- *India*: In an era where information is power, the Indian military is harnessing the potential of big data analytics to transform intelligence gathering. As the forces of developed countries, in the Indian Armed forces too, intelligence is at the heart of all defense planning and implementation. The major need of the hour is Big Data Strategy as well as recognition of its crucial importance from the top echelons to the front line soldier. Big data provides the Indian Army with advanced tools (analytics and algorithms) to reveal critical information. Handling of logistics data is a nightmare for the Indian Army [17]. Big data analytics is a game-changer in modern military intelligence, and the Indian Armed Forces are at the forefront of leveraging this technology. Through continuous innovation and strategic investment, the Indian military is poised to lead the way in leveraging big data analytics for national defense and security.

- *Ukraine*: Ukrainian military officials are evaluating whether to launch a cyber-operation to delete large quantities of data stored on a server run by a Russian company, located in Russia. Some of the data feeds into Russian weapons systems that operate within the armed conflict in Ukraine. But the proposed operation would also likely delete some civilian data that is stored on the same server. How would the existing rules apply to the data-deletion operation? Consider the efforts by Ukrainian officials to investigate and prosecute war crimes. Large quantities of data retrieved from a variety of sources such as satellites, social media, and crowdsourced information might be used to build a case against a particular perpetrator. Yet, private companies might own significant quantities of this data, creating challenges for prosecutors seeking to access it [18].

- *South Korea*: The Ministry of Defense is teaming up with the Ministry of Science, ICT, and Future Planning for a big data research project that will make use of the medical information of 600,000 South Korean military personnel. Currently, there are 19 military hospitals and some 1,200 medical detachments across the country, treating on average 2,500 soldiers daily. Regarding privacy concerns for the soldiers whose data will be utilized, the ministry emphasizes that protection of private information will be its foremost priority, and that all private information will be encrypted before being used for analysis [19]. South Korean military authorities have decided to add new food choices at military cafeterias based on a big data analysis of military food services. As illustrated in Figure 12.8, South Korean military uses big data for food service management [20].

Figure 12.8 South Korean military uses big data for food service management [20].

- *China*: China has wealth of data on what individuals are doing at a micro level. Pretty much everything about you is known or easily can be known by the government. There is an entire network, the Internet inside China's Great Firewall, designed to gather the information. Every picture posted, every comment made, every driving infraction or incident of rowdiness would go into a central database. Much of the data seems to come from companies like telecom providers and hotels. The approach is a far cry from what many Western governments still consider an appropriate balance between privacy and "national security."

Technically, privacy is protected by the constitution and the law in China [21]. China is building up its arsenal of missiles, jets, and ships. Beijing's new missiles, aircraft carriers, and hypersonic glide vehicles threaten US military assets in China's littoral waters and beyond. Figure 12.9 shows ranges of Chinese land-based missiles [22]. Beijing developed at least two interrelated operational concepts aimed at dominating the information environment: system destruction warfare and multi-domain precision warfare. System destruction warfare targets vulnerable links between sensors and platforms. The system allows militaries to communicate, process battlefield information, and carry out strikes. Chinese strategists believe that the enemy will lose "the will and ability to resist." Multi-domain precision warfare aims to integrate AI and big data analysis with precision strikes to identify and target enemy weaknesses [23].

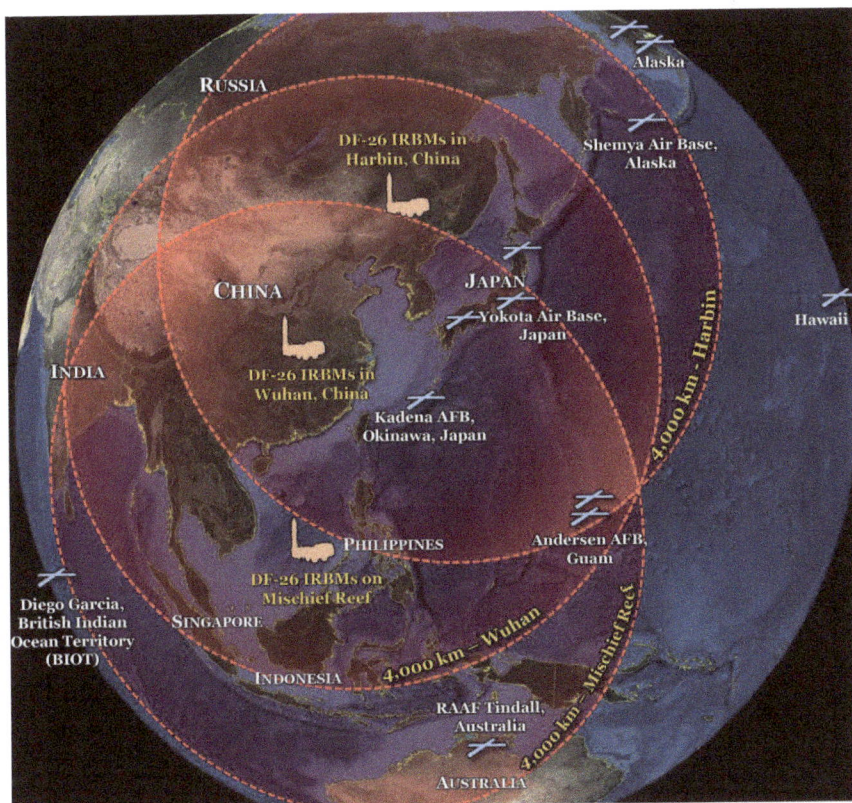

Figure 12.9 Ranges of Chinese land-based missiles [22].

12.6 BENEFITS

Big data is used in a variety of battlefield functions, such as targeted killing operations and intelligence collection and analysis. It is used to improve the procurement, transportation, and redeployment of personnel and material. Skillful deployment of big data analytics has the potential to confer a competitive edge amid complex and ever-evolving operational environments. Other benefits of big data in the military include the following:

- *Flexible Decision-making*: Data-driven decision-making enables military personnel to utilize real-time information to make decisions while personnel are in the field or on the base waiting for assignments. Big Data provides decision-makers with timely and accurate information for effective decision-making. Considering the rise of big data, decision-makers and commanders must grasp the potential of this data and its inherent utility on the battlefield. The abundance of available data can significantly augment intelligence analysis and bolster more knowledgeable and flexible decision-making processes during military operations. Army decision-making must remain widely distributed to maintain tactical flexibility.

- *Logistics*: Big Data will also play an important part in the fields of human resources and logistics. Big data aids in optimizing military logistics. Logistics is the backbone of any military; without it, the military is rendered inoperable. By analyzing historical data on supply chains, transportation routes, and maintenance records, military planners can identify bottlenecks, streamline operations, and improve resource utilization and logistics.

- *Democratization of Data*: This is the act of making the data easily accessible to those who need it. It is another internal push driving the utilization of big data in defense. However, more easily accessed data comes with its own set of challenges, primarily revolving around security concerns and system innovation.

- *Faster Response Time*: Big data can help the military respond quickly to threats by identifying them before they escalate.

- *Optimized Operations*: Big data can help the military optimize operations by analyzing data on logistics, resource allocation, and troop deployment. It can help the military understand the enemy by analyzing their communication, movement patterns, and social media activity. It can help the military develop more effective weapons by analyzing data to identify specific threats.

- *Improved Surveillance*: Big data can help the military develop sophisticated surveillance systems that can monitor in real-time.

12.7 CHALLENGES

While big data holds significant potential for revolutionizing defense intelligence, its exploration necessitates a nuanced consideration of both limitations and ethical considerations. It is crucial to address challenges related to data security, interoperability, and ethical considerations to ensure responsible and effective utilization of big data for military purposes. Other challenges of big data in military operations include the following [16]:

- *Ethical Concerns*: Ethical considerations arise regarding the use of data in military operations. Questions of proportionality, accountability, and the potential for biased decision-making require careful attention to ensure the responsible and ethical use of big data in warfare. The expanding influence of big data analytics on strategic decision-making within military operations necessitates a robust dedication to ethical considerations and methodological precision. Ethical concerns revolve around potential safety hazards, the responsible use of data, safeguarding privacy, and ensuring data protection. Successfully harnessing the transformative potential of big data within defense intelligence management requires a comprehensive approach that addresses ethical principles.

- *Expertise*: The precise understanding and effective utilization of data analytics require skilled professionals. Analysis needs expert analysts. Data-intensive fusion and analysis always require expert analysts to make sense of outputs. Even puzzles require expert analysts—to frame the puzzles in the first place, solve them, and then to make them relevant. For mysteries, data may offer valuable piecemeal insights, but expert analysts need to do even more heavy lifting to translate those insights into meaningful assessments for customers. Expertise is critical for inferring a target commander's intent.

- *Inefficiency*: The US military has staff that attempts to tackle processing their data. However, a human being can work at a human speed. This is a huge limitation and inefficiency. Between the joint headquarters and a battalion, there are six tiers of leadership at minimum. Before they can decide, a joint capability request will need to travel through every tier of leadership, which again, is at least six.

- *Data Security and Privacy Concern*: This remains the paramount concern as militaries collect and store vast amounts of sensitive information. Safeguarding this data against cyber threats and unauthorized access is crucial.

- *Interoperability*: Another challenge is the integration and interoperability of diverse data sources. Different military branches and agencies may use disparate systems, making it essential to establish data standards and frameworks for seamless data sharing and collaboration. In order for both industry and DoD officials to be successful in leveraging big data successfully, it is increasingly clear that open standards and interoperability will be key, especially with the push toward more cross-domain access to that data.

- *Information Overload*: The US military is struggling with information overload. Big data in the military comes from many sources and information overload is a very real problem. Increasingly, weapons systems depend on unfathomably large quantities of data to operate. Technologies that process and analyze large quantities of data, including artificial intelligence and machine learning, can exponentially increase military capabilities.

- *Bias*: The role of big data on the battlefield also raises important questions about privacy rights, discrimination, and bias

12.8 CONCLUSION

Big data refers to data that is too large or complex, grows, or changes at such a high velocity that traditional methods can no longer analyze it. It is emerging as a key component of military operations, both on and off the battlefield. On the battlefield, big data is being deployed, and has the potential to be deployed, for an astonishing array of purposes. Big data is also increasingly essential to military detention operations. It is now a key tool to investigate and prosecute those responsible for wartime atrocities. Big data therefore has the potential not only to revolutionize the tools armed forces use to fight, but to transform members of the armed forces themselves. More information about big data in military operations can be found in the books in [24-29] and the following related journals:

- *Military Review*
- *Journal of Military Learning*
- *Journal of Defence & Security Technologies*
- *The Cyber Defense Review*
- *Application of Big Data for National Security*

REFERENCES

[1] R. Delgado, "The challenges of bringing BYOD to the military," https://socpub.com/articles/the-challenges-of-bringing-byod-to-the-military-11272

[2] J. Moorthy et al., "Big data: Prospects and challenges," *The Journal for Decision Makers*, vol. 40, no. 1, 2015, pp. 74–96.

[3] "How does big data promise to transform the battlefield?" https://euro-sd.com/2024/06/articles/technology/38672/how-does-big-data-promise-to-transform-the-battlefield/#:~:text=By%20leveraging%20advanced%20analytics%20techniques,competitive%20edge%20on%20the%20battlefield.

[4] M. N. O. Sadiku, C. M. M. Kotteti, and J. O. Sadiku, "Big data in the military," *International Journal of Trend in Research and Development*, vol. 11, no. 5, September-October 2024, pp. 58-65.

[5] M. Swan, "Philosophy of big data," *Proceeding of IEEE First International Conference on Big Data Computing Service and Applications*, 2015, pp. 468-4712.

[6] "The complete overview of big data," https://intellipaat.com/blog/tutorial/hadoop-tutorial/big-data-overview/

[7] R. Allen, "Types of big data | Understanding & Interacting with key types (2024)," https://investguiding-com.custommapposter.com/article/types-of-big-data-understanding-amp-interacting-with-key-types

[8] A. K. Tiwari, H. Chaudhary, and S. Yadav, "A review on big data and its security," *Proceedings of IEEE Sponsored 2nd International Conference on Innovations in Information Embedded and Communication Systems*, 2015.

[9] M. B. Hoy, "Big data: An introduction for librarians," *Medical Reference Services Quarterly*, vol. 33, no 3. 2014, pp. 320-326.

[10] M. Viceconti, P. Hunter, and R. Hose, "Big data, big knowledge: Big data for personalized healthcare," *IEEE Journal of Medical and Health Informatics*, vol. 19, no. 4, July 2015, pp. 1209-1215.

[11] M. N.O. Sadiku, M. Tembely, and S.M. Musa, "Big data: An introduction for engineers," *Journal of Scientific and Engineering Research*, vol. 3, no. 2, 2016, pp. 106-108.

[12] X. Wu et al., "Knowledge engineering with big data," *IEEE Intelligent Systems*, September/October 2015, pp.46-55.

[13] "Big data | Effective collecting, analyzing, using data critical for success on the battlefield," November 2023, https://www.army.mil/article/270894/big_data_effective_collecting_analyzing_using_data_critical_for_success_on_the_battlefield#:~:text=United%20States%20Army-,Big%20Data%20%7C%20Effective%20Collecting%2C%20Analyzing%2C%20Using%20Data%20Critical,for%20Success%20on%20the%20Battlefield&text=Over%20the%20past%20few%20decades,and%20improve%20decision%2Dmaking%20processes.

[14] "The role of data analytics in defense strategies," March 2024, https://medium.com/@analyticsemergingindia/the-role-of-data-analytics-in-defense-strategies-7810ed837848

[15] "The role of big data in military operations: A game-changer in modern warfare," https://globmill.com/the-role-of-big-data-in-military-operations-a-game-changer-in-modern-warfare/

[16] S. Jang, "The role of data collection and big data in military war planning," November 2023, https://medium.com/ciss-al-big-data/data-is-constantly-generated-a-collected-in-the-modern-era-by-everything-3738f0d8ac10

[17] P. K. Chakravorty, "Big data: Implications for the Indian army," January 2020, https://bharatshakti.in/big-data-implications-for-the-indian-army/#:~:text=Big%20data%20provides%20the%20Indian,operations%2C%20training%20and%20other%20activities.

[18] L. A. Dickinson, "Lieber studies big data volume – Big data and armed conflict – Legal issues above and below the armed conflict threshold," January 2024, https://lieber.westpoint.edu/big-data-armed-conflict-legal-issues-above-below-armed-conflict-threshold/

[19] K. Bizwire, "Military uses big data for disease control and prevention," December 2016, http://koreabizwire.com/military-uses-big-data-for-disease-control-and-prevention/71669

[20] K. Bizwire, "S. Korean military uses big data for food service management," December 2019, http://koreabizwire.com/s-korean-military-uses-big-data-for-food-service-management/150341

[21] "Big Brother collecting big data — and in China, it's all for sale," January 2017, https://www.cbc.ca/news/world/china-data-for-sale-privacy-1.3927137

[22] "Big data for big wars: JEDI vs. China & Russia," August 2019, https://breakingdefense.com/2019/08/big-data-for-big-wars-jedi-vs-china-russia/

[23] S. Bresnick, "China bets big on military AI," https://cepa.org/article/china-bets-big-on-military-ai/

[24] M. N. O. Sadiku, U. C. Chukwu, and P. O. Adebo, *Big Data and Its Applications*. Moldova, Europe: Lambert Academic Publishing, 2024.

[25] L. A. Dickinson and E. W. Berg (eds.), *Big Data and Armed Conflict: Legal Issues Above and Below the Armed Conflict Threshold (The Lieber Studies Series)*. Oxford University Press, 2024.

[26] K. Huggins (ed.), *Military Applications of Data Analytics*. Boca Raton, FL: CRC Press, 2023.

[27] G. Galdorisi and S. J. Tangredi (eds.), *AI at War: How Big Data, Artificial Intelligence, and Machine Learning Are Changing Naval Warfare*. Naval Institute Press, 2021.

[28] N. Lim, B. R. Orvis, and K. C. Hall, *Leveraging Big Data Analytics to Improve Military Recruiting*. RAND Corporation, 2019.

[29] E. Berman, J. H. Felter, and J. N. Shapiro, *Small Wars, Big Data: The Information Revolution in Modern Conflict*. Princeton University Press, 2018.

APPENDIX

SHORT TABLE OF CONTENTS +

+M. N. O. Sadiku, U. C. Chukwu, and P. O. Adebo, *Big Data and Its Applications*. Moldova, Europe: Lambert Academic Publishing, 2024.

INDEX